Linux

LINUX

Ritu Choudhary

CENTRUM PRESS
NEW DELHI-110002 (INDIA)

CENTRUM PRESS
H.O.: 4360/4, Ansari Road, Daryaganj,
New Delhi-110002 (India)
Tel: 23278000, 23261597, 23255577, 23286875
B.O.: No. 1015, Ist Main Road, BSK IIIrd Stage,
IIIrd Phase, IIIrd Block, Bangalore-560085 (INDIA)
Tel: 080-41723429
Email: centrumpress@gmail.com
Visit us at: www.centrumpress.com

Linux

First Edition, 2011

PRINTED IN INDIA

Printed at Tarun Offset Printers, Delhi-110053

Contents

Preface

Linux is well-known as a stable and reliable platform, providing database and trading services for companies like Amazon, the well-known online bookshop, US Post Office, the German army and such. Especially Internet providers and Internet service providers have grown fond of Linux as firewall, proxy-and web server, and you will find a Linux box within reach of every UNIX system administrator who appreciates a comfortable management station.

It is also worth to note that modern Linux not only runs on workstations, mid-and high-end servers, but also on "gadgets" like PDA's, mobiles, a shipload of embedded applications and even on experimental wristwatches. This makes Linux the only operating system in the world covering such a wide range of hardware.

Author

1

Introduction to Linux

INTRODUCTION

WHY THIS GUIDE

Many people still believe that learning Linux is difficult, or that only experts can understand how a Linux system works. Though there is a lot of free documentation available, the documentation is widely scattered on the Web, and often confusing, since it is usually oriented towards experienced UNIX or Linux users. Today, thanks to the advancements in development, Linux has grown in popularity both at home and at work. The goal of this guide is to show people of all ages that Linux can be simple and fun, and used for all kinds of purposes.

WHO SHOULD READ THIS BOOK

This guide was created as an overview of the Linux Operating System, geared towards new users as an exploration tour and getting started guide, with exercises at the end of each chapter.

For more advanced trainees it can be a desktop reference, and a collection of the base knowledge needed to proceed with system and network administration. This book contains many real life examples derived from the author's experience as a Linux system and network administrator, trainer and consultant. We hope these examples will help you to get a better understanding of the Linux system and that you feel encouraged to try out things on your own.

NEW VERSIONS AND AVAILABILITY

This document is published in the Guides section of the Linux Documentation Project collection at; you can also download PDF and PostScript formatted versions here. The second edition of this guide is available in print from Fultus.com Books as paperback Print On Demand (POD) book.

Fultus distributes this document through Ingram and Baker and Taylor to many bookstores, including Amazon.com, Amazon.co.uk, BarnesAndNoble.com and Google's Froogle global shopping portal andGoogle Book Search.

Fig. Introduction to Linux Front Cover

The guide has been translated into Hindi by:

- Alok Kumar
- Dhananjay Sharma
- Kapil
- Puneet Goel
- Ravikant Yuyutsu

CONTRIBUTIONS

Many thanks to all the people who shared their experiences. And especially to the Belgian Linux users for hearing me out every day and always being generous in their comments. Also a special thought for Tabatha Marshall for doing a really thorough revision, spell check and styling, and to Eugene Crosser for spotting the errors that we two overlooked. And thanks to all the readers who notified me about missing topics and who helped to pick out the last errors, unclear definitions and typos by going through the trouble of mailing me all their remarks. These are also the people who help me keep this guide up to date, like Filipus Klutiero who did a complete review in 2005 and 2006 and helps me getting the guide into the Debian docs collection, and Alexey Eremenko who sent me the foundation for chapter 11. In 2006, Suresh Rajashekara created a Debian package of this documentation. Finally, a big thank you for the volunteers who are currently translating this document in French, Swedish, German, Farsi, Hindi and more. It is a big work that should not be underestimated; I admire your courage.

COPYRIGHT INFORMATION

WHAT DO YOU NEED

You will require a computer and a medium containing a Linux distribution. Most of this guide applies to all Linux distributions-and UNIX in general. Apart from time, there are no further specific requirements. The Installation HOWTO contains helpful information on how to obtain Linux software and install it on your computer. Hardware requirements and coexistence with other operating systems are also discussed. An interesting alternative for those who don't dare to take the step of an actual Linux installation on their machine are the Linux distributions that you can run from a CD, such as the Knoppix distribution.

WHAT IS LINUX

HISTORY

UNIX

In order to understand the popularity of Linux, we need

to travel back in time, about 30 years ago... Imagine computers as big as houses, even stadiums. While the sizes of those computers posed substantial problems, there was one thing that made this even worse: every computer had a different operating system. Software was always customised to serve a specific purpose, and software for one given system didn't run on another system. Being able to work with one system didn't automatically mean that you could work with another. It was difficult, both for the users and the system administrators.

Computers were extremely expensive then, and sacrifices had to be made even after the original purchase just to get the users to understand how they worked. The total cost per unit of computing power was enormous. Technologically the world was not quite that advanced, so they had to live with the size for another decade. In 1969, a team of developers in the Bell Labs laboratories started working on a solution for the software problem, to address these compatibility issues.

They developed a new operating system, which was

- Simple and elegant.
- Written in the C programming language instead of in assembly code.
- Able to recycle code.

The Bell Labs developers named their project "UNIX."

The code recycling features were very important. Until then, all commercially available computer systems were written in a code specifically developed for one system. UNIX on the other hand needed only a small piece of that special code, which is now commonly named the kernel. This kernel is the only piece of code that needs to be adapted for every specific system and forms the base of the UNIX system. The operating system and all other functions were built around this kernel and written in a higher programming language, C. This language was especially developed for creating the UNIX system. Using this new technique, it was much easier to develop an operating system that could run on many different types of hardware.

The software vendors were quick to adapt, since they could sell ten times more software almost effortlessly. Weird new situations came in existence: imagine for instance computers from different vendors communicating in the same network, or users working on different systems without the need for extra education to use another computer. UNIX did a great deal to help users become compatible with different systems.

Throughout the next couple of decades the development of UNIX continued. More things became possible to do and more hardware and software vendors added support for UNIX to their products.

UNIX was initially found only in very large environments with mainframes and minicomputers (note that a PC is a "micro" computer). You had to work at a university, for the government or for large financial corporations in order to get your hands on a UNIX system.

But smaller computers were being developed, and by the end of the 80's, many people had home computers. By that time, there were several versions of UNIX available for the PC architecture, but none of them were truly free and more important: they were all terribly slow, so most people ran MS DOS or Windows 3.1 on their home PCs.

Linus and Linux

By the beginning of the 90s home PCs were finally powerful enough to run a full blown UNIX. Linus Torvalds, a young man studying computer science at the university of Helsinki, thought it would be a good idea to have some sort of freely available academic version of UNIX, and promptly started to code.

He started to ask questions, looking for answers and solutions that would help him get UNIX on his PC.

Below is one of his first posts in comp.os.minix, dating from 1991:

```
From: torvalds@klaava.Helsinki.FI (Linus Benedict
Torvalds)
Newsgroups: comp.os.minix
Subject: Gcc-1.40 and a posix-question Message-
ID: <1991Jul3.100050.9886@klaava.Helsinki.FI>
```

```
Date: 3 Jul 91 10:00:50 GMT
Hello netlanders,
Due to a project I'm working on (in minix), I'm
interested in the posix
standard definition. Could somebody please point
me to a (preferably)
machine-readable format of the latest posix rules?
Ftp-sites would be
nice.
```

From the start, it was Linus' goal to have a free system that was completely compliant with the original UNIX. That is why he asked for POSIX standards, POSIX still being the standard for UNIX.

In those days plug-and-play wasn't invented yet, but so many people were interested in having a UNIX system of their own, that this was only a small obstacle. New drivers became available for all kinds of new hardware, at a continuously rising speed. Almost as soon as a new piece of hardware became available, someone bought it and submitted it to the Linux test, as the system was gradually being called, releasing more free code for an ever wider range of hardware. These coders didn't stop at their PC's; every piece of hardware they could find was useful for Linux.

Back then, those people were called "nerds" or "freaks", but it didn't matter to them, as long as the supported hardware list grew longer and longer. Thanks to these people, Linux is now not only ideal to run on new PC's, but is also the system of choice for old and exotic hardware that would be useless if Linux didn't exist.

Two years after Linus' post, there were 12000 Linux users. The project, popular with hobbyists, grew steadily, all the while staying within the bounds of the POSIX standard. All the features of UNIX were added over the next couple of years, resulting in the mature operating system Linux has become today. Linux is a full UNIX clone, fit for use on workstations as well as on middle-range and high-end servers. Today, a lot of the important players on the hard- and software market each have their team of Linux developers; at your local dealer's you can even buy pre-installed Linux systems with official support-eventhough there is still a lot of hard- and software that is not supported, too.

Current Application of Linux Systems

Today Linux has joined the desktop market. Linux developers concentrated on networking and services in the beginning, and office applications have been the last barrier to be taken down. We don't like to admit that Microsoft is ruling this market, so plenty of alternatives have been started over the last couple of years to make Linux an acceptable choice as a workstation, providing an easy user interface and MS compatible office applications like word processors, spreadsheets, presentations and the like.

On the server side, Linux is well-known as a stable and reliable platform, providing database and trading services for companies like Amazon, the well-known online bookshop, US Post Office, the German army and many others. Especially Internet providers and Internet service providers have grown fond of Linux as firewall, proxy- and web server, and you will find a Linux box within reach of every UNIX system administrator who appreciates a comfortable management station. Clusters of Linux machines are used in the creation of movies such as "Titanic", "Shrek" and others. In post offices, they are the nerve centers that route mail and in large search engine, clusters are used to perform internet searches.These are only a few of the thousands of heavy-duty jobs that Linux is performing day-to-day across the world.

It is also worth to note that modern Linux not only runs on workstations, mid- and high-end servers, but also on "gadgets" like PDA's, mobiles, a shipload of embedded applications and even on experimental wristwatches. This makes Linux the only operating system in the world covering such a wide range of hardware.

THE USER INTERFACE

Linux Difficult

Whether Linux is difficult to learn depends on the person

you're asking. Experienced UNIX users will say no, because Linux is an ideal operating system for power-users and programmers, because it has been and is being developed by such people. Everything a good programmer can wish for is available: compilers, libraries, development and debugging tools. These packages come with every standard Linux distribution.

The C-compiler is included for free-as opposed to many UNIX distributions demanding licensing fees for this tool. All the documentation and manuals are there, and examples are often included to help you get started in no time. It feels like UNIX and switching between UNIX and Linux is a natural thing. In the early days of Linux, being an expert was kind of required to start using the system. Those who mastered Linux felt better than the rest of the "lusers" who hadn't seen the light yet. It was common practice to tell a beginning user to "RTFM" (read the manuals). While the manuals were on every system, it was difficult to find the documentation, and even if someone did, explanations were in such technical terms that the new user became easily discouraged from learning the system.

The Linux-using community started to realise that if Linux was ever to be an important player on the operating system market, there had to be some serious changes in the accessibility of the system.

Linux for non-Experienced Users

Companies such as RedHat, SuSE and Mandriva have sprung up, providing packaged Linux distributions suitable for mass consumption. They integrated a great deal of graphical user interfaces (GUIs), developed by the community, in order to ease management of programs and services. As a Linux user today you have all the means of getting to know your system inside out, but it is no longer necessary to have that knowledge in order to make the system comply to your requests.

Nowadays you can log in graphically and start all required applications without even having to type a single character, while you still have the ability to access the core of the system if needed. Because of its structure, Linux allows a user to grow into the system: it equally fits new and experienced users. New users are not forced to do difficult things, while experienced users are not forced to work in the same way they did when they first started learning Linux.

While development in the service area continues, great things are being done for desktop users, generally considered as the group least likely to know how a system works. Developers of desktop applications are making incredible efforts to make the most beautiful desktops you've ever seen, or to make your Linux machine look just like your former MS Windows or an Apple workstation. The latest developments also include 3D acceleration support and support for USB devices, single-click updates of system and packages, and so on. Linux has these, and tries to present all available services in a logical form that ordinary people can understand. Below is a short list containing some great examples; these sites have a lot of screenshots that will give you a glimpse of what Linux on the desktop can be like:

DOES LINUX HAVE A FUTURE

Open Source

The idea behind Open Source software is rather simple: when programmers can read, distribute and change code, the code will mature. People can adapt it, fix it, debug it, and they can do it at a speed that dwarfs the performance of software developers at conventional companies. This software will be more flexible and of a better quality than software that has been developed using the conventional channels, because more people have tested it in more different conditions than the closed software developer ever can.

The Open Source initiative started to make this clear to the commercial world, and very slowly, commercial vendors are starting to see the point. While lots of academics and technical people have already been convinced for 20 years now that this is the way to go, commercial vendors needed applications like the Internet to make them realise they can profit from Open Source.

Now Linux has grown past the stage where it was almost exclusively an academic system, useful only to a handful of people with a technical background. Now Linux provides more than the operating system: there is an entire infrastructure supporting the chain of effort of creating an operating system, of making and testing programs for it, of bringing everything to the users, of supplying maintenance, updates and support and customizations, etcetera. Today, Linux is ready to accept the challenge of a fast-changing world.

Ten Years of Experience at Your Service

While Linux is probably the most well-known Open Source initiative, there is another project that contributed enormously to the popularity of the Linux operating system. This project is called SAMBA, and its achievement is the reverse engineering of the Server Message Block (SMB)/ Common Internet File System (CIFS) protocol used for file- and print-serving on PC-related machines, natively supported by MS Windows NT and OS/2, and Linux. Packages are now available for almost every system and provide interconnection solutions in mixed environments using MS Windows protocols: Windows-compatible (up to and includingWinXP) file- and print-servers.

Maybe even more successful than the SAMBA project is the Apache HTTP server project. The server runs on UNIX, Windows NT and many other operating systems. Originally known as "A PAtCHy server", based on existing code and a series of "patch files", the name for the matured code deserves to be connoted with the native American tribe of the Apache, well-known for their superior skills in warfare strategy and inexhaustible endurance.

Apache has been shown to be substantially faster, more stable and more feature-full than many other web servers. Apache is run on sites that get millions of visitors per day, and while no official support is provided by the developers, the Apache user community provides answers to all your questions. Commercial support is now being provided by a number of third parties.

In the category of office applications, a choice of MS Office suite clones is available, ranging from partial to full implementations of the applications available on MS Windows workstations. These initiatives helped a great deal to make Linux acceptable for the desktop market, because the users don't need extra training to learn how to work with new systems. With the desktop comes the praise of the common users, and not only their praise, but also their specific requirements, which are growing more intricate and demanding by the day.

The Open Source community, consisting largely of people who have been contributing for over half a decade, assures Linux' position as an important player on the desktop market as well as in general IT application. Paid employees and volunteers alike are working diligently so that Linux can maintain a position in the market. The more users, the more questions. The Open Source community makes sure answers keep coming, and watches the quality of the answers with a suspicious eye, resulting in ever more stability and accessibility.

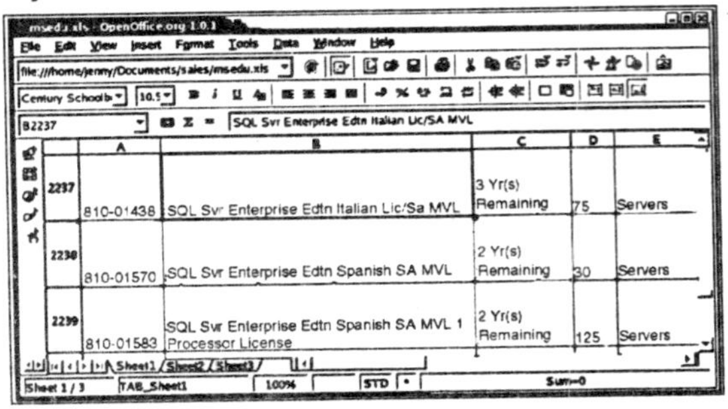

Fig. Open Office MS-Compatible Spreadsheet

Listing all the available Linux software is beyond the scope of this guide, as there are tens of thousands of packages. Throughout this course we will present you with the most common packages, which are almost all freely available. In order to take away some of the fear of the beginning user, here's a screenshot of one of your most-wanted programs. You can see for yourself that no effort has been spared to make users who are switching from Windows feel at home:

PROPERTIES OF LINUX

Linux Pros

A lot of the advantages of Linux are a consequence of Linux' origins, deeply rooted in UNIX, except for the first advantage, of course:

Linux is Free

As in free beer, they say. If you want to spend absolutely nothing, you don't even have to pay the price of a CD. Linux can be downloaded in its entirety from the Internet completely for free. No registration fees, no costs per user, free updates, and freely available source code in case you want to change the behaviour of your system.

Most of all, Linux is Free as in Free Speech

The license commonly used is the GNU Public License (GPL). The license says that anybody who may want to do so, has the right to change Linux and eventually to redistribute a changed version, on the one condition that the code is still available after redistribution. In practice, you are free to grab a kernel image, for instance to add support for teletransportation machines or time travel and sell your new code, as long as your customers can still have a copy of that code.

Linux is Portable to any Hardware Platform [

A vendor who wants to sell a new type of computer and who doesn't know what kind of OS his new machine will run (say the CPU in your car or washing machine), can take a Linux kernel and make it work on his hardware, because documentation related to this activity is freely available.

Linux was Made to Keep on Running

As with UNIX, a Linux system expects to run without

rebooting all the time. That is why a lot of tasks are being executed at night or scheduled automatically for other calm moments, resulting in higher availability during busier periods and a more balanced use of the hardware. This property allows for Linux to be applicable also in environments where people don't have the time or the possibility to control their systems night and day.

Linux is Secure and Uersatile

The security model used in Linux is based on the UNIX idea of security, which is known to be robust and of proven quality. But Linux is not only fit for use as a fort against enemy attacks from the Internet: it will adapt equally to other situations, utilizing the same high standards for security. Your development machine or control station will be as secure as your firewall.

Linux is Scalable

From a Palmtop with 2 MB of memory to a petabyte storage cluster with hundreds of nodes: add or remove the appropriate packages and Linux fits all. You don't need a supercomputer anymore, because you can use Linux to do big things using the building blocks provided with the system. If you want to do little things, such as making an operating system for an embedded processor or just recycling your old 486, Linux will do that as well.

The Linux OS and Most Linux Applications have Very Short Debug-Times

Because Linux has been developed and tested by thousands of people, both errors and people to fix them are usually found rather quickly. It sometimes happens that there are only a couple of hours between discovery and fixing of a bug.

Linux Cons

There are Far too Many Different Distributions

"Quot capites, tot rationes", as the Romans already said:

the more people, the more opinions. At first glance, the amount of Linux distributions can be frightening, or ridiculous, depending on your point of view. But it also means that everyone will find what he or she needs. You don't need to be an expert to find a suitable release.

When asked, generally every Linux user will say that the best distribution is the specific version he is using. So which one should you choose? Don't worry too much about that: all releases contain more or less the same set of basic packages. On top of the basics, special third party software is added making, for example, TurboLinux more suitable for the small and medium enterprise, RedHat for servers and SuSE for workstations.

However, the differences are likely to be very superficial. The best strategy is to test a couple of distributions; unfortunately not everybody has the time for this. Luckily, there is plenty of advice on the subject of choosing your Linux. A quick search on Google, using the keywords "choosing your distribution" brings up tens of links to good advise. TheInstallation HOWTO also discusses choosing your distribution.

Linux is not Very user Friendly and Confusing for Beginners

It must be said that Linux, at least the core system, is less userfriendly to use than MS Windows and certainly more difficult than MacOS, but... In light of its popularity, considerable effort has been made to make Linux even easier to use, especially for new users. More information is being released daily, such as this guide, to help fill the gap for documentation available to users at all levels.

Is an Open Source Product Trustworthy

How can something that is free also be reliable? Linux users have the choice whether to use Linux or not, which gives them an enormous advantage compared to users of proprietary software, who don't have that kind of freedom. After long periods of testing, most Linux users come to the conclusion that Linux is not only as good, but in many cases better and faster that the traditional solutions. If Linux were not trustworthy, it would have been long gone, never knowing the popularity it has now, with millions of users. Now users can influence their systems and share their remarks with the community, so the system gets better and better every day. It is a project that is never finished, that is true, but in an ever changing environment, Linux is also a project that continues to strive for perfection.

LINUX FLAVOURS

Linux and GNU

Although there are a large number of Linux implementations, you will find a lot of similarities in the different distributions, if only because every Linux machine is a box with building blocks that you may put together following your own needs and views. Installing the system is only the beginning of a longterm relationship. Just when you think you have a nice running system, Linux will stimulate your imagination and creativeness, and the more you realise what power the system can give you, the more you will try to redefine its limits.

Linux may appear different depending on the distribution, your hardware and personal taste, but the fundamentals on which all graphical and other interfaces are built, remain the same. The Linux system is based on GNU tools (Gnu's Not UNIX), which provide a set of standard ways to handle and use the system. All GNU tools are open source, so they can be installed on any system. Most distributions offer pre-compiled packages of most common tools, such as RPM packages on RedHat and Debian packages (also called deb or dpkg) on Debian, so you needn't be a programmer to install a package on your system. However, if you are and like doing things yourself, you will enjoy Linux all the better, since most distributions come with a complete set of development tools, allowing installation of new software purely from source code. This setup also allows you to install software even if it does not exist in a pre-packaged form suitable for your system.

A list of common GNU software:

- *Bash:* The GNU shell
- *GCC:* The GNU C Compiler
- *GDB:* The GNU Debugger
- *Coreutils:* A set of basic UNIX-style utilities, such as ls, cat and chmod
- *Findutils:* To search and find files
- *Fontutils:* To convert fonts from one format to another or make new fonts
- *The Gimp:* GNU Image Manipulation Program
- *Gnome:* The GNU desktop environment
- *Emacs:* A very powerful editor
- Ghostscript and Ghostview: interpreter and graphical frontend for PostScript files.
- *GNU Photo:* Software for interaction with digital cameras
- *Octave:* A programming language, primarily intended to perform numerical computations and image processing.
- *GNU SQL:* Relational database system
- *Radius:* A remote authentication and accounting server

Many commercial applications are available for Linux, and for more information about these packages we refer to their specific documentation. Throughout this guide we will only discuss freely available software, which comes (in most cases) with a GNU license.

To install missing or new packages, you will need some form of software management. The most common implementations include RPM and dpkg. RPM is the RedHat Package Manager, which is used on a variety of Linux systems, eventhough the name does not suggest this. Dpkg is the Debian package management system, which uses an interface called apt-get, that can manage RPM packages as well. Novell Ximian Red Carpet is a third party implementation of RPM with a graphical front-end. Other third party software vendors may have their own installation procedures, sometimes resembling the InstallShield and such, as known on MS Windows and other platforms. As you advance into Linux, you will likely get in touch with one or more of these programs.

GNU/Linux

The Linux kernel (the bones of your system, is not part of the GNU project but uses the same license as GNU software. A great majority of utilities and development tools (the meat or your system), which are not Linux-specific, are taken from the GNU project. Because any usable system must contain both the kernel and at least a minimal set of utilities, some people argue that such a system should be called a GNU/Linux system.

In order to obtain the highest possible degree of independence between distributions, this is the sort of Linux that we will discuss throughout this course. If we are not talking about a GNU/Linux system, the specific distribution, version or program name will be mentioned.

Which Distribution Should I Install

Prior to installation, the most important factor is your hardware. Since every Linux distribution contains the basic packages and can be built to meet almost any requirement (because they all use the Linux kernel), you only need to consider if the distribution will run on your hardware.

LinuxPPC for example has been made to run on Apple and other PowerPCs and does not run on an ordinary x86 based PC. LinuxPPC does run on the new Macs, but you can't use it for some of the older ones with ancient bus technology. Another tricky case is Sun hardware, which could be an old SPARC CPU or a newer UltraSparc, both requiring different versions of Linux.

Some Linux distributions are optimized for certain processors, such as Athlon CPUs, while they will at the same time run decent enough on the standard 486, 586 and 686 Intel processors.

Sometimes distributions for special CPUs are not as reliable, since they are tested by fewer people. Most Linux distributions offer a set of programs for generic PCs with special packages containing optimized kernels for the x86 Intel based CPUs.

These distributions are well-tested and maintained on a regular basis, focusing on reliant server implementation and easy installation and update procedures.

Examples are Debian, Ubuntu, Fedora, SuSE and Mandriva, which are by far the most popular Linux systems and generally considered easy to handle for the beginning user, while not blocking professionals from getting the most out of their Linux machines. Linux also runs decently on laptops and middle-range servers.

Drivers for new hardware are included only after extensive testing, which adds to the stability of a system. While the standard desktop might be Gnome on one system, another might offer KDE by default. Generally, both Gnome and KDE are available for all major Linux distributions. Other window and desktop managers are available for more advanced users.

The standard installation process allows users to choose between different basic setups, such as a workstation, where all packages needed for everyday use and development are installed, or a server installation, where different network services can be selected.

Expert users can install every combination of packages they want during the initial installation process. The goal of this guide is to apply to all Linux distributions. For your own convenience, however, it is strongly advised that beginners stick to a mainstream distribution, supporting all common hardware and applications by default.

The following are very good choices for novices:

- Fedora Core
- Debian
- SuSE Linux
- Mandriva (former MandrakeSoft)
- *Knoppix:* An operating system that runs from your CD-ROM, you don't need to install anything.

Downloadable ISO-images can be obtained from LinuxISO.org. The main distributions can be purchased in any decent computer shop.

2

Processes

PROCESSES INSIDE OUT

MULTI-USER AND MULTI-TASKING

Now that we are more used to our environment and we are able to communicate a little bit with our system, it is time to study the processes we can start in more detail. Not every command starts a single process. Some commands initiate a series of processes, such as mozilla; others, like ls, are executed as a single command.

Furthermore, Linux is based on UNIX, where it has been common policy to have multiple users running multiple commands, at the same time and on the same system. It is obvious that measures have to be taken to have the CPU manage all these processes, and that functionality has to be provided so users can switch between processes. In some cases, processes will have to continue to run even when the user who started them logs out. And users need a means to reactivate interrupted processes. We will explain the structure of Linux processes in the next sections.

PROCESS TYPES

Interactive Processes

Interactive processes are initialized and controlled through a terminal session. In other words, there has to be someone connected to the system to start these processes; they are not started automatically as part of the system functions.

These processes can run in the foreground, occupying the terminal that started the program, and you can't start other applications as long as this process is running in the foreground. Alternatively, they can run in the background, so that the terminal in which you started the program can accept new commands while the program is running. Until now, we only used programs running in the foreground-the length of time taken to run them was too short to notice-but viewing a file with the less command is a good example of a command occupying the terminal session.

In this case, the activated program is waiting for you to do something. The program is still connected to the terminal from where it was started, and the terminal is only useful for entering commands this program can understand. Other commands will just result in errors or unresponsiveness of the system. While a process runs in the background, however, the user is not prevented from doing other things in the terminal in which he started the program, while it is running.

The shell offers a feature called job control which allows easy handling of multiple processes. This mechanism switches processes between the foreground and the background. Using this system, programs can also be started in the background immediately. Running a process in the background is only useful for programs that don't need user input (via the shell). Putting a job in the background is typically done when execution of a job is expected to take a long time. In order to free the issuing terminal after entering the command, a trailing ampersand is added.

In the example, using graphical mode, we open an extra terminal window from the existing one:

```
billy:~> xterm &
billy:~> xterm &
[1] 26558
billy:~> jobs
[1]+ Running xterm &
```

The full job control features are explained in detail in the bash Info pages, so only the frequently used job control applications are listed here:

Table. Controlling Processes:

(Part of) Command	Meaning
Regular_Command	Runs this command in the foreground.
Command &	Run this command in the background (release the terminal)
Jobs	Show commands running in the background.
Ctrl+Z	Suspend (stop, but not quit) a process running in the foreground (suspend).
Ctrl+C	Interrupt (terminate and quit) a process running in the foreground.
%n	Every process running in the background gets a number assigned to it. By using the % expression a job can be referred to using its number, for instance fg %2.
Bg	Reactivate a suspended program in the background.
Fg	Puts the job back in the foreground.
Kill	End a process (also see Shell Builtin Commands in the Info pages of bash)

More practical examples can be found in the exercises. Most UNIX systems are likely to be able to run screen, which is useful when you actually want another shell to execute commands.

Upon calling screen, a new session is created with an accompanying shell and/or commands as specified, which you can then put out of the way.

In this new session you may do whatever it is you want to do. All programs and operations will run independent of the issuing shell. You can then detach this session, while the programs you started in it continue to run, even when you log out of the originating shell, and pick your *screen* up again any time you like.

This program originates from a time when virtual consoles were not invented yet, and everything needed to be done using one text terminal. To addicts, it still has meaning in Linux, even though we've had virtual consoles for almost ten years.

Automatic Processes

Automatic or batch processes are not connected to a terminal. Rather, these are tasks that can be queued into a spooler area, where they wait to be executed on a FIFO (first-in, first-out) basis.

Such tasks can be executed using one of two criteria:

- At a certain date and time: done using the at command, which we will discuss in the second part of this chapter.
- At times when the total system load is low enough to accept extra jobs: done using the batch command. By default, tasks are put in a queue where they wait to be executed until the system load is lower than 0.8. In large environments, the system administrator may prefer batch processing when large amounts of data have to be processed or when tasks demanding a lot of system resources have to be executed on an already loaded system. Batch processing is also used for optimizing system performance.

Daemons

Daemons are server processes that run continuously. Most of the time, they are initialized at system startup and then wait in the background until their service is required. A typical example is the networking daemon, *xinetd,* which is started in almost every boot procedure.

After the system is booted, the network daemon just sits and waits until a client program, such as an FTP client, needs to connect.

PROCESS ATTRIBUTES

A process has a series of characteristics:

- *The Process ID or PID:* A unique identification number used to refer to the process.
- *The Parent Process ID or PPID:* The number of the process that started this process.
- *Nice Number:* The degree of friendliness of this process towards other processes (not to be confused

with process priority, which is calculated based on this nice number and recent CPU usage of the process).

- *Terminal or TTY:* Terminal to which the process is connected.
- *User Name of the Real and Effective user (RUID and EUID):* The owner of the process. The real owner is the user issuing the command, the effective user is the one determining access to system resources. RUID and EUID are usually the same, and the process has the same access rights the issuing user would have. An example to clarify this: the browsermozilla in/usr/bin is owned by user root:

```
theo:~> ls -l/usr/bin/mozilla
-rwxr-xr-x 1 root root 4996 Nov 20 18:28/usr/
bin/mozilla*
theo:~> mozilla &
[1] 26595
theo:~> ps -af
UID PID PPID C STIME TTY TIME CMD
theo 26601 26599 0 15:04 pts/5 00:00:00/usr/lib/
mozilla/mozilla-bin
theo 26613 26569 0 15:04 pts/5 00:00:00 ps -af
```

When user *theo* starts this program, the process itself and all processes started by the initial process, will be owned by user *theo* and not by the system administrator.

When mozilla needs access to certain files, that access will be determined by *theo*'s permissions and not by *root*'s.

- *Real and Effective Group Owner (RGID and EGID):* The real group owner of a process is the primary group of the user who started the process. The effective group owner is usually the same, except when SGID access mode has been applied to a file.

DISPLAYING PRO^ESS INFORMATION

The ps command is one of the tools for visualizing processes. This command has several options which can be combined to display different process attributes.

With no options specified, ps only gives information about the current shell and eventual processes:

```
theo:~> ps
  PID TTY          TIME CMD
4245 pts/7  00:00:00 bash
5314 pts/7  00:00:00 ps
```

Since this does not give enough information-generally, at least a hundred processes are running on your system-we will usually select particular processes out of the list of all processes, using the grep command in a *pipe*, as in this line, which will select and display all processes owned by a particular user:

```
ps -ef | grep username
```

This example shows all processes with a process name of bash, the most common login shell on Linux systems:

```
theo:> ps auxw | grep bash
brenda 31970 0.0 0.3 6080 1556 tty2 S Feb23 0:00
-bash
root 32043 0.0 0.3 6112 1600 tty4 S Feb23 0:00 -
bash
theo 32581 0.0 0.3 6384 1864 pts/1 S Feb23 0:00
bash
theo 32616 0.0 0.3 6396 1896 pts/2 S Feb23 0:00
bash
theo 32629 0.0 0.3 6380 1856 pts/3 S Feb23 0:00
bash
theo 2214 0.0 0.3 6412 1944 pts/5 S 16:18 0:02
bash
theo 4245 0.0 0.3 6392 1888 pts/7 S 17:26 0:00
bash
theo 5427 0.0 0.1 3720 548 pts/7 S 19:22 0:00
grep bash
```

In these cases, the grep command finding lines containing the string *bash* is often displayed as well on systems that have a lot of idletime. If you don't want this to happen, use the pgrep command. Bash shells are a special case: this process list also shows which ones are login shells (where you have to give your username and password, such as when you log in in textmode or do a remote login, as opposed to non-login shells, started up for instance by clicking a terminal window icon). Such login shells are preceded with a dash (-). More info can be found the usual way: ps —help or man *ps*. GNU ps supports different styles of option formats; the above examples don't contain errors.

Note that ps only gives a momentary state of the active processes, it is a one-time recording. The top program displays a more precise view by updating the results given by ps (with a bunch of options) once every five seconds, generating a new list of the processes causing the heaviest load periodically, meanwhile integrating more information about the swap space in use and the state of the CPU, from the proc file system:

```
12:40pm up 9 days, 6:00, 4 users, load average:
0.21, 0.11, 0.03
89 processes: 86 sleeping, 3 running, 0 zombie,
0 stopped
CPU states: 2.5% user, 1.7% system, 0.0% nice,
95.6% idle
Mem: 255120K av, 239412K used, 15708K free, 756K
shrd, 22620K buff
Swap: 1050176K av, 76428K used, 973748K free,
82756K cached
PID USER PRI NI SIZE RSS SHARE STAT %CPU %MEM
  TIME COMMAND
5005 root 14 0 91572 15M 11580 R 1.9 6.0 7:53 X
19599 jeff 14 0 1024 1024 796 R 1.1 0.4 0:01 top
19100 jeff 9 0 5288 4948 3888 R 0.5 1.9 0:24
gnome-terminal
19328 jeff 9 0 37884 36M 14724 S 0.5 14.8 1:30
mozilla-bin
1 root 8 0 516 472 464 S 0.0 0.1 0:06 init
2 root 9 0 0 0 0 SW 0.0 0.0 0:02 keventd
3 root 9 0 0 0 0 SW 0.0 0.0 0:00 kapm-idled
4 root 19 19 0 0 0 SWN 0.0 0.0 0:00 ksoftirqd_CPU0
5 root 9 0 0 0 0 SW 0.0 0.0 0:33 kswapd
6 root 9 0 0 0 0 SW 0.0 0.0 0:00 kreclaimd
7 root 9 0 0 0 0 SW 0.0 0.0 0:00 bdflush
```

```
8 root 9 0 0 0 0 SW 0.0 0.0 0:05 kupdated
9 root -1-20 0 0 0 SW< 0.0 0.0 0:00 mdrecoveryd
13 root 9 0 0 0 0 SW 0.0 0.0 0:01 kjournald
89 root 9 0 0 0 0 SW 0.0 0.0 0:00 khubd
219 root 9 0 0 0 0 SW 0.0 0.0 0:00 kjournald
220 root 9 0 0 0 0 SW 0.0 0.0 0:00 kjournald
```

The first line of top contains the same information displayed by the uptime command:

```
jeff:~> uptime
  3:30pm, up 12 days, 23:29, 6 users, load average:
0.01, 0.02, 0.00
```

The data for these programs is stored among others in/ var/run/utmp (information about currently connected users) and in the virtual file system/proc, for example/proc/loadavg (average load information). There are all sorts of graphical applications to view this data, such as the *Gnome System Monitor* and *lavaps*. Open Source initiatives like Big Brother centralize this information along with other server data and logs from multiple servers on one web server, allowing monitoring of the entire IT infrastructure from one workstation.

The relations between processes can be visualized using the pstree command:

```
sophie:~> pstree
init-+-amd
|-apmd
|-2*[artsd]
|-atd
|-crond
|-deskguide_apple
|-eth0
|-gdm—gdm-+-X
|  '-gnome-session-+-Gnome
|  |-ssh-agent
|  '-true
|-geyes_applet
|-gkb_applet
|-gnome-name-serv
```

```
|-gnome-smproxy
|-gnome-terminal-+-bash—vim
|  |-bash
|  |-bash—pstree
|  |-bash—ssh
|  |-bash—mozilla-bin—mozilla-bin—3*[mozilla-bin]
|  `-gnome-pty-helper
|-gpm
|-gweather
|-kapm-idled
|-3*[kdeinit]
|-keventd
|-khubd
|-5*[kjournald]
|-klogd
|-lockd—rpciod
|-lpd
|-mdrecoveryd
|-6*[mingetty]
|-8*[nfsd]
|-nscd—nscd—5*[nscd]
|-ntpd
|-3*[oafd]
|-panel
|-portmap
|-rhnsd
|-rpc.mountd
|-rpc.rquotad
|-rpc.statd
|-sawfish
|-screenshooter_a
|-sendmail
|-sshd—sshd—bash—su—bash
|-syslogd
|-tasklist_applet
|-vmnet-bridge
|-xfs
`-xinetd-ipv6
```

The -u and -a options give additional information, and for more, refer to the Info pages.

In the next section, we will see how one process can create another.

LIFE AND DEATH OF A PROCESS

Ending Processes

When a process ends normally (it is not killed or otherwise unexpectedly interrupted), the program returns its exit status to the parent. This exit status is a number returned by the program providing the results of the program's execution. The system of returning information upon executing a job has its origin in the C programming language in which UNIX has been written.

The return codes can then be interpreted by the parent, or in scripts. The values of the return codes are program-specific. This information can usually be found in the man pages of the specified program, for example the grep command returns -1 if no matches are found, upon which a message on the lines of "No files found" can be printed. Another example is the Bash Builtin command true, which does nothing except return an exit status of 0, meaning success.

Signals

Processes end because they receive a signal. There are multiple signals that you can send to a process. Use the kill command to send a signal to a process. The command kill -l shows a list of signals. Most signals are for internal use by the system, or for programmers when they write code.

As a user, you will need the following signals:

```
Table. Common signals
Signal name
Signal number
Meaning
SIGTERM
15
Terminate the process in an orderly way.
```

```
SIGINT
2
Interrupt the process. A process can ignore this
signal.
SIGKILL
9
Interrupt the process. A process can not ignore
this signal.
SIGHUP
1
For daemons: reread the configuration file.
```

You can read more about default actions that are taken when sending a signal to a process in man 7 *signal*.

SUID AND SGID

As promised in the previous chapter, we will now discuss the special modes SUID and SGID in more detail. These modes exist to provide normal users the ability to execute tasks they would normally not be able to do because of the tight file permission scheme used on UNIX based systems. In the ideal situation special modes are used as sparsely as possible, since they include security risks. Linux developers have generally tried to avoid them as much as possible.

The Linux ps version, for example, uses the information stored in the/proc file system, which is accessible to everyone, thus avoiding exposition of sensitive system data and resources to the general public. Before that, and still on older UNIX systems, the ps program needed access to files such as/ dev/mem and/dev/kmem, which had disadvantages because of the permissions and ownerships on these files:

```
rita:~> ls -l/dev/*mem
crw-r—    1 root kmem 1, 2 Aug 30 22:30/dev/kmem
crw-r—    1 root kmem 1, 1 Aug 30 22:30/dev/mem
```

With older versions of ps, it was not possible to start the program as a common user, unless special modes were applied to it. While we generally try to avoid applying any special modes, it is sometimes necessary to use an SUID. An example is the mechanism for changing passwords. Of course users will want to do this themselves instead of having their password set by the system administrator.

As we know, user names and passwords are listed in the/etc/ passwd file, which has these access permissions and owners:

```
bea:~> ls -l/etc/passwd
-rw-r—r— 1 root root 1267 Jan 16 14:43/etc/passwd
```

Still, users need to be able to change their own information in this file.

This is achieved by giving the passwd program special permissions:

```
mia:~> which passwd
passwd is/usr/bin/passwd mia:~> ls -l/usr/bin/
passwd
-r-s—x—x 1 root root 13476 Aug 7 06:03/usr/bin/
passwd*
```

When called, the passwd command will run using the access permissions of *root,* thus enabling a common user to edit the password file which is owned by the system admin. SGID modes on a file don't occur nearly as frequently as SUID, because SGID often involves the creation of extra groups.

In some cases, however, we have to go through this trouble in order to build an elegant solution (don't worry about this too much-the necessary groups are usually created upon installation).

This is the case for the write and wall programs, which are used to send messages to other users' terminals (ttys). The write command writes a message to a single user, while wall writes to all connected users.

Sending text to another user's terminal or graphical display is normally not allowed. In order to bypass this problem, a group has been created, which owns all terminal devices. When the write and wall commands are granted SGID permissions, the commands will run using the access rights as applicable to this group, *tty* in the example. Since this group has write access to the destination terminal, also a user having no permissions to use that terminal in any way can send messages to it.

In the example below, user *joe* first finds out on which terminal his correspondent is connected, using the who command. Then he sends her a message using the write command.

Also illustrated are the access rights on the write program and on the terminals occupied by the receiving user: it is clear that others than the user owner have no permissions on the device, except for the group owner, which can write to it.

```
joe:~> which write
write is/usr/bin/write
joe:~> ls -l/usr/bin/write
-rwxr-sr-x 1 root tty 8744 Dec 5 00:55/usr/bin/
write*
joe:~> who
jenny tty1 Jan 23 11:41
jenny pts/1 Jan 23 12:21 (:0)
jenny pts/2 Jan 23 12:22 (:0)
jenny pts/3 Jan 23 12:22 (:0)
joe pts/0 Jan 20 10:13 (lo.callhost.org)
joe:~> ls -l/dev/tty1
crw—w— 1 jenny tty 4, 1 Jan 23 11:41/dev/tty1
joe:~> write jenny tty1
hey Jenny, shall we have lunch together?
^C
User jenny gets this on her screen:
Message from joe@lo.callhost.org on ptys/1 at
12:36...
hey Jenny, shall we have lunch together?
EOF
```

After receiving a message, the terminal can be cleared using the Ctrl+L key combination. In order to receive no messages at all (except from the system administrator), use the mesg command.

To see which connected users accept messages from others use who -w. All features are fully explained in the Info pages of each command. Group names may vary The group scheme is specific to the distribution. Other distributions may use other names or other solutions.

BOOT PROCESS, INIT AND SHUTDOWN

INTRODUCTION

One of the most powerful aspects of Linux concerns its open method of starting and stopping the operating system, where it loads specified programs using their particular configurations, permits you to change those configurations to control the boot process, and shuts down in a graceful and organized way.

Beyond the question of controlling the boot or shutdown process, the open nature of Linux makes it much easier to determine the exact source of most problems associated with starting up or shutting down your system. A basic understanding of this process is quite beneficial to everybody who uses a Linux system.

A lot of Linux systems use lilo, the LInux LOader for booting operating systems. We will only discuss GRUB, however, which is easier to use and more flexible. Should you need information about lilo, refer to the man pages and HOWTOs. Both systems support dual boot installations, we refer to the HOWTOs on this subject for practical examples and background information.

THE BOOT PROCESS

When an x86 computer is booted, the processor looks at the end of the system memory for the BIOS (Basic Input/ Output System) and runs it. The BIOS program is written into permanent read-only memory and is always available for use. The BIOS provides the lowest level interface to peripheral devices and controls the first step of the boot process.

The BIOS tests the system, looks for and checks peripherals, and then looks for a drive to use to boot the system. Usually it checks the floppy drive (or CD-ROM drive on many newer systems) for bootable media, if present, and then it looks to the hard drive. The order of the drives used for booting is usually controlled by a particular BIOS setting on the system. Once Linux is installed on the hard drive of a system, the BIOS looks for a Master Boot Record (MBR) starting at the first sector on the first hard drive, loads its contents into memory, then passes control to it.

This MBR contains instructions on how to load the GRUB (or LILO) boot-loader, using a pre-selected operating system. The MBR then loads the boot-loader, which takes over the process (if the boot-loader is installed in the MBR). In the default Red Hat Linux configuration, GRUB uses the settings in the MBR to display boot options in a menu. Once GRUB has received the correct instructions for the operating system to start, either from its command line or configuration file, it finds the necessary boot file and hands off control of the machine to that operating system.

GRUB FEATURES

This boot method is called direct loading because instructions are used to directly load the operating system, with no intermediary code between the boot-loaders and the operating system's main files (such as the kernel). The boot process used by other operating systems may differ slightly from the above, however. For example, Microsoft's DOS and Windows operating systems completely overwrite anything on the MBR when they are installed without incorporating any of the current MBR's configuration.

This destroys any other information stored in the MBR by other operating systems, such as Linux. The Microsoft operating systems, as well as various other proprietary operating systems, are loaded using a chain loading boot method. With this method, the MBR points to the first sector of the partition holding the operating system, where it finds the special files necessary to actually boot that operating system.

GRUB supports both boot methods, allowing you to use it with almost any operating system, most popular file systems, and almost any hard disk your BIOS can recognize.

GRUB contains a number of other features; the most important include:

- GRUB provides a true command-based, pre-OS environment on x86 machines to allow maximum flexibility in loading operating systems with certain options or gathering information about the system.

- GRUB supports Logical Block Addressing (LBA) mode, needed to access many IDE and all SCSI hard disks. Before LBA, hard drives could encounter a 1024-cylinder limit, where the BIOS could not find a file after that point.
- GRUB's configuration file is read from the disk every time the system boots, preventing you from having to write over the MBR every time you change the boot options.

A full description of GRUB may be found by issuing the info grub command or at the GRUB site. The Linux Documentation Project has a Multiboot with GRUB Mini-HOWTO.

INIT

The kernel, once it is loaded, finds init in sbin and executes it. When init starts, it becomes the parent or grandparent of all of the processes that start up automatically on your Linux system. The first thing init does, is reading its initialization file,/etc/inittab. This instructs init to read an initial configuration script for the environment, which sets the path, starts swapping, checks the file systems, and so on. Basically, this step takes care of everything that your system needs to have done at system initialization: setting the clock, initializing serial ports and so forth.

Then init continues to read the/etc/inittab file, which describes how the system should be set up in each run level and sets the default run level. A run level is a configuration of processes. All UNIX-like systems can be run in different process configurations, such as the single user mode, which is referred to as run level 1 or run level S (or s). In this mode, only the system administrator can connect to the system. It is used to perform maintenance tasks without risks of damaging the system or user data. Naturally, in this configuration we don't need to offer user services, so they will all be disabled. Another run level is the reboot run level, or run level 6, which shuts down all running services according to the appropriate procedures and then restarts the system.

Commonly, run level 3 is configured to be text mode on a Linux machine, and run level 5 initializes the graphical login and environment. More about run levels in the next section. After having determined the default run level for your system, init starts all of the background processes necessary for the system to run by looking in the appropriate rc directory for that run level. init runs each of the kill scripts (their file names start with a K) with a stop parameter. It then runs all of the start scripts (their file names start with an S) in the appropriate run level directory so that all services and applications are started correctly. In fact, you can execute these same scripts manually after the system is finished booting with a command like/etc/rc.d/init.d/httpd stop or service httpd stop *logged in as* root, *in this case stopping the web server.*

None of the scripts that actually start and stop the services are located in/etc/rc.d/rc<x>.d. Rather, all of the files in/etc/rc.d/rc<x>.d are symbolic links that point to the actual scripts located in/etc/rc.d/init.d. A symbolic link is nothing more than a file that points to another file, and is used in this case because it can be created and deleted without affecting the actual scripts that kill or start the services. The symbolic links to the various scripts are numbered in a particular order so that they start in that order.

You can change the order in which the services start up or are killed by changing the name of the symbolic link that refers to the script that actually controls the service. You can use the same number multiple times if you want a particular service started or stopped right before or after another service.

Below a sample of/etc/rc5.d content, which lists the *services started up in run level 5:*

```
[jean@blub/etc/rc5.d] ls
K15httpd@    K45named@  S08ipchains@  S25netfs@
S85gpm@
K16rarpd@    K46radvd@  S08iptables@  S26apmd@
S90crond@
K20nfs@      K61ldap@   S09isdn@   S28autofs@
```

```
S90xfs@
K20rstatd@   K65identd@ S10network@  S30nscd@
S95anacron@
K20rusersd@ K74ntpd@  S12syslog@ S55sshd@ S95atd@
K20rwalld@   K74ypserv@ S13portmap@ S56rawdevices@
S97rhnsd@
K20rwhod@    K74ypxfrd@  S14nfslock@  S56xinetd@
S99local@
K25squid@    K89bcm5820@ S17keytable@ S60lpd@
K34yppasswdd@ S05kudzu@ S20random@ S80sendmail@
```

After init has progressed through the run levels to get to the default run level, the/etc/inittab script forks a getty process for each virtual console (login prompt in text mode). getty opens tty lines, sets their modes, prints the login prompt, gets the user's name, and then initiates a login process for that user. This allows users to authenticate themselves to the system and use it. By default, most systems offer 6 virtual consoles, but as you can see from the inittab file, this is configurable.

/etc/inittab can also tell init how it should handle a user pressing Ctrl+Alt+Delete at the console. As the system should be properly shut down and restarted rather than immediately power-cycled, init is told to execute the command/sbin/shutdown -t3 -r *now,* for instance, when a user hits those keys. In addition,/etc/inittab states what init should do in case of power failures, if your system has a UPS unit attached to it.

In run level 5,/etc/inittab runs a script called/etc/X11/prefdm. The prefdm script runs the preferred X display manager, based on the contents of the/etc/sysconfig/desktop directory. This is typically gdm if you run GNOME orkdm if you run KDE, but they can be mixed, and there's also the xdm that comes with a standard X installation.

The/etc/sysconfig directory contains entries for a range of functions and services, these are all read at boot time. This last part, however, might be somewhat different depending on your Linux distribution.

Besides the graphical user environment, a lot of other services may be started as well. But if all goes well, you should be looking at a login prompt or login screen when the boot process has finished.

Other Procedures

We explained how SysV init works on x86 based machines. Startup procedures may vary on other architectures and distributions. Other systems may use the BSD-style init, where startup files are not split up into multiple/etc/rc.d/ rc<LEVEL>.d directories. It might also be possible that your system uses/etc/init.d instead of/etc/rc.d/init.d.

INIT RUN LEVELS

The idea behind operating different services at different run levels essentially revolves around the fact that different systems can be used in different ways. Some services cannot be used until the system is in a particular state, or mode, such as being ready for more than one user or having networking available.

There are times in which you may want to operate the system in a lower mode. Examples are fixing disk corruption problems in run level 1 so no other users can possibly be on the system, or leaving a server in run level 3 without an X session running. In these cases, running services that depend upon a higher system mode to function does not make sense because they will not work correctly anyway. By already having each service assigned to start when its particular run level is reached, you ensure an orderly start up process, and you can quickly change the mode of the machine without worrying about which services to manually start or stop.

Available run levels are generally described in/etc/inittab, which is partially shown below:

```
#
# Inittab This file describes how the INIT process
# should set up the system in a certain run-level.
#
# Default runlevel. The runlevels are:
# 0-halt (Do NOT set initdefault to this)
# 1-Single user mode
# 2-Multiuser, without NFS
```

```
# (The same as 3, if you do not have networking)
# 3-Full multiuser mode
# 4-unused
# 5-X11
# 6-reboot (Do NOT set initdefault to this)
#
id:5:initdefault:
<—cut—>
```

Feel free to configure runlevels 2 and 4 as you see fit. Many users configure those runlevels in a way that makes the most sense for them while leaving the standard runlevels 3 and 5 alone. This allows them to quickly move in and out of their custom configuration without disturbing the normal set of features at the standard runlevels.

If your machine gets into a state where it will not boot due to a bad/etc/inittab or will not let you log in because you have a corrupted/etc/passwd file (or if you have simply forgotten your password), boot into single-user mode.

No Graphics

When you are working in text mode because you didn't get presented a graphical login screen on the console of your machine, you can normally switch to console 7 or up to have a graphical login. If this is not the case, check the current run level using the command who -r. If it is set to something else than 5, chances are that the system does not start up in graphical mode by default. Contact your system administrator or read man init in that case. Note that switching run levels is done using the init command; switching from a text to a graphical console or vice versa does not involve a run level switch.

TOOLS

The chkconfig utility in/sbin provides a simple command-line tool for maintaining the/etc/rc.d/init.d directory hierarchy. It relieves system administrators from having to directly manipulate the numerous symbolic links in the directories under/etc/rc.d.

In addition, some systems offer the ntsysv tool, which provides a text-based interface; you may find this easier to use thanchkconfig's command-line interface. On SuSE Linux, you will find the yast and insserv tools. For Mandrake easy configuration, you may want to try *DrakConf,* which allows among other features switching between run levels 3 and 5.

Most distributions provide a graphical user interface for configuring processes, check with your system documentation. All of these utilities must be run as root. The system administrator may also manually create the appropriate links in each run level directory in order to start or stop a service in a certain run level.

SHUTDOWN

UNIX was not made to be shut down, but if you really must, use the shutdown command. After completing the shutdown procedure, the -h option will halt the system, while -r will reboot it. The reboot and halt commands are now able to invoke shutdown if run when the system is in runlevels 1-5, and thus ensure proper shutdown of the system,but it is a bad habit to get into, as not all UNIX/Linux versions have this feature.

If your computer does not power itself down, you should not turn off the computer until you see a message indicating that the system is halted or finished shutting down, in order to give the system the time to unmount all partitions. Being impatient may cause data loss.

MANAGING PROCESSES

WORK FOR THE SYSTEM ADMIN

While managing system resources, including processes, is a task for the local system administrator, it doesn't hurt a common user to know something about it, especially where his or her own processes and their optimal execution are concerned. We will explain a little bit on a theoretical level about system performance, though not as far as hardware optimization and such. Instead, we will study the daily problems a common user is confronted with, and actions such a user can take to optimally use the resources available. As we learn in the next section, this is mainly a matter of thinking before acting.

HOW LONG DOES IT TAKE

Bash offers a built-in time command that displays how long a command takes to execute. The timing is highly accurate and can be used on any command.

In the example below, it takes about a minute and a half to make this book:

```
billy:~/xml/src> time make
Output written on abook.pdf (222 pages, 1619861
bytes).
Transcript written on abook.log.
real 1m41.056s
user 1m31.190s
sys  0m1.880s
```

The GNU time command in/usr/bin (as opposed to the shell built-in version) displays more information that can be formatted in different ways. It also shows the exit status of the command, and the total elapsed time.

```
billy:~/xml/src>/usr/bin/time make
Output written on abook.pdf (222 pages, 1595027
bytes).
Transcript written on abook.log.
Command exited with non-zero status 2
88.87user 1.74system 1:36.21elapsed 94%CP
                (0avgtext+0avgdata 0maxresident)k
0inputs+0outputs (2192major+30002minor)pagefaults
0swaps
Refer again to the Info pages for all the
information.
```

PERFORMANCE

To a user, performance means quick execution of commands. To a system manager, on the other hand, it means much more: the system admin has to optimize system performance for the whole system, including users, all programs and daemons.

System performance can depend on a thousand tiny things which are not accounted for with the time command:

- The program executing is badly written or doesn't use the computer appropriately
- Access to disks, controllers, display, all kinds of interfaces, etc.
- Reachability of remote systems (network performance)
- Amount of users on the system, amount of users actually working simultaneously
- Time of day
- ...

LOAD

In Short: The load depends on what is normal for your system. My old P133 running a firewall, SSH server, file server, a route daemon, a sendmail server, a proxy server and some other services doesn't complain with 7 users connected; the load is still 0 on average. Some (multi-CPU) systems I've seen were quite happy with a load of 67. There is only one way to find out-check the load regularly if you want to know what's normal. If you don't, you will only be able to measure system load from the response time of the command line, which is a very rough measurement since this speed is influenced by a hundred other factors.

Keep in mind that different systems will behave different with the same load average. For example, a system with a graphics card supporting hardware acceleration will have no problem rendering 3D images, while the same system with a cheap VGA card will slow down tremendously while rendering. My old P133 will become quite uncomfortable when I start the X server, but on a modern system you hardly notice the difference in the system load.

CAN I DO ANYTHING AS A USER

A big environment can slow you down. If you have lots

of environment variables set (instead of shell variables), long search paths that are not optimized (errors in setting the path environment variable) and such, the system will need more time to search and read data. In X, window managers and desktop environments can be real CPU-eaters. A really fancy desktop comes with a price, even when you can download it for free, since most desktops provide add-ons ad infinitum. Modesty is a virtue if you don't buy a new computer every year.

Priority

The priority or importance of a job is defined by it's nice number. A program with a high nice number is friendly to other programs, other users and the system; it is not an important job. The lower the nice number, the more important a job is and the more resources it will take without sharing them. Making a job nicer by increasing its nice number is only useful for processes that use a lot of CPU time (compilers, math applications and such). Processes that always use a lot of I/O time are automatically rewarded by the system and given a higher priority (a lower nice number), for example keyboard input always gets highest priority on a system.

Defining the priority of a program is done with the nice command. Most systems also provide the BSD renice command, which allows you to change the niceness of a running command. Again, read the man page for your system-specific information. Interactive programs

It is NOT a good idea to nice or renice an interactive program or a job running in the foreground. Use of these commands is usually a task for the system administrator.

CPU Resources

On every Linux system, many programs want to use the CPU(s) at the same time, even if you are the only user on the system. Every program needs a certain amount of cycles on the CPU to run. There may be times when there are not enough cycles because the CPU is too busy. The uptime command is wildly inaccurate (it only displays averages, you have to know what is normal), but far from being useless.

There are some actions you can undertake if you think your CPU is to blame for the unresponsiveness of your system:

- Run heavy programs when the load is low. This may be the case on your system during the night. See next section for scheduling.
- Prevent the system from doing unnecessary work: stop daemons and programs that you don't use, use locate instead of a heavy find...
- Run big jobs with a low priority

If none of these solutions are an option in your particular situation, you may want to upgrade your CPU. On a UNIX machine this is a job for the system admin.

Memory Resources

When the currently running processes expect more memory than the system has physically available, a Linux system will not crash; it will start paging, or *swapping*, meaning the process uses the memory on disk or in swap space, moving contents of the physical memory (pieces of running programs or entire programs in the case of swapping) to disk, thus reclaiming the physical memory to handle more processes. This slows the system down enormously since access to disk is much slower than access to memory. The top command can be used to display memory and swap use. Systems using glibc offer the memusage andmemusagestat commands to visualize memory usage.

If you find that a lot of memory and swap space are being used, you can try:

- Killing, stopping or renicing those programs that use a big chunk of memory
- Adding more memory (and in some cases more swap space) to the system.
- Tuning system performance, which is beyond the scope of this document. See the reading list in for more.

I/O Resources

While I/O limitations are a major cause of stress for system admins, the Linux system offers rather poor utilities to measure I/O performance. The ps, vmstat and top tools give some indication about how many programs are waiting for I/O; netstatdisplays network interface statistics, but there are virtually no tools available to measure the I/O response to system load, and the iostat command gives a brief overview of general I/O usage. Various graphical front-ends exist to put the output of these commands in a humanly understandable form.

Each device has its own problems, but the bandwidth available to network interfaces and the bandwidth available to disks are the two primary causes of bottlenecks in I/O performance.

Network I/O Problems

The amount of data transported over the network is larger than the network's capacity, resulting in slow execution of every network related task for all users. They can be solved by cleaning up the network (which mainly involves disabling protocols and services that you don't need) or by reconfiguring the network (for example use of subnets, replacing hubs with switches, upgrading interfaces and equipment).

Network Integrity Problems

Occurs when data is transferred incorrectly. Solving this kind of problem can only be done by isolating the faulty element and replacing it.

Disk I/O Problems

- *Per-Process Transfer Rate too Low:*
  - Read or write speed for a single process is not sufficient.
- *Aggregate Transfer Rate too Low:*
  - The maximum total bandwidth that the system can provide to all programs that run is not enough.

This kind of problem is more difficult to detect, and usually takes extra hardware in order to re-divide data streams over buses, controlers and disks, if overloaded hardware is cause of the problem. One solution to solve this is a RAID array configuration optimized for input and output actions. This way, you get to keep the same hardware. An upgrade to faster buses, controlers and disks is usually the other option.

If overload is not the cause, maybe your hardware is gradually failing, or not well connected to the system. Check contacts, connectors and plugs to start with.

Users

Users can be divided in several classes, depending on their behaviour with resource usage:

- *Users who Run a (large) Number of Small Jobs:* you, the beginning Linux user, for instance.
- *Users who run Relatively few but Large Jobs:* users running simulations, calculations, emulators or other programs that eat a lot of memory, and usually these users have accompanying large data files.
- Users who run few jobs but use a lot of CPU time (developers and the like).

You can see that system requirements may vary for each class of users, and that it can be hard to satisfy everyone. If you are on a multi-user system, it is useful (and fun) to find out habits of other users and the system, in order to get the most out of it for your specific purposes.

Interrupting Your Processes

As a non-privileged user, you can only influence your own processes. We already saw how you can display processes and filter out processes that belong to a particular user, and what possible restrictions can occur. When you see that one of your processes is eating too much of the system's resources,

There are two things that you can do:

1. Make the process use less resources without interrupting it;
2. Stop the process altogether.

In the case that you want the process to continue to run, but you also want to give the other processes on the system a chance, you can renice the process. Appart from using the nice or renice commands, top is an easy way of spotting the troublesome process(es) and reducing priority.

Identify the process in the "NI" column, it will most likely have a negative priority. Type r and enter the process ID of the process that you want to renice. Then enter the nice value, for instance "20". That means that from now on, this process will take 1/5 of the CPU cycles at the most.

Examples of processes that you want to keep on running are emulators, virtual machines, compilers and so on. If you want to stop a process because it hangs or is going totally berserk in the way of I/O consumption, file creation or use of other system resources, use the kill. If you have the opportunity, first try to kill the process softly, sending it the *SIGTERM*signal.

This is an instruction to terminate whatever it is doing, according to procedures as described in the code of the program:

```
joe:~> ps -ef | grep mozilla
joe 258221 0 Mar11 ?00:34:04/usr/lib/mozilla-
1.4.1/mozilla-
joe:~> kill -15 25822
```

In the example above, user *joe* stopped his Mozilla browser because it hung.

Some processes are a little bit harder to get rid of. If you have the time, you might want to send them the SIGINT signal to interrupt them. If that does not do the trick either, use the strongest signal, SIGKILL.

In the example below, joe stops a Mozilla that is frozen:

```
joe:~> ps -ef | grep mozilla
joe 259151 0 Mar11 ?00:15:06/usr/lib/mozilla-
1.4.1/mozilla-
joe:~> kill -9 25915
joe:~> ps -ef | grep 25915
joe2634 32273 0 18:09 pts/4 00:00:00 grep 25915
```

In such cases, you might want to check that the process is really dead, using the grep filter again on the PID. If this only returns the grep process, you can be sure that you succeeded in stopping the process.

Among processes that are hard to kill is your shell. And that is a good thing: if they would be easy to kill, you woud loose your shell every time you type Ctrl-C on the command line accidentally, since this is equivalent to sending a SIGINT.

UNIX without pipes is almost unthinkable. The usage of pipes (|) for using output of one command as input of another is explained in the next chapter. In a graphical environment, the xkill program is very easy to use. Just type the name of the command, followed by an Enterand select the window of the application that you want to stop. It is rather dangerous because it sends a SIGKILL by default, so only use it when an application hangs.

SCHEDULING PROCESSES

USE THAT IDLE TIME

A Linux system can have a lot to suffer from, but it usually suffers only during office hours. Whether in an office environment, a server room or at home, most Linux systems are just idling away during the morning, the evening, the nights and weekends.

Using this idle time can be a lot cheaper than buying those machines you'd absolutely need if you want everything done at the same time.

There are three types of delayed execution:

- Waiting a little while and then resuming job execution, using the sleep command. Execution time depends on the system time at the moment of submission.
- Running a command at a specified time, using the at command. Execution of the job(s) depends on system time, not the time of submission.
- Regularly running a command on a monthly, weekly, daily or hourly basis, using the cron facilities.

The following sections discuss each possibility.

THE SLEEP COMMAND

The Info page on sleep is probably one of the shortest there is. All sleep does is wait. By default the time to wait is expressed in seconds.

So why does it exist? Some practical examples:

- Somebody calls you on the phone, you say "Yes I'll be with you in half an hour" but you're about drowned in work as it is and bound to forget your lunch:

  `(sleep 1800; echo "Lunch time..") &`

- When you can't use the at command for some reason, it's five o'clock, you want to go home but there's still work to do and right now somebody is eating system resources:

  `(sleep 10000; myprogram) &`

- Make sure there's an auto-logout on your system, and that you log out or lock your desktop/office when submitting this kind of job, or run it in a screen session.
- When you run a series of printouts of large files, but you want other users to be able to print in between:

  `lp lotoftext; sleep 900; lp hugefile; sleep 900; lp anotherlargefile`

- Programmers often use the sleep command to halt script or program execution for a certain time.

THE AT COMMAND

The at command executes commands at a given time, using your default shell unless you tell the command otherwise. The options to at are rather user-friendly, which is demonstrated in the examples below:

```
steven@home:~> at tomorrow + 2 days
warning: commands will be executed using (in order)
a) $SHELL
  b) login shell c)/bin/sh
at> cat reports | mail myboss@mycompany
at> <EOT>
job 1 at 2001-06-16 12:36
Typing Ctrl+D quits the at utility and generates
the "EOT" message.
```

```
User steven does a strange thing here combining
two commands; we will study this sort of practice
in, Redirecting Input and Output.
steven@home:~> at 0237
warning: commands will be executed using (in order)
a) $SHELL
   b) login shell c)/bin/sh
at> cd new-programs
at>./configure; make
at> <EOT>
job 2 at 2001-06-14 02:00
```

The -m option sends mail to the user when the job is done, or explains when a job can't be done. The command atq lists jobs; perform this command before submitting jobs in order prevent them from starting at the same time as others. With the atrmcommand you can remove scheduled jobs if you change your mind.

It is a good idea to pick strange execution times, because system jobs are often run at "round" hours, as you can the next section. For example, jobs are often run at exactly 1 o'clock in the morning (*e.g.* system indexing to update a standard locate database), so entering a time of 0100 may easily slow your system down rather than fire it up. To prevent jobs from running all at the same time, you may also use the batch command, which queues processes and feeds the work in the queue to the system in an evenly balanced way, preventing excessive bursts of system resource usage. See the Info pages for more information.

CRON AND CRONTAB

The cron system is managed by the cron daemon. It gets information about which programs and when they should run from the system's and users' crontab entries. Only the root user has access to the system crontabs, while each user should only have access to his own crontabs. On some systems (some) users may not have access to the cron facility.

At system startup the cron daemon searches/var/spool/ cron/for crontab entries which are named after accounts in/

etc/passwd, it searches/etc/cron.d/and it searches/etc/crontab, then uses this information every minute to check if there is something to be done. It executes commands as the user who owns the crontab file and mails any output of commands to the owner.

On systems using Vixie cron, jobs that occur hourly, daily, weekly and monthly are kept in separate directories in/etc to keep an overview, as opposed to the standard UNIX cron function, where all tasks are entered into one big file.

Example of a Vixie crontab file:

```
[root@blob/etc]# more crontab
SHELL=/bin/bash
PATH=/sbin:/bin:/usr/sbin:/usr/bin
MAILTO=root
HOME=/
# run-parts
# commands to execute every hour
01 * * * * root run-parts/etc/cron.hourly
# commands to execute every day
02 4 * * * root run-parts/etc/cron.daily
# commands to execute every week
22 4 * * 0 root run-parts/etc/cron.weekly
commands to execute every month 42 4 1 * * root
run-parts/etc/cron.monthly
```

Some variables are set, and after that there's the actual scheduling, one line per job, starting with 5 time and date fields. The first field contains the minutes (from 0 to 59), the second defines the hour of execution (0-23), the third is day of the month (1-31), then the number of the month (1-12), the last is day of the week (0-7, both 0 and 7 are Sunday). An asterisk in these fields represents the total acceptable range for the field. Lists are allowed; to execute a job from Monday to Friday enter 1-5 in the last field, to execute a job on Monday, Wednesday and Friday enter 1,3,5.

Then comes the user who should run the processes which are listed in the last column. The example above is from a Vixie cron configuration where root runs the program run-parts on regular intervals, with the appropriate directories as options.

In these directories, the actual jobs to be executed at the scheduled time are stored as shell scripts, like this little script that is run daily to update the database used by the locate command:

```
billy@ahost cron.daily]$ cat slocate.cron
#!/bin/sh
renice +19 -p $$ >/dev/null 2>&1
/usr/bin/updatedb -f "nfs,smbfs,ncpfs,proc,devpts"
-e \
"/tmp,/var/tmp,/usr/tmp,/afs,/net"
```

Users are supposed to edit their crontabs in a safe way using the crontab -e command. This will prevent a user from accidentally opening more than one copy of his/her crontab file. The default editor is vi, but you can use any text editor, such as gvim or gedit if you feel more comfortable with a GUI editor. When you quit, the system will tell you that a new crontab is installed.

This crontab entry reminds billy to go to his sports club every Thursday night:

```
billy:~> crontab -l
# DO NOT EDIT THIS FILE-edit the master and
reinstall.
# (/tmp/crontab.20264 installed on Sun Jul 20
22:35:14 2003)
# (Cron version—$Id: chap4.xml,v 1.16 2004/07/09
05:34:22 tille Exp $)
38 16 * * 3 mail -s "sports evening" billy
```

After adding a new scheduled task, the system will tell you that a new crontab is installed. You do not need to restart the cronddaemon for the changes to take effect.

In the example, billy added a new line pointing to a backup script:

```
billy:~> crontab -e
45 15 * * 3 mail -s "sports evening" billy
4 4 * * 4,7/home/billy/bin/backup.sh
<—write and quit—>
crontab: installing new crontab
billy:~>
```

The backup.sh script is executed every Thursday and Sunday. for an introduction to shell scripting. Keep in mind that output of commands, if any, is mailed to the owner of the crontab file. If no mail service is configured, you might find the output of your commands in your local mailbox,/var/spool/mail/<your_username>, a plain text file. Who runs my commands? You don't have to specify the user who should run the commands. They are executed with the user's own permissions by default.

EXERCISES

These are some exercises that will help you get the feel for processes running on your system.

General

- Run top in one terminal while you do the exercises in another.
- Run the ps command.
- Read the man pages to find out how to display all your processes.
- Run the command find/. What effect does it have on system load? Stop this command.
- In graphical mode, start the xclock program in the foreground. Then let it run in the background. Stop the program using the kill command.
- What does kill -9 -1 do?
- Open two terminals or terminal windows again and use write to send a message from one to the other.
- Issue the dmesg command. What does it tell?
- How long does it take to execute ls in the current directory?
- Based on process entries in/proc, owned by your UID, how would you work to find out which processes these actually represent?
- How long has your system been running?
- Which is your current TTY?
- Name 3 processes that couldn't have had init as an initial parent.

- Name 3 commands which use SUID mode. Explain why this is so.
- Name the commands that are generally causing the highest load on your system.

Booting, Init etc

- Can you reboot the system as a normal user? Why is that?
- According to your current runlevel, name the steps that are taken during shutdown.
- How do you change the system runlevel? Switch from 3 to 5 and vice versa.
- Which kernel is currently load at startup?
- Suppose you have to start some exotic server at boot time. Up until now, you logged in after booting the system and started this server manually using a script named deliver_pizza in your home directory. What do you have to do in order to have the service start up automatically in run level 4, which you defined for this purpose only?

Scheduling

- Use sleep to create a reminder that your pasta is ready in ten minutes.
- Create an at job that copies all files in your home directory to/var/tmp within half an hour. You may want to create a sub-directory in/var/tmp.
- Make a cronjob that does this task every Monday to Friday during lunch.
- Check that it works.
- Make a mistake in the crontab entry, like issuing the nonexistent command coppy instead of cp. What happens upon execution of the task?

3

Introduction to Clusters

INTRODUCTION TO CLUSTER

"Cluster" is an ambiguous term in computer industry. Depending on the vendor and specific contexts, a cluster may refer to wide a variety of environments. In general a cluster refers to a set of computer systems connected together. For the purposes of this book a *cluster* is set of computers which are connected to each other, and are physically located close to each other, in order to solve problems more efficiently. These types of clusters are also referred to as High Performance Computing (HPC) clusters, or simply Compute clusters.

Another popular usage of the term *cluster* is to describe High Availability environments. In this environment a computer system acts as the *backup* system to one or more *primary* systems. When there is a failure in a primary system, the critical applications running on that system are *failed over* to its designated backup system. Detailed usage and technology behind these types of clusters is outside the scope of this book. Nevertheless, we will touch upon specific usage of high availability technology within the context of compute clusters.

Clusters are becoming increasingly popular as computational resources both in research and commercial organizations. These organizations are favouring clusters over single large servers (Wė will be referring to the set of processing elements within the boundaries of single instantiation of an operating system as comprising a *single server* or a *shared-memory* system) for a wide variety of problems. The increasing popularity of the Linux operating system is adding fuel to this fire. Linux provides a very cost effective and open environment to build a cluster. Since its conception in the early nineties, Linux has been very popular with researchers. The open-source code of Linux allows researchers to customise the system to best suit their specific problems, and to do advanced computing research without getting tied to any specific system vendor. Starting in 1999 many system vendors started offering full production-level support on Linux platforms. This took Linux systems, and their clusters, out of the realm of *early adopters* into mainstream usage. In this chapter we will begin by delineating various approaches to building parallel computing environments and compare and contrast them with clusters. We will go over benefits of deploying clusters as well as expose their downsides. We will then discuss two broad categories of compute clusters and their usage to solve problems from various fields. We will end the chapter by giving a high level description of the architecture of a cluster and introduce terminology to be used throughout the book.

APPROACHES IN BUILDING A PARALLEL COMPUTING ENVIRONMENT

Before discussing clusters in detail, let us examine different ways of putting various computational resources together to solve problems. As explained in a subsection below, the boundaries between various types of parallel systems have been blurred significantly, both because of new technologies as well as vendor marketing efforts. The simplified taxonomy in next sections will help us discuss various trade-offs between different technologies.

SINGLE OPERATING SYSTEM IMAGE

This class of systems have multiple CPUs within the boundary of a single operating system (OS) image. Design emphasis is put on scaling the OS to increasing number of CPUs, and providing an environment which allows a single application instance to scale on multiple CPUs. Symmetric multiprocessor (SMP) machines and implementations of Non-Uniform Memory Access (NUMA) systems in the late nineties belong to this category. All CPUs within the system can directly access the physical memory as well as any peripherals installed in the system.

MASSIVELY PARALLEL PROCESSORS

Designers of Massively Parallel Processor (MPP) systems put emphasis on the scalability of the hardware. MPP systems have been designed to go up to hundreds, in some cases thousands, of processors. Processing elements (sometimes referred to as nodes) are connected together using a proprietary interconnect. Each node runs its own copy of the OS kernel (or microkernel).

Programmers view an MPP as having distributed memory. A processor cannot directly access the physical memory located in a remote node. The programmer or the compiler has to instruct the machine to transfer data from one node to another node on need basis. Faster and well controlled interconnects in MPPs have led to some attempts in providing a shared memory look-alike programming model on these machines. However, these attempts suffer from scalability and availability concerns.

NETWORK OF WORKSTATIONS (NOWS)

In many organizations, especially those with some engineering design intent, individual users have powerful workstations on their desks. These workstations usually sit idle during off-work hours. Various innovative technologies make it possible to harness these idle cycles, hence providing an optimal use of the computing infrastructure.

In most environments these workstations are simply connected to the building local area network (LAN) and don't have a special high speed interconnect between them. A distributed resource manager controls the jobs submitted by users, and attempts to execute them on idle workstation(s). The Condor system developed at University of Wisconsin is an example of one such resource manager.

CLUSTERS

Given the ambiguity in the usage of terminology and blurred boundaries between various technologies, we will stick to the definition of clusters given by Pfister:

A cluster is a type of parallel or distributed system that:

- Consists of a collection of interconnected whole computers
- And is used as single, unified computing resource.

The "whole computer" in above definition can have one or more processors built into a single operating system image.

Clusters vs. NOWs

The key differences between a cluster and a NOW are:

- All of the compute nodes in a cluster are dedicated only for cluster usage. Whereas, individual workstation in NOWs may or may not be participating in the parallel computing environment, depending on whether that workstation is idle at that time or not. Thus on a cluster a parallel algorithm can assume certain amout of computational resources in a node to be available for its exclusive use, but on a NOW the parallel algorithm needs to take into account possible significant changes in available resources on a participating workstation.
- A cluster has a dedicated interconnect fabric connecting its compute nodes. This interconnect fabric can be highly optimized to work best for the needs of parallel applications being run on the cluster. A NOW typically uses the building LAN network for the communication requirements of parallel algorithms running on its workstations. Since the building LAN is used for a very broad set of applications for various users, it cannot be optimized just for the use within a NOW.
- A workstation participating in a NOW is optimized for interactive usage of the workstation user. A cluster nodes, on the other hand, can be fully optimized for the parallel algorithms being run on them.

- A cluster is managed as a single entity located in a single computer center. A NOW consists of entities managed by multiple personnel, often by individual workstation owners.

Clusters vs. MPPs

The key differences between a cluster and an MPP system are:

- In a cluster various components or layers can change relatively independently of each other, whereas components in MPP systems are much more tightly integrated. For example, a cluster administrator can choose to upgrade the interconnect, say from fast ethernet to gigabit ethernet, just by adding new network interface cards (NICs) and switches to the cluster. On the other hand, in most cases the administrator for an MPP system cannot do such upgrades without upgrading the whole machine.
  A cluster decouples the development of system software from innovations in underlying hardware. Cluster management tools and parallel programming libraries can be optimized independent of the changes in the node hardware itself. This results in more mature and reliable cluster middleware software as compared to the system software layer in an MPP class system, which requires at least a major rewrite with each generation of the system hardware.
- An MPP usually has a single system serial number used for software licensing and support tracking. Clusters and NOW have multiple serial numbers, one for each of their constituent nodes.

BEOWULF AND ITS PHILOSOPHY

Beowulf is a popular term to describe Linux compute clusters. The term originated as the name of a project at NASA Goddard, which resulted in creation of a cluster system comprising of 16 nodes in 1994. From that time on Beowulf has evolved into a broader term, describing a genre of high performance computer systems with a very enthusiastic (and vocal!) community of supporters.

What exactly constitues a Beowulf is a subject of debate. Some people characterize any Linux compute cluster as being a Beowulf. Other folks deem the exclusive use of commodity hardware, open-source software and open & standard protocols as key for a system to be called Beowulf. According to the latter view the Beowulf philosophy is to not get tied to any particular vendor for any component of the system. The extreme form of this view supports building even the individual cluster nodes themselves from pieces parts by separately buying motherboards, CPUs, memory chips etc.

The authors of this book very much subscribe to the Beowulf philosopy, and support using commodity off-the-shelf components whenever appropriate. But we also believe that many organizations will benefit significantly by deploying advanced technologies, which are not commodity yet, in their Linux clusters. Some organizations will also find it more cost effective to deploy vendor integrated nodes, even integrated clusters, instead of building their own expertise to do so.

BLURRING BOUNDARIES

Many developments have blurred the boundaries between above mentioned types of systems. Their distinction, or lack thereof, is sometimes the subject of heated debates.

This is a brief list of developments indicating the foray of one type of architecture into another architecture's domain:

- As vendors building NUMA based systems design their hardware to scale to the levels earlier only available in MPP domain, they hit operating system or application scalability issues. Therefore these vendors have to provide distributed memory style programming models on their systems.
- Fast cluster interconnects are coming close and even exceeding the performance of some of the proprietary interconnects used in MPP systems
- Various vendors are beginning to provide pre-packaged clusters with fast interconnects and cluster

wide management tools, thus creating almost an MPP like experience for users and administrators.

WHY A CLUSTER

The two key reasons for using clusters instead of a large system are price/performance and scalability. As system size becomes larger, the size of its installed base decreases quite rapidly. Thus the cost of producing technology to scale the system to higher number of processors is amortized to a relatively fewer number of systems. Hence single systems reach a point of diminishing returns beyond which it is not cost-effective to scale them except for a limited set of special applications.

Some benefits of clusters include:

Lower Cost

In general smaller sized systems benefit the most from commoditization of technology. Both hardware and software acquisition costs tend to be significantly lower for smaller systems. However you should consider the total cost of ownership of your computing environment while making a purchase decision. Next subsection points to some factors which may offset some of the advantages of initial cost of acquisition of a cluster.

Scalability

In many environments the problem workload is so large that it simply cannot be processed on a single system within the time constraints of the organization. Clusters also provide an easier path for increasing the computational resources as the workload increases over time. Most large systems scale to a certain number of processors and require a costly fork-lift upgrade.

Vendor Independence

Although it is generally advisable to use similar components across various servers in a cluster, it is good to maintain a certain degree of vendor independence, especially if the cluster is being deployed for long term usage. A Linux cluster based on mostly commodity hardware allows for much greater vendor independence than a large multi-processor system running a proprietary operating system.

AdaptAbility

It is much more easier to adapt the topology, *i.e.* pattern of connecting the compute nodes together, of a cluster to best suit the application requirements of a computer center. Vendors typically support very restricted topologies of MPPs because of design, or sometimes testing, issues.

Reliability, Availability and Serviceability (RAS)

A larger system is typically more susceptible to failure than a smaller system. A major hardware or software component failure brings the whole system down. Hence if a large single system is deployed as the computational resource, a component failure will bring down significant computing power. In case of a cluster, a single component failure only affects a small proportion of the overall computational resources.

A system in the cluster can be serviced without bringing rest of the cluster down. Also, additional computational resources can be added to a cluster while it is running the user workload. Hence a cluster maintains continuity of user operations in both of these cases. In similar situations a SMP system will require a complete shutdown and a restart.

Faster Technology Innovation

Clusters benefit from thousands of researchers around the world, who typically work on smaller systems rather than expensive high end systems.

DOWNSIDES OF CLUSTERS

It is important to mention some disadvantages of using clusters as opposed to a single large system. These should be closely considered while deciding an optimal computational resource for an organization. System administrators and programmers of the organization should actively take part in evaluating the following trade-offs.

A cluster increases the number of individual components in a computer center. Every server in a cluster has its own independent power supplies, network ports etc. The increased number of components and cables going across servers in a cluster partially offsets some of the RAS advantages mentioned above. It is easier to manage a single system as opposed to multiple servers in a cluster.

There are a lot more system utilities available to manage computing resources within a single system than those which can help manage a cluster. As clusters increasingly find their way into commercial organizations, more cluster savvy tools will become available over time, which will bridge some of this gap.

In order for a cluster to scale to make effective use of multiple CPUs, the workload needs to be properly balanced on the cluster. Workload imbalance is easier to handle in a shared memory environment, because switching tasks across processors doesn't require too much data movement. On the other hand, on a cluster it tends to be very hard to move an already running task from one node to another. If the environment is such that workload balance cannot be controlled, a cluster may not provide good parallel efficiency.

Programming paradigms used on a cluster are usually different from those used on shared-memory systems. It is relatively easier to use parallelism in a shared-memory system, since the shared data is readily available. On a cluster, as in an MPP system, either the programmer or the compiler has to explicitly transport data from one node to another. Before deploying a cluster as a key resource in your environment, you should make sure that your system administrators and programmers are comfortable in working in a cluster environment.

CLUSTER TYPES

There are two broad categories of compute clusters based on the computational resource usage characteristics of problem(s) being solved them: Throughput clusters and Capability clusters.

THROUGHPUT CLUSTERS

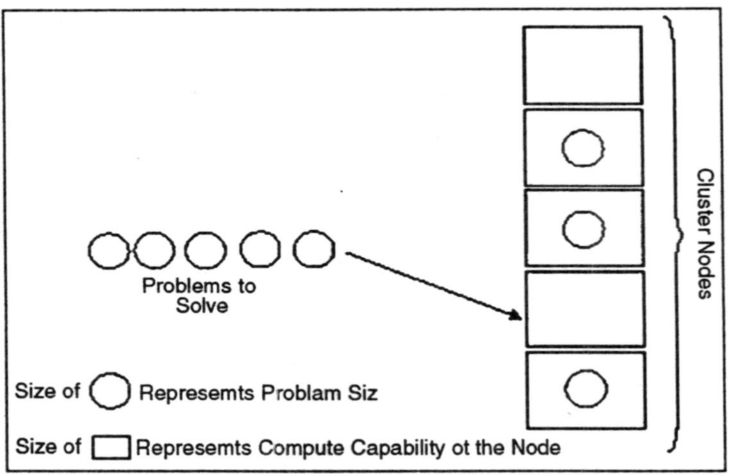

Fig: Throughput Cluster

A throughput cluster is deployed to solve a lot of relatively small problems. A single compute node is capable of providing sufficient computational resources to solve any of these problems. These could be independent applications (We will be referring to the program developed by a software developer to solve a problem as an *application,* and a particular instantiation of the application will be referred to as a *job.* A job may be composed of one or more *processes/threads.*) or multiple instantiations of the same application.

A cluster is deployed to optimally spread these problems on multiple compute nodes so that the overall workload can be executed on in parallel (see fig 1.1). A load balancing tool is used to optimally allocate compute nodes to address the needs of the users.

CAPABILITY CLUSTERS

A capability cluster is deployed when a problem cannot be cost-effectively solved using a single server. As mentioned earlier, a set of small servers is significantly cheaper than a single system with same number of aggregate CPUs. So, a cluster is more cost-effective to deploy if it can execute the application at a comparable level of performance of a similar sized single system. In some extreme cases the resource requirements of a problem could be so large that a single system image cannot effectively scale to meet the demand.

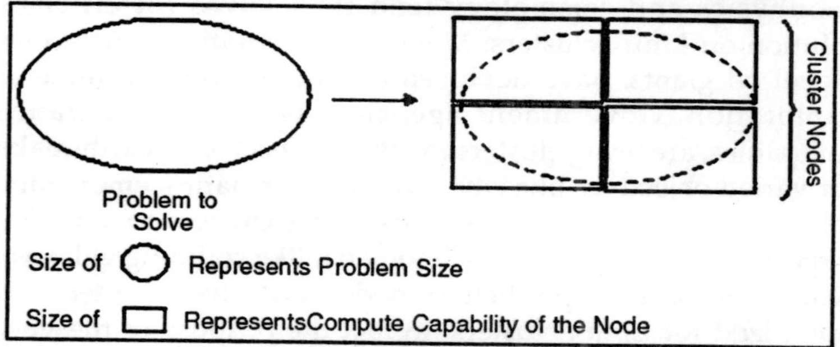

Fig: Capability Cluster

Multiple nodes, in a capability cluster, coordinate with each other to solve the problem concurrently (see fig 1.2). A parallel programming technique is used to spread the load of a problem across compute nodes.

PROBLEMS BEING SOLVED ON LINUX CLUSTERS

Scientists and engineers have been the predominant users of Linux clusters. These users range from an aerospace engineer simulating a trajectory to a financial engineer performing economic scenario analysis. New applications are getting ported to Linux clusters every day. Clusters are now finding aggressive acceptance into data mining applications, where a lot of largely independent data, *e.g.* clicks on a website, needs to be crunched for finding interesting and useful patterns.

Clusters are sometimes used as development or intermediary tools to assist specialized supercomputers. In many environments parallel programs are designed and tested on clusters and then deployed on, *e.g.*, an MPP machine. Linux clusters are very popular in universities and research labs for teaching and experimenting with parallel and distributed computing technologies. In next sections we provide some examples of clusters usage in specific areas and point out reasons for their preference.

EARTH AND SPACE SCIENCE

Many of the computing problems in the areas of geophysics and seismology lend themselves for efficient solution on Linux clusters. Many big corporations, including global oil giants, have deployed clusters for oil and mineral exploration. Government agencies, as well as insurance companies, are using clusters to model effects of an earthquake for varied objectives like city planning, evaluating emergency readiness, etc. Astrophysicists are using clusters to simulate large and complex cosmic phenomena, like colliding galaxies. Numerical weather prediction models have been ported and optimized for Linux clusters. In fact the purpose of the very first Beowulf system built at NASA Goddard was to operate on the large data sets typically associated with applications in earth and space sciences.

Space, earth's core and its surface can be divided into smaller chunks and for some of these problems each chunk can be processed independent of the other. For example, an oil exploration project can divide the sea-floor into various areas. Nodes in a throughput cluster can then process the seismic data from these areas in parallel.

BIOINFORMATICS AND CHEMISTRY

Linux clusters are widely used in established and emerging areas in the fields of bioinformatics and computational chemistry. Scientists can use numerical simulation of electronic structures of molecules to predict various chemical phenomena, without actual laboratory experimentation. This simulation can be highly computationally intensive, and benefits significantly from scalability of a cluster. Another exciting usage of Linux clusters is in the areas of gene sequencing and protein modeling. Applications in these clusters are used for such crucial areas as understanding diseases, designing drugs and improving agricultural output.

Many popular computational chemistry applications have been ported and tuned for Linux clusters. Examples include Gaussian[], GAMESS[], CHARMM[] etc. A typical computational chemistry environment has a mix of both sequential jobs (requiring a throughput cluster) and parallel jobs (requiring a capability cluster). Therefore the deployed clusters are hybrid in nature, providing tools for both throughput and capability requirements.

Clusters deployed in bioinformatics applications require not only the scalability of their number crunching capabilities, but also the scalability of their data storage and retrieval. For example, a system meant for sequencing of genomes requires access to a large amount of pre-existing sequence knowledge along with the capability of adding numerous new entries. Special databases have been designed to serve the purposes of such clusters.

RENDERING

Rendering refers to the process of transforming software scene descriptions into coloured pixels. Rendering a sequence of frames to create an animation is one of the so called embarrassingly parallel applications. A cluster meant for rendering a set of frames is referred to as a Render farm.

A render farm is a throughput cluster, with each node capable of running a rendering algorithm. Even a small animation contains thousands of frames, and a single frame may take hours to get rendered. A render farm renders an animation in parallel, hence cutting down on production time. A Linux cluster was used to render the visual effects in the movie Titanic.

Artists submit the scenes of a film to a control server. The control server monitors the various nodes in the cluster to see availability of idle computing resources. It then submits the frame to an available CPU. The computing node renders the frame and sends it to a storage server (which may or may not be the same as the control server). The storage server makes sure that the frames are kept in the correct order as desired by the artists.

An advanced technique for exploiting the parallelism of rendering is to break a single frame into multiple segments, and spread these segments onto different nodes of the cluster. These nodes then send the rendered segments back to a master server. The master server usually has to do some post-processing on the frame after assembling all the segments. This technique is useful when fast rendering of an individual frame is desired.

CLUSTER OVERVIEW AND TERMINOLOGY

A compute cluster consists of a lot of different hardware and software components with complex interactions between various components. In we show a simplified abstraction of the key layers that form a cluster. Following sections give a brief overview of these layers.

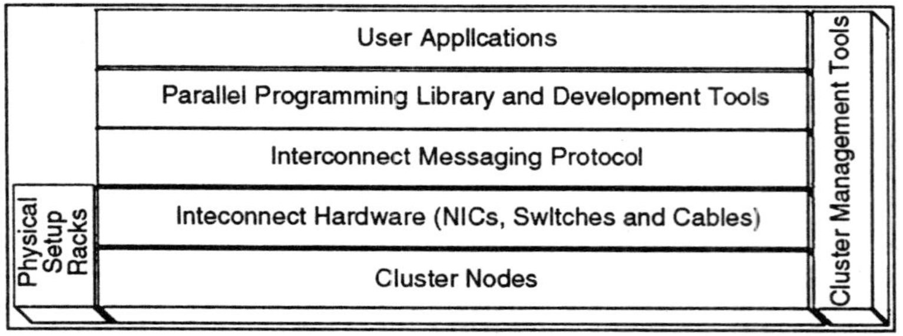

Fig: Layers in a Typical Cluster

CLUSTER NODES AND INTERCONNECT HARDWARE

A cluster consists of a set of *cluster nodes,* or simply *nodes.* A node can be a server, which is dedicated to the cluster, or it can be a workstation (Note that in our definition of a cluster, a workstation cannot be a compute node) participating in cluster activities on a need basis. In this section we will introduce various types of nodes in a cluster. Some of these nodes are optional and in some configurations one computer system may have the functionality of more than one type of node.

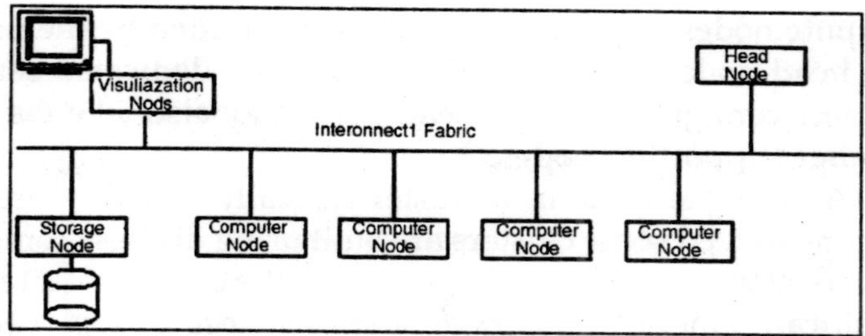

Fig: Hardware Architecture of a Typical Cluster

A typical compute cluster (see fig 1.4) consists of a set of nodes designated as *compute nodes,* and other nodes which provide various support functions for the compute nodes. These supporting nodes include head nodes, management nodes, storage nodes and visualization nodes. The compute nodes form the core of a cluster. Compute nodes are dedicated servers which constitute the processing power of the cluster. Compute nodes are connected using a dedicated *interconnect fabric.* This fabric is used for communicating data and control messages between the compute nodes. Some environments may require multiple interconnects to be used within a single cluster, *E.g.,* an interconnect for fast data messages (usually connecting only the compute nodes), and another for slower control messages.

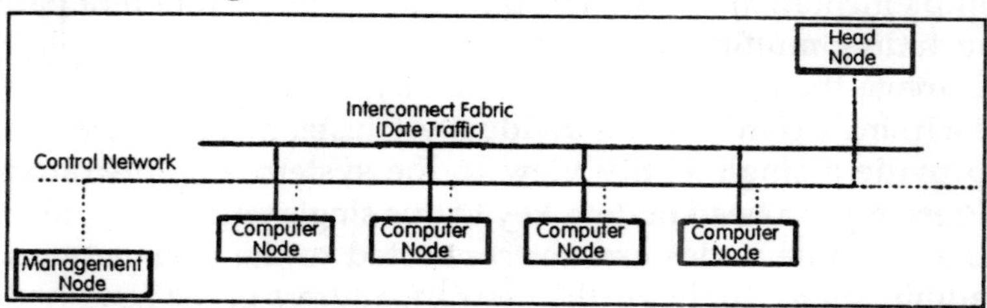

Fig: A Cluster with two Interconnect Fabrics

Compute nodes do not directly connect to the user network, instead a *head node* of the cluster is connected to the user network. The head node provides the interface of the cluster to the outside world. The users only communicate with the head node for solving their problems, or to check the status of their problem. The head node in turn coordinates the compute nodes to solve the problems submitted by the users. The head node in most configurations is a dedicated server. In some configurations the head node may also take the role of other supporting nodes.

A compute node in a cluster typically has very limited storage. Indeed some clusters are built using diskless compute servers. If the applications being run on the cluster require any significant amount of storage, a *storage node* is deployed. A storage node is a dedicated server and has the capability of storing and serving data for rest of the cluster nodes.

Many applications being deployed on a cluster may have a visualization component to them. This could be either real time visualization where the processed data gets visualized concurrently while the computation is going on, or based on post-processing where the processed data gets collected on a storage node and is visualized later on need basis. In both of these cases, a *visualization node* is deployed to provide the required capability of viewing the data. The visualization node is a workstation with good graphics capabilities.

CLUSTER MANAGEMENT TOOLS

Intuitive and effective management of a cluster tends to be of great importance in the overall success of a cluster implementation. Since a cluster is sum of many different parts including multiple computer systems, it is vital to be able to manage the cluster as a single entity, rather than managing each single component individually. Cluster management tools provide a single entity view to the system administrators. Presence of a head node is key to this single entity view. Since the compute nodes are not connected to the user network, administrators only see the network address of the head node as the address of the cluster. All the compute nodes are hidden behind the head node. Hence, administrators don't need any reconfiguration of the public network whenever a change is made to the topology of compute nodes. Access and security of the cluster is also controlled solely through the head node.

Most clusters have a dedicated management node, which has the capability of providing critical control of other nodes of the cluster (see fig 1.6). These controls include ability to get to the system console, ability to monitor the software and hardware of other nodes and ability to power-cycle any node on need basis. A management node is typically a workstation with a serial multiplexer device attached to it. This serial device enables the management node to communicate with rest of the nodes in the cluster even if the building network is down.

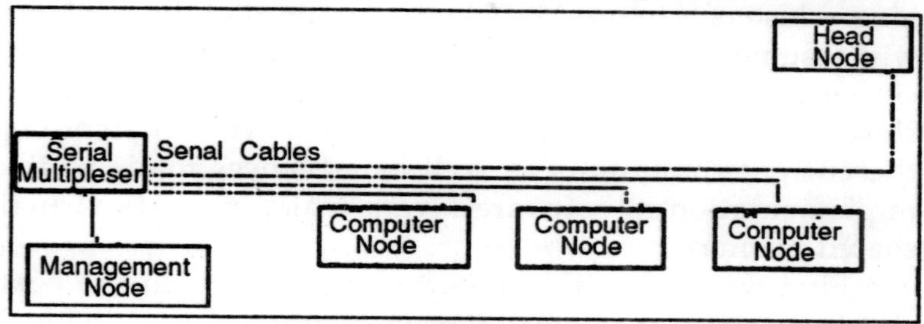

Fig: Management Node

DISTRIBUTED MESSAGING AND PROGRAMMING ENVIRONMENT

A capability cluster relies on ability of programmers to create distributed applications and ability of these applications to efficiently run on the cluster. There are many different parallel programming techniques deployed by programmers for their development purposes. If a cluster has compute nodes with more than one processor, the application developer must consider two levels of parallelism: Parallelism within a node (intra-node parallelism) and parallelism across nodes (inter-node parallelism). Intra-node parallelism uses the shared memory within a node, hence does not require explicit movement of data. Inter-node parallelism, on the other hand, requires data to be shipped across the interconnect fabric.

There are three ways of implementing inter-node message traffic:

- By making ad hoc use of a lower level communication protocol, *e.g.* by using sockets interface
- By using a portable distributed communication library, *e.g.* Message Passing Interface (MPI) library

- By deploying a software layer which hides the interconnect from the programmer, essentially providing a virtual shared memory environment.

While the first approach can provide opportunities of very low level tuning, the code thus generated is very hard to maintain, and is not easily portable to different platforms. Currently the most popular mechanism of programming on Linux clusters is to use MPI library. For most of this book we will assume MPI based programming model for capability clusters. The concepts discussed will in general apply to other cluster programming approaches as well. We will point out the current limitations as well as advances made in the implementation of software layers which provide virtual shared memory.

First we start with the bottommost layer. In the next chapter we explore in detail the key features of an individual cluster node and discuss the trade-offs between various choices.

CLUSTER NODES

OVERVIEW

This chapter contains an expansion of the definitions presented in the first chapter, and lays groundwork for the following sections.

Processor and Memory Choices

This section contains an overview of the different processors that are available for use in a beowulf cluster. This section contains a brief overview of x86 compatible and other than x86 CPUs. A more in depth analysis of IA-32 CPUs by Intel and AMD and IA-64 are also presented. Low level processor, and memory subsystem performance are discussed briefly. An overview of memory architecture is also presented.

COMMON PROCESSOR ARCHITECTURES

Intel 32 bit Processors

The IA-32 is sometimes generically called x86 or even x86-

32. The term means Intel Architecture, 32 bit which distinguishes it from the 16 bit versions that preceded it and the 64 bit version referred to as IA-64 that followed it. Within various programming language directives it is also referred to as *i386*; this directive would inform the compiler to generate code only for the IA-32 instruction set. This instruction set was introduced in the *Intel 80386* microprocessor in 1985. Even though the basic instruction set has remained intact the successive generation of microprocessors that run it have become much faster at running it.

The biggest supplier and inventor of this class of processors is Intel. However it is not the only supplier of this family of processors. The second biggest supplier is AMD and there are also numerous even smaller specialized supplier of these processors. The following sections will briefly describe the various features of the IA-32 family of processors.

MODES OF OPERATIONS

The IA-32 supports three basic operating modes refered to as the *Real Mode*, the *Protected Mode* and the *Syetm Management mode*. The operating mode determines which instructions and architectural features are accessible to the processor. For example in the Real Mode the processor is limited to accessing just 1Mb of memory, while in the Protected Mode it can access all its memory.

REAL MODE

Once the machine is booted the processor initiates itself into the Real Mode and then starts loading programs automatically into RAM from ROM and disk.A program inserted somewhere along the boot sequence maybe used to put the processor into the Protected Mode.

PROTECTED MODE

This mode is the native state of the processor. In this mode all instructions and architectural features are available providing the highest performance and capability. Besides having the additional memory addressability ability various other advantageous features get activated as well. One of them is the *protected memory* which prevents programs from corrupting each other. another one is the *virtual memory,* which lets programs use more memory than is physically installed on the machine. And the third feature is task switching known as *multitasking,* which lets a computer juggle multiple programs all at once to look like they are running at the same time. Another important feature of the Protected mode is the ability to directly execute "real address mode" 8086 software in a protected, multitasking environment. This feature is called te *virtual-8086 mode,* though strictly speaking it is not an actual processor mode. It is infact a protected mode attribute that can be enabled for any task. The size of the memory in Protected mode is limited to 4Gb. But this isnt the limit of the memory size in IA-32 processors. Using tricks in the processors' page and segment memory management systems (for example Physical address extension or PAE), IA-32 maybe able to access much more than the 32 bits address space, even without switchover to the 64 bit family of processors.

SYSTEM MANAGEMENT MODE (SMM)

This mode provides an operating system or executive with a transparent mechanism for implementing platform specific fucntions such as power management and system security. The processor enters SMM when the external SMM interrupt pin (SMI#) is activated or an SMI is received from the advanced programmable interrupt controller (APIC). In SMM, the processor switches to a separate address space while saving the basic context of the currently running program or task. SIMM-specific code may then be executed transparently. Upon returning from SMM, the processor is placed back into its state prior to the system management interrupt. SMM was introduced with the Intel386 SL and Intel486 SL processors and is a standard IA-32 feature.

REGISTERS

The 386 has eight 32 bit *general purpose* registers for application use. There are 8 floating point stack registers. Other processors added new registers with various SIMD instruction sets such as MMX, 3DNow! and SSE. There are also system registers that are used mostly by operating systems but not by applications. These include segment, control, debug and test registers. There are 6 segment registers used mainly for memory management. The number of control, debug or test registers varies from model to model.

GENERAL PURPOSE REGISTERS

The x86 general purpose registers are not really as general purpose as their name implies. That is because these general purpose registers have some highly specialized tasks that can often only be done by using one or two specific registers. These registers further subdivide into registers specializing in data and others in addressing.

8 BIT AND 16 BIT REGISTER SUBSETS

8 bit and 16 bit substes of these registers are also accessible. For example the lower 16 bits and 32 bit EAX registers can be accessed by calling it the AX register. Some of the 16 bit registers can be further subdivided into 8 bit subsets, for example, the upper 8 bit half of AX is called AH and the lower half is called AL. Similarly EBX is subdivided into BX (16 bit) and BH and BL (8 bit each).

GENERAL DATA REGISTERS

These include:

- EAX Accumulator (with a special interpretation for arithmetic instructions;a for accumulator).
- EBX base register (used for addressing data in the data segment)
- ECX counter (with a special interpretation for loops, c for counter)
- EDX data register

GENERAL ADDRESS REGISTERS

These are used for address pointing and include:

- EBP stack base pointer (holds base address of stack)

- ESI source index (for string operations)
- EDI destination index (for string operations)
- ESP stack pointer (holds top address of stack)
- EIP instruction pointer (holds current instruction address)

FLOATING POINT STACK REGISTERS

There are 8x87 floating point registers known as ST(0) to ST(7). these registers are accessible like a FIFO stack. The register numbers are not fixed but are relative to the top of the stack; ST(0) being the top of the stack, ST(1) is the next one below the top and so on. That means that data is always pushed down from the top of the stack and operations are always done against the top of the stack. As a result these registers can only be accessed in the stack order and not randomly.

SIMD REGISTERS

These include the MMX, 3DNow! and SSE registers.

MMX REGISTERS

MMX added 8 registers to the architecture known as MM0 through to MM7. These registers are just aliases for existing x87 FPU stack registers. Hence anything that is done to the floating point stack would also affect the MMX registers. Unlike the FP stack, the MMn registers are fixed and not relative so that they are randomly accessible. Each of these registers are 64 bit integers. However one of the main concepts of the MMX instruction set is that of packed data types, which means that instead of using the whole register for a single 64 bit integer two 32 bits or four 16 bits or eight 8 bits integers may be used.

3DNOW! REGISTERS

3DNow! was designed to be a natural evolution of MMX from integer to floating point. It uses the same name convention as MMX registers (MM0 to MM7), the only difference being that one could pack single precision floating points into these registers. Due to the aliasing with the FPU registers, same instruction and data structures which are used to save the state of the FPU registers can be used for these registers.

SSE REGISTERS

SSE is a SIMD instruction set that works only on floating point values, like 3DNow!. However unlike 3DNow! it has no connection with the FPU stack. It has larger registers than 3DNow! and can pack twice the number of single precision floats. The original SSE was designed for handling single precision only, but then the SSE2 was introduced for double precision numbers, which the 3DNow! could not handle as a double precision number is 64 bit in size which would be the full size of a single 3DNow! MMn register. At 128 bit the SSE2 can pack two double precision floats into one register. Thus SSE2 is much more suitable for scientific calculations than either SSE1 or 3DNow!.

MEMORY MANAGEMENT

The memory that the processor addresses on its bus is called the physical memory. Physical memory is organized as a sequence of 8-bit bytes. Each byte has an unique address called physical address which ranges frm 0 to 64 Gb. Any operating system designed to work with the IA-32 will use its processor memory management facilities which provides features like segmentation, paging etc. With the flat memory model, memory appears to a program as a single continous address space called linear address space. This is byte addressable. With the segmented memory model, memory appears to a program as a group of independent address spaces called segments.

sWhen using this model, code, data and stacks are typically contained in separate segments. To address a byte in a segment, a program muct issue a logical address or far pointer. The programs running on an IA-32 processor can address upto 16383 segments of different sizes and types. The primary reason for using a segmented memory is to increase the reliability of programs and systems. For example placing a program's stack in a separate segment prevents the stack from growing into the code or data space and overwriting instructions or data.

With either the flat or segmented memory model, the linear address space is mapped into the processor's physical address space either directly or through paging. When using direct mapping, each linear address has a one-to-one correspondence with a physical address. On the other hand when using the IA-32's paging mechanism, the linear address space is divided into pages which are mapped into virtual memory. The pages of virtual memory are then mapped as needed into physical memory.

The real address mode memory model uses the memory model for the Intel 8086 processor. This memory model is supported in the IA-32 architecture for compatibility with existing programs written to run on 8086 processors. The real address mode uses a specific implementation of segmented memory in which the linear address space for the program and the operating system/executive consists of an array of segments of upto 64 KB in size each.

Intel IA-64 Processors

IA-64 is a 64 bit processor architecture developed in cooperation by Intel and Hewlett-Packard for processors such as Itanium and Itanium 2.

The goal of Itanium is to produce a post-RISC era of architecture using a very long instruction word (VLIW) design. Unlike previous Intel x86 processors the Itanium is not geared towards high performance exceution of the IA-32 (x86) instruction set.

ARCHITECTURE

A key feature of the IA 64 is that it features a revolutionary 64 bit instruction set architecture which applies a new processor architecture technology known as EPIC (Explicit Parallel Instruction Computing). Another key feature is that it is fully compatible with the IA-32 instruction set. In a maninstream design, a complex decoder system examines each instruction as they flow through the pipeline and sees which can be operated on parallel across different execution units. This ability to extracct instruction level parallelism (ILP) from the instruction stream is essential to good performance in a modern CPU. However predicting which code can and cannot be split up this way is a complex task. For instance with an *IF* statement the inputs to one line is dependent on the output from another. The calculations although independent of one another, due to the presence of the *IF* statement, the *THEN* following the *IF* requires the result from the *IF* to know whether it should proceed at all or not.

Usually in these cases the circuitry on the CPU typically "guesses" what the condition will be. However if the guesses are wrong then it causes a significant performance problem as the wrong result has to be discarded and the CPU needs to wait for the right result. The IA-64 relies on the compiler for this task. The complier examines the code and makes these decisions that would happen during run time on the chip itself. Once it decides which path to take it gathers up all the instructions and stores it in the VLIW form in the program.

This strategy of moving the task from the CPU to the complier is one of the major advantages of the IA-64. Offloading the whole prediction task to the compiler reduces the complexity of the circuitry greatly as the prediction can be very complicated. Further the compiler can spend more time examining the code, which the chip itself cannot do as it has to complete the task as quickly as possible.

The Itanium architectire provides mechanisms such as instruction templates, branch hints and cache hints to enable the compiler to communicate compile-time information to the processor. It also allows compiled code to manage the processor hardware using run-time information. These compiler to processor communication mechanisms are vital in minimizing the performance penalties associated with branches and cache misses.

The disadvantage of this however is that the program's run time behaviour is sometimes not obvious in the code. It also makes the VLIW strategy heavily dependent on the performance of the compilers, thus there is a trade off between reducing microprocessor complexity and increasing the compiler software complexity.

REGISTERS

This section briefly reviews some of the registers available in IA 64. The IA 64 includes 128 64 bit integer and 82 bit floating point registers. Besides the sheer number of the registers the IA 64, also adds in a register rotation mechanism that is controlled by the Register Stack Engine which allows the processor to rotate in a set of new registers to accomodate for new function parameters or temporaries.

GENERAL REGISTERS

A set of 128 (64 bit) general registers provide the resource for all integer and integer multimedia computation. These are numberes GR0 through to GR127. Each general register has 64 bits of normal data storage plus an additional bit called the *NaT* bit to track deferred speculative exceptions. The general registers are partitioned into two sets GR0 to GR31 are termed static general registers, while GR32 to GR127 are called stacked general registers. GR8 to GR31 contain the IA 32 integer, segment selector and segment descriptor registers.

FLOATING POINT REGISTERS

There are 128 (82 bit) floating point registers. Again these are numbered FR0 to FR127 and partitioned into two subsets. FR0 to FR31 are called static floating point registers, while FR32 to FR127 are called rotating floating point registers. Floating point registers FR8 to FR31 contain IA 32 floating point and multi-media registers while executing IA 32 instructions.

REGISTER STACK CONFIGURATION REGISTERS

The RSC register is a 64 bit register used to control the operation of the Register Stack engine (RSE). Instructions that modify RSC can never set the privilege level field to a more privileged level than the currently executing process.

PREDICATE REGISTERS

A set of 64 (1 bit) predicate registers are used to hold the results of comparable instructions. These are numbered PR0 to PR63 and are used for conditional execution of instructions. These are further partitioned into two subsets static predicate registers (PR0 to PR15) and rotating predicate registers (PR16 to PR63).

BRANCH REGISTERS

A set of 8 (64 bit) registers are used for holding branch information and are numbered from BR0 to BR7.

INSTRUCTION SET

The architecture provides a CISC like complement of instructions where there are explicit instructions for both floating point operations and multimedia operations. The Itanium supports several bundle mappings to allow for more instruction mixing possibility and includes a balance between serial and parallel execution modes. There is also room left in the initial bundle encodings to allow additional mappings to be added in future versions of IA 64.

Despite the huge capabilities in IA 64 instruction set, it is notoriously difficult to program directly. Intel discourages against the practise of assembly programming on Itanium and instead urges the use of the Intel C++ compiler which has platform specific heuristics.

AMD X86 COMPATIBLE PROCESSORS

The AMD x86-64 or AMD64 is a 64 bit pricessor architecture invented by AMD. Its is a superset of the x86 architecture (discussed in 2.1.2) which it natively supports. The AMD64 instruction set is currently being used in AMD's Athlon 64, Athlon 64 FX and Opteron processors. An important part of AMD64 is tht it allows the latest in processor innovation to be brought to the existing installed base of 32 bit applications and operating systems, while establishing an installed base of systems that are 64 bit capable. For example the IA-64 offers no native x86 compatibility, meaning that existing 32 bit applications are not anticipated ti run with leading edge performance on IA-64 technology based processors. Instaed the AMD64 provides extensions to the reliable, proven and high performance x86 instruction set and preserver full compatibility between 32 and 64 bit environments.

AMD64 Architecture Overview

The AMD64 architecture extends the x86 architecture by introducing two major features: a 64 bit extension called long mode and register extensions. The new modes are encoded using two flags in the segment decsriptor. The first flag in the existing "D" bit that controls the size of operands, a second bit is a previously unused "L" bit which is used for determining if specific applications are 64 bit enabled or are run in compatibility mode.

Long Mode

Long mode is enabled by a global control bit called LMA (Long mode Active). When LMA is disabled, the processor operates as a standard x86 processor and is compatible with all existing 16 and 32 bit operating systems and applications. When LMA is activated (LMA = 1), the 64 bit processor extensions are enables. Thus the system can auto configure according to the capabilities of the machine and the processor. Long mode consists of two sub modes:

64 Bit Mode

This mode supports the following new features:

- 64 bit virtual addresses (implementations can have less)
- Register extensions through a new prefix (REX) which adds eight GPR (R8-R15), widens GPRs to 64 bits and adds eight 128 bit Streaming SIMD extension (SSE) registers (XMM8-XMM15)
- 64 bit instruction pointer (RIP)
- new RIP data addressing mode
- Flat address space with single code, data and stack space. Since the 64 bit mode supports a 64 bit virtual

address space, it requires a 64 bit operating system and tool chain. A few instruction opcodes and prefix bytes are redefined to allow the register extensions and 64 bit addressing.

The default address size is 64 bits and the default operand size is 32 bits. The defaults can be overriden on an instruction-by-instruction basis using prefixes. A new REX prefix is introduced for specifying 64 bit operand size and the new registers. This mode is enabled by the OS on an individual code segment basis. The new register extensions added via the new REX prefix add eight 64 bit GPRs (R8-R15), eight 128 bit streamimg SIMD Extensions registers (XMM8-XMM15) and widens all GPRs and the instruction pointer to 64 bits. The instruction pointer is also widened to 64 bits.

Compatibility Mode

Compatibility mode supports binary compatibility with existing 16 and 32 bit applications within a 64 bit environment.In compatibility mode the applications can only access the first 4 GB of virtual address space. As with the 64 bit mode, compatibility mode is enabled by the OS on an individual code segment basis. However unlike the 64 bit mode, x86 segmentation functions normally using either the 16 bit or 32 bit protected mode semantics. From the application's point of view the compatibility mode looks like a legacy x86 protected mode environment. From the OS's point of view, address translation, interrupt and exception handling and system data structures use the 64 bit long mode mechanisms.

In addition to the long mode the architecture also supports a pure x86 legacy mode, which preserves binary compatibility not only with existing 16 and 32 bit applications but also with such 16 bit and 32 bit OS. None of the 64 bit features are available when the processor operates as a standard x86 processor. The Legacy mode is completely compatible with existing 32 bit implementations of the x86 architecture. This includes support for current technologies like segmented memory and 32 bit GPRs and instruction pointer.

Register Extensions

To define the addressing logic for the registers, the AMD64 architecture simply extends the addressing scheme currently used for 16 and 32 bit instructions. For example for 16 bit operations, the two bytes of register A are addressed as AX, for 32 bit operations four bytes of register A are addressed as EAX and for 64 bit operations the eight bytes are addresses as RAX. In 64 bit mode the general purpose registers (GPRs) are extended to 64 bits. The 64 bit registers are called RAX,RBX,RCX,RDX,RDI,RSI,RBP,RSP,RIP and RFLAGS. The new 64 bit registers overlay and extend the existing registers. Besides 8 new 64 bit GPRs are added for a total of 16 GPRs. There are also eight new streaming SIMD registers for a total of 16 SIMD registers. These new SIMD registers are called XMM8 through XMM15. Segment registers (ES, DS, FS, GS and SS) are ignored in the 64 bit mode. Code segments still exist however.

The CS is needed to encapsulate the defult mode of the processor as well as the execution privilege level. When performing 32 bit operations the destination register being a GPR, the 32 bit value will be zero extended into the full 64 bit GPR. 8 bit and 16 bit operations on GPRs preserve all unwritten upper bits. This preserves the 16 and 32 bit semantics for partial width results. The final step is to simply define a set of instructions prefixes that specify a 64 bit operand size and allow access to the new registers. This is similar to the the method used to extend the x86 architecture for other funtionalities such as AMD's 3DNOW! technology.

Thus by extending the x86 core rather than replacing it with a new, entirely different instruction set, AMD64 makes the transition to 64 bit much easier, faster and less expensive. The problem of migrating to a new architecture is greatly reduced, without limitung the forward compatibility and future performance of existing applications.

MOTHERBOARDS AND SYSTEM BUSSES

In this section the different choices for motherboards will be given. Distinctions between workstation and server chasis will be presented. This will include an introduction to system busses. Most of the detailed information will be about the PCI bus. The two next generation of buses that will replace PCI will also be introduced.

MOTHERBOARDS

The motherboard is the main circuit board inside the PC which holds the processor, memory and expansion slots and connects directly or indirectly to every part of the PC. It is made up of a chipset, some ROM code and various interconnections known as buses. The physical layout of the motherboard itself varies greatly from PC to PC, two different boards can have very similar performance even though they might be laid out completely differently. This is more true because of the large number of vendors available who manufacture a variety of motherboards. But the basic function of the motherboard is to provide a useful working place for all the components of the PC. The following sections give a brief overview of the basic functionality and layout of the motherboard.

Motherboard Form Factors

The form factor of the motherboard describes its general shape, the kind of power supply used, its physical organization and the kind of cses it uses. The two most common form factors in motherboards are the AT and the Baby AT form factors. These two forms differ mainly in the width, the older AT board being 12" wide, while the Baby AT board is 8.5" wide and nominally 13". The AT form is the much older version and is usually found in older machines (386 or older).

Another troublesome feature of this board is that a good percentage of the board overlaps with the drive bays which makes installation and upgrading difficult and cumbersome. For the Baby AT form. the reduced width allows much less overlap with drive bays. IT has three rows of mounting holies, the first running along the back of the board where the bus slots and key connectors reside, the second running through the middle of the board and the third along the fron of the board near to where the drivers are mounted. One problem with the Baby AT is that many of its newer versions try and reduce cost by reducing the board size (for example 10" to 11" long). This often leads to mounting problems as the third row of holes might now line up with rows on the case. Both the AT and Baby AT form factors places the processor sockets, slots amd memory sockets at the front of the motherboard and long expansion cards were designed to extend over them.

This design was introduced over a decade ago. However presently the processors need bigger heat sinks and fans mounted on them, the result is that the processor, heat sink and fan combination can often block as many as three of the expansion slots on the motherboard. Besides there are also SIMM/DIMM sockets. Although the newer Baby AT motherboards move the SIMM/DIMM sockets out of the way but the processors still remain a problem. The ATX was designed to solve this problem.

ATX and Mini ATX Form Factors

The ATX form was invented by Intel in 1995. The Pentium Pro and Pentium II are the most common users of this kind of motherboards.

The ATX has many advantages over the older motherboards which include:

- *Integrated I/O Port Connectors:* Baby AT motherboards use headers which stick up from the board, and a cable that goes from them to the physical serial and parallel port connectors mounted on to the case. The ATX has these connectors soldered directly onto the motherboard. This improvement reduces cost, saves installation time, improves reliability (since the ports can be tested before the motherboard is shipped) and makes the board more standardized.
- *Integrated PS/2 Mouse Connector:* On most retail baby AT style motherboards, there is either no PS/2 mouse port, or to get one you need to use a cable from the PS/2 header on the motherboard, just like the serial and parallel ports. (Of course most large OEMs have

PS/2 ports built in to their machines, since their boards are custom built in large quantities). ATX motherboards have the PS/2 port built into the motherboard.

- *Reduced Drive Bay Interference:* Since the board is essentially "rotated" 90 degrees from the baby AT style, there is much less "overlap" between where the board is and where the drives are. This means easier access to the board, and fewer cooling problems.
- *Reduced Expansion Card Interference:* The processor socket/slot and memory sockets are moved from the front of the board to the back right side, near the power supply. This eliminates the clearance problem with baby AT style motherboards and allows full length cards to be used in most (if not all) of the system bus slots.
- *3.3V Power Support:* The ATX style motherboard has support for 3.3V power from the ATX power supply. This voltage (or lower) is used on almost all newer processors, and this saves cost because the need for voltage regulation to go from 5V to 3.3V is removed.
- *Soft Power Support:* The ATX power supply is turned on and off using signalling from the motherboard, not a physical toggle switch. This allows the PC to be turned on and off under software control, allowing much improved power management. For example, with an ATX system you can configure Windows 95 so that it will actually turn the PC off when you tell it to shut down.

LPX and Mini LPX

The primary design goal behind the LPX form factor is reducing space usage (and cost). This can be seen in its most distinguishing feature: the riser card that is used to hold expansion slots. Instead of having the expansion cards go into system bus slots on the motherboard, like on the AT or ATX motherboards, LPX form factor motherboards put the system bus on a riser card that plugs into the motherboard. Then, the expansion cards plug into the riser card; usually, a maximum of just three. This means that the expansion cards are parallel to the plane of the motherboard. This allows the height of the case to be greatly reduced, since the height of the expansion cards is the main reason full-sized desktop cases are as tall as they are.

LPX form factor motherboards also often come with video display adapter cards built into the motherboard. If the card built in is of good quality, this can save the manufacturer money and provide the user with a good quality display. However, if the user wants to upgrade to a new video card, this can cause a problem unless the integrated video can be disabled. LPX motherboards also usually come with serial, parallel and mouse connectors attached to them, like ATX.

NLX Form Factor

The need for a modern, small motherboard standard has lead to the development of the new NLX form factor. In many ways, NLX is to LPX what ATX is to AT: it is generally the same idea as LPX, but with improvements and updates to make it more appropriate for the latest PC technologies. Also like ATX, the NLX standard was developed by Intel Corporation and is being promoted by Intel. Intel of course is a major producer of large-volume motherboards for the big PC companies. NLX still uses the same general design as LPX, with a smaller motherboard footprint and a riser card for expansion cards.

The NLX form factor is, like the LPX, designed primarily for commercial PC makers mass-producing machines for the retail market. Many of the changes made to it are based on improving flexibility to allow for various PC options and flavours, and to allow easier assembly and reduced cost. For homebuilders and small PC shops, the ATX form factor is the design of choice heading into the future.

PCI BUS

PCI or Peripheral Component Interface is a 32 bit bus

architecture (64 bit with multiplexing) developed by DEC, IBM, Intel and others, that is widely used in Pentium bases PCs. A PCI bus provides a high bandwidth data channel between system board components such as the CPU and devices such as hard disks and video adapters. The PCI superseded the VL-bus which as widely in use till the early 1990s. The essential purpose of introducing the PCI bus was to make expansion easier to implement by offering plug and play (PnP) hardware, *i.e.* a system that would enable the PC to adjust automatically to new cards as they are plugged in, thus making redundant the need to check jumper settings and interrupt levels. By 1994 PCI was established as the dominant Local Bus standard.

Unlike the VL-bus, which was essentially an extension of the bus that the CPU uses to access the main memory, the PCI is a separate bus isolated from the CPU but having access to the main memory. Besides the VL-bus was designed to run at system bus speeds, whereas since the PCI bus is linked to the system bus through special bridge circuitry, the speed of the PCI bus can be set synchronously or asynchronously depending on the chipset and the motherboard. In a synchronous setup (used in most PCs), the PCI bus runs at half the memory bus speed, which is usually 25 or 30 or 33 MHZ.

In an asynchronous setup the speed of the PCI bus can be set independent of the memory bus speed, controlled through jumpers on the motherboard or BIOS settings. The PCI is also limited to five connectors, although each can be replaced by two devices built into the motherboard. It is also possible for a processor to support more than one bridge chip. The PCI is more tightly specified than the VL-bus and offers a number of additional features. For example it cab support cards running from both 5 volts and 3.3 volt supplies using different key slots to prevent the wrong card being put into the wrong slot.

In its original implementation the PCI ran at 33MHz, but was then raised to 66MHz by the later PCI 2.1 specification. As a result the theoretical thoroughput was increased to 266

MBps. The PCI can also be configured both as a 32 bit and a 64 bit bus and both kinds of cards can be used as well in either configuration.

PCI Bus Performance

The PCI is the highest performance general I/O bus currently used on PCs.

This superior performance of the PCI bus is due to several factors:

- *Burst mode:* The PCI bus can transfer information in a burst mode, where after an initial address is provided multiple sets of data can be transmitted in a row. This works in a manner similar to how cache bursting works
- *Bus Mastering:* PCI supports full bus mastering, which leads to improved performance.
- *High Bandwidth Options:* The PCI 2.1 version is expanded to 64 bits and 66 MHz, thus quadrupling the bandwidth.

PCI Internal Interrupts

The PCI bus uses its own interrupt system for dealing with requests from the cards on the bus. These interrupts are often called "#A", "#B", "#C", "#D" to avoid confusion with the normal sytem IRQs (they are sometimes called "#1" to "#4" as well). These interrupts if needed by cards in the alots are mapped to regular interrupts, normally IRQ9 through IRQ12. The PCI slots in most systems can be mapped to at most 4 regular IRQs. In systems having more than 4 PCI slots two or more PCI devices share an IRQ.

PCI Bus Mastering

Bus mastering is the ability of devices on the PCI bus (other than the system chipset) to take control of the bus and perform transfers directly. The PCI bus is the first bus to popularize bus mastering. PCI's design allows bus mastering of multiple devices on the bus simultaneously, with the arbitration circuitry working to ensure that no device on the bus (including the processor) locks out any other device. At the same time it allows any given device to use the full bus thoroughput if no other device needs to transfer anything. Thus it acts as a tiny local network within the computer in which multiple devices can talk to each other through a communication channel managed by the chipset. The PCI bus also allows you to setup compatible IDE/ATA hard disk drives to be bus masters. This can increase the performance over the use of PIO modes, which are the default way of data transfering used by IDE/ATA.

However for IDE bus mastering to work properly and correctly all of the following are needed:

- *Bus Mastering Capable System Hardware:* This includes the motherboard, chipset, bus and BIOS. Most of the newer motherboards using Intel 430 PEntium chipset family will support bus mastering IDE.
- *Bus Mastering hard Disk:* All Ultra ATA hard disks support bus mastering
- 32 bit Multitasking OS
- Bus Mastering drivers: A special driver must be provided to the OS to enable bus mastering to work.

The PCI Protocol

The PCI bus uses an intermediate protocol rather than a register to register protocol.

With a conventional PCI device, the following steps occur when the device switches a control signal:

- On the rising clock edge, the device switches the signal to a high or low state onto the PCI bus.
- The signal propagates across the bus (propagation delay).
- during the same clock cycle, the receiving device decodes the signal to determine whether the signal is for the receiving device and to determine if ir must respond by switching one of its outputs.
- The receiving device responds immediately, that is in the next clock cycle.

With a 33MHz clock frequency the time allocated to the decode logic is of the order of 7 nanoseconds of the total 30ns clock cycle time. At 33MHz this is sufficient time for the receiving device to respond on the next rising clock edge. However an important bottleneck or problem with this protocol is that when the clock frequency is doubled to 66MHz (thus reducing the clock cycle time to 15ns), the number of nanoseconds available for the receiving device to respond is cut down to 3ns. Thus there is a severe time constraint for the conventional PCI bus which makes it difficult for the PCI bus to adapt to 66MHz. Dating from the mid 1995s, the main performance critical components of the PC communicated with each other across the PCI bus. Most common of these PCI devices were the disk and graphics controllers which were either mounted onto the motherboard or on expansion cards in PCI slots. Moreover by the late 1990s new processors and I/O devices were demanding much higher I/O bandwidth than PCI could deliver. This resulted in creation of higher bandwidth buses like the PCI-X bus.

PCI-X BUS

The PCI-X is a high performance addendum to the PCI local bus specification developed in collaboration by IBM, HP and Compaq. The PCI-X is generally viewed as an immediate solution to the increased I/O requirements for high bandwidth enterprise applications such as Gigabit ethernet, fibre channel and high performance graphics. The PCI-X technology increases bus capacity to more than eight times that of the conventional PCI bus bandwidth, from 133 Mbps with the 32 bit 33 MHz PCI bus to 1066Mbps with the 64 bit 133MHz PCI-X bus. It also enhances the PCI protocol to develop an interconnect that exceeds raw bandwidth of 1 Gbps. The following sections briefly describe some of the key elements of the PCI-X technology:

Register to Register Protocol

With the PCI-X register-to register protocol the following steps occur:

- On the rising clock edge, the device switches the signal to a high or low state onto the PCI-C bus.

- The signal propagates across the bus.
- 'The signal is sent to a register or flip-flop, that holds the signal until the nexy clock cycle.
- The receiving device has a full clock cycle to decode the signal and determine the proper response.
- The receiving device responds two full clock cycles after the sending device first switched the signal.

Thus the PCI-X considerably eases the time constraints that were a bottleneck for the PCI bus by providing an entire clock cycle for the decoding logic to occur. The net difference is that the PCI-X transactions will require an additional clock cycle more than the conventional PCI transaction. With the timing constraint reduced it is much easier to design and implement adapters and systems to operate at 66MHz and greater.

Enhanced Bus Efficiency

The PCI-X bus incorporates the following technologies to improve the bus efficiency:

Attribute Phase

The PCI-C includes a new transaction phase called the attribute phase that uses a 36 bit attribute field to decsribe bus transactions in more detail than conventional PCI allows. The following enhancements are included in the attribute phase:

Relaxed Ordering

IF the device driver or the controlling software sets this bit, then the transaction is permitted to pass previously posted transactions from other devices. Relaxed ordering is especially important in applications such as audio or video streaming, where a delay in information would cause a noticeable interruption.

Non-Cache-Coherent Transactions

This refers to maintaining a consistent view of memory during a transaction between the processors and I/O subsystem. For the PCI bus whenever a device writes or reads to main memory, the processor has to perform a snoop operation to make sure that the data does not exist in the cache memory.

These snoop cycles limits the performance of the system by adding traffic. In the PCI-X non-cache-coherrent transactions are allowed by using a dont snoop bit. If any device driver or software sets this bit, then the PCI-X device informs the system cache controllers that no query is needed.

Transaction Byte Count

In PCI protocol the bridge fetches a default number of cache lines (one or two) for every data request as it has no way knowing how much data will be requested. With the PCI-X the bridge knows exactly how much data to fetch because the byte count is included in the attribute field.

Each PCI-X transaction in a sequence identifies the total number of bytes remaining to be read or written in its associated sequence. This enables more efficient buffer management schemes in the bridge as well as more efficient utilization of bus and other system resources.

Sequence Number

The sequence number uniquely identifies transactions that are part of the same sequence. The sequence number is used to increase efficiency in the buffer management algorithms.

Split Transaction Support

Conveentional PCI protocol supports delayed transactions. With a delayed transaction, the device requesting data must poll the target to determine when the request has been completed. But with split transaction in PCI-X the device requesting data sends a signal to the target. The target device informs the requester that is accepted the request so that the requester is free to process other jobs, thus increasing the efficiency.

Optimized Wait States

PCI-X eliminatesthe use of wait states, excepr for initial

target latency. When a PCI-X device does not have data to transfer, it will remove itself from the bus so that another device can use the bus bandwidth. This provides more efficient use of bus and memory resources.

Standard Block Size Movements

With PCI-X, adapters and bridges are permitted to disconnect transactions only on natural aligned 128 byte boundaries. This encourages longer bursts and enables more efficient use of cache line based resources such as the processor bus and main memory.

The operating mode and the frequency of the PCI-X bus depends on the type of adapters installed on the bus and on the number of adapters installed on it. A PCI-X system automatically adjusts the bus frequency to match the frequency of the slowest adapter on that bus segment. PCI-X supports upto 256 bus segments and each segment is initialized separately so that different operating frequencies can be used. Also as with conventional PCI, system designers can optimize a PCI-X system for particular I/O bandwidth needs. An important point about the PCI-X bus is that even if it operates as a conventional PCI bus, it still provides a significant performance enhancement.

INFINIBAND BUS

To meet the increasing I/O demands of the computer industry, major technology leaders including Compaq, Dell, HP, IBM, Intel, Microsoft and Sun codeveloped the Infiniband architecture and released it in the year 2000. The Infiniband architecture was developed as a means to connect servers with remote storage, networking devices and other servers as well as for use inside servers for interprocessor communications. The Infiniband architecture offers many advantages over the existing PCI architecture and other I/O architecture which include:

- Provides bandwidths which are an order of magnitude greater rthan existing I/O capabilities.
- Provides improved connection flexibility and

scalability as storage and I/O are separated from processor and memory

- It offloads communications processing from the OS and CPU,thus eliminating traditional communications overhead.
- It can also do simultaneous device communication, rather than waiting for other devices to complete their communication.
- Provides support for up to 64,000 addressable devices and support for Internet Protocol version 6 (IPv6) for effective communications between IBA fabrics and the Internet or intranets.

INFINIBAND ARCHITECTURE

InfiniBand is a point-to-point, switched I/O fabric architecture. Each end point, or node, can vary from an inexpensive single SCSI chip or Ethernet adapter to complex host systems. Point-to-point means that each communication link extends between only two devices. Both devices at each end of a link have full and exclusive access to the communication path. To go beyond a point and traverse the network, switches come into play. By adding switches, multiple points can be interconnected to create a fabric. As more switches are added to a network, aggregated bandwidth of the fabric increases. By adding multiple paths between devices, switches also provide a greater level of redundancy. There are five primary components that make up an InfiniBand fabric:

Host Channel Adapter (HCA)

An HCA is an interface that resides within a server and communicates directly with the server's memory and processor as well as the IBA fabric. The HCA guarantees delivery of data, performs advanced memory access and can recover from transmission errors. HCAs can communicate with a target channel adapter or a switch.

An HCA can be a PCI to InfiniBand card or it can be integrated on a system motherboard:

- *Target Channel Adapter (TCA):*A TCA enables I/O

devices, such as disk or tape storage, to be located within the network independent of a host computer. The TCA includes an I/O controller that is specific to its particular device's protocol. TCAs can communicate with an HCA or a switch.

- *Switch:* The switch allows many HCAs and TCAs to connect to it and handles network traffic. The switch looks at the local route header on each packet of data that passes through it and forwards it to the appropriate location. A group of switches is referred to as a fabric. The switch also frees up servers and other devices by handling network traffic.
- *Router:* A router forwards data packets from a local network (called a subnet) to other external subnets. The router reads the global route header and forwards packets based on the IPv6 network layer address. The router rebuilds each packet with the proper local address header as it passes it to the new subnet.
- *Subnet Manager:* The subnet manager is an application responsible for configuring the local subnet and ensuring its continued operation. Configuration responsibilities include managing switch and router setups and reconfiguring the subnet if a link goes down or a new one is added.

Infiniband Layers

The Inifiniband is comprised of four primary layers that describe communication devices and methodology. These layers are briefly described below:

Physical Layer

The InfiniBand physical layer defines its electrical and mechanical characteristics, including cables, connectors and hot-swap characteristics. Connectors include fibre, copper and backplane connectors. There are three link speeds specified as 1X, 4X and 12X. The speeds are a function of the pin counts or wires within each cable. With a 1X link cable, there are four wires, two for each direction of communication (read and write). The 4X speed has four times as many pins and wires and the 12X has twelve times as many pins and wires as a 1X link cable. he bandwidth for a 1X InfiniBand link is 2.5 Gb/s, which can achieve an actual raw data bandwidth of 2 Gb/s because 8b/10b data encryption is used on all transmissions, resulting in a 20% performance overhead. Because all links are bidirectional, the aggregate bandwidth can be doubled. Many InfiniBand products have multiple ports, further increasing I/O bandwidth.

Link Layer

The link layer is central to the Infiniband and includes packet layout, point-topoint link instructions, switching within a local subnet and data integrity. There are two types of packets, management and data. Management packets handle link configurations and maintenance. Data packets carry up to 4 kilobytes of transaction payload. Packet forwarding and switching within a local subnet is also part of the link layer's responsibilities. Every device in a local subnet has a local ID (LID).

Packets of data are forwarded to the appropriate LID by reading the local route header found in each packet of data. Virtual lanes are also part of the link layer. A virtual lane is a unique logical communication link that shares a single physical link. Each link can have up to 15 virtual lanes and a management lane. As a packet travels through the subnet, it can be assigned a priority or service level. Higher-priority packets are sent down special virtual lanes ahead of other packets.

Network Layer

The network layer is responsible for routing packets from one subnet to another. The global route header located within a packet includes an IPv6 address for the source and destination of each packet. Using a router, packets are forwarded through different subnets. For singlesubnet environments, the network layer information is not used.

Transport Layer

The transport layer handles the order of packet delivery as well as partitioning, multiplexing and transport services that determine reliable connections. The Infiniband bus represents a significant improvement in reliability, availability and serviceability over the PCI bus. The bascic Infiniband link is comprised of only 4 signal wires compared to more than 100 on a PCI bus. IT can also accomodate multiple ports for each I/O unit.

The Inifiniband also incluses a gailover mechanism that allows network to heal itself if a link fails, further it removes the I/O from the server, thus breaking the one-to-one relation between the server and the I/O elements. Thus if an I/O device fails, communication simply falls over to another redundant I/O device. This is unlike the PCI bus and so saves much time, resources and helps keep the server online.

CLUSTER INTERCONNECTS

The network fabric connecting the compute nodes in a cluster to carry inter-node message traffic is referred to as cluster interconnect or simply interconnect. The term System Area Network(SAN) is also sometimes used to denote a cluster interconnect. Although the scope of SANs is somewhat broader than cluster interconnects. Note that an interconnect does not hook up to the user LAN.

It is completely under the administrative domain of the cluster administrator. The LAN administrator need not be even aware of the type of interconnect being used in a cluster, unless of course the same person is playing both roles. The user connectivity of the cluster is simply through a LAN connection on the head node of the cluster and does not require much design consideration.

The choice of optimal interconnect for a cluster is very important and can be very difficult to make. If the right balance is not struck between the processing power of the nodes in a cluster and the communication ability of its interconnect, the nodes will potentially waste their computing resources while waiting for data. On the other hand depending on the interconnect that you choose, it may turn out to be a significant percentage of the cost of the cluster.

The research and practice in the area of high performance cluster interconnect techonology lies interestingly between MPP interconnect technologies and generic LAN technologies. A cluster interconnect is much more specialized than a generic LAN, hence providing many opportunities for performance optimization as well as ability to use network equipment without the bells and whistles needed to support a general purpose network.

On the other hand a cluster interconnect, by its very nature, is more flexible than an MPP interconnect and thus *e.g.* cannot use highly optimized routing algorithms which assume fixed topology.

In this chapter we will present an overview of the most popular networking hardware and software packages that are being used as cluster interconnects. We will also share practical experiences with many of these technologies. Before we start talking about the particular technologies in detail, let us first go over an abstract introduction which is needed to compare and contrast various technologies.

Following is not offered as Networking 101, indeed we assume basic networking knowledge, but we go over the aspects of networking most relevant to cluster interconnects.

INTERCONNECT BASICS

Fig shows the path of a packet in a cluster from one compute node to another. We have simplified this model in order to explain the relevant concepts in this section, *e.g.* we have not shown all the various layers within the interconnect fabric itself.

A process, which is part of a parallel application is running on node A and is attempting to send a message to another process running on node B. The sending process initiates the message by making a call to a parallel programming library, *e.g.* an MPI library.

The MPI library transfers the message down to the particular protocol layer being used to implement the MPI library. This protocol layer then either passes the message directly or through the operating system on to the physical network.

On the receiving side events happen in the reverse chronological order as on the sending host, ultimately providing the packet to the application process. At a physical level the packet passes from sending host's memory onto the NIC, then to the network cable, going through any switches, reaching the NIC of the receiving host, finally into the memory of the receiving host.

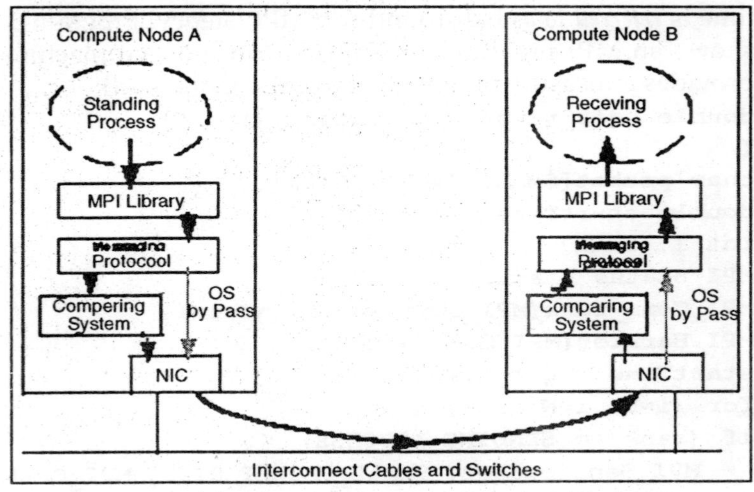

Fig: Path of a Packet Between two Compute Nodes

When designing the interconnect fabric for a Linux compute cluster the choice of Network Interface Cards (NICs) and their corresponding switches, if necessary, depends highly on the application(s) for which the cluster is being built. The key parameters of the network type that affect this choice are: Latency, Bandwidth, CPU overhead, Multithreading and, of course, cost of the network devices and required software packages.

In the following sections we define each of these parameters and describe ways of comparing various choices along these parameters.

Latency

Latency refers to the time it takes for a single packet to leave the source and reach the destination. It is measured from the time the sending process sends the packet to the time the destination process starts receiving the packet.

A popular way of measuring the latency of an interconnect is to have a pair of machines repeatedly send a small message back and forth. If the packet was able to make N round-trips in time T, the one-way latency of the network will be T/2N.

If MPI is the programming API being used, this measured time is *referred to as* half-round-trip MPI latency. Program 3.1 shows an MPI program which when run on two machines provides a measure of the latency of the fabric used.

```
double half_round_trip_latency(int N)
{
char packet[SMALL_PACKET_SIZE];
double startTime, endTime;
int i, rank;
MPI_Status status;
MPI_Comm_rank(MPI_COMM_WORLD, \&rank)
MPI_Barrier(MPI_COMM_WORLD);
startTime = get_time();
for (i=0; i<N; i++) {
if (rank == SENDING_PROCESS)
   MPI_Send(packet, SMALL_PACKET_SIZE, MPI_CHAR,
RECEIVING_PROCESS, i,
     MPI_COMM_WORLD);
 if (rank == RECEIVING_PROCESS)
   MPI_Recv(packet, SMALL_PACKET_SIZE, MPI_CHAR,
 SENDING_PROCESS, i,
     MPI_COMM_WORLD, &status);
}
endTime = get_time();
if (rank == SENDING_PROCESS)
return((endTime-startTime)/(2*N));
else
return(0);
}
```

Program: Procedure to compute half-round-trip MPI latency.

It is important to measure the latency of a fabric at an API level. Even if the underlying physical media can support very fast exchange of messages, the protocol implementation on top of the physical media can make a significant difference in the effective latency for the application.

For example if the parallel programming library is implemented on top of a general-purpose protocol like TCP/ IP, the packet will take a significant time to go through the various layers of the protocol to reach the physical media itself. *E.g.* in MPI implementations over TCP/IP data is first copied from NIC to kernel space and then from kernel space to user space. Although Linux has an excellent TCP/IP implementation, for many MPI application environments use of a *light-weight* protocol is desired. In sections ? and ? we go in detail of some of these light-weight protocols and their implementations.

It is also important to account the affect of switches on the latency between two machines in the cluster. If messages have to go through multiple switches before reaching their destination node, the latency for these messages could be significantly higher compared to point-to-point connected nodes. Such configurations also introduce different latency numbers between different pairs of nodes. For example, in fig 3.1 nodes 1 and 2 would likely have better latency between them, as compared to nodes 1 and 6, especially if the intermediate switches introduce significant latency.

Implementation and scheduling of many parallel programs can benefit from knowledge of such non-uniformities, especially since many parallel algorithms have a significant amount of communication between neighbours.

How a message is viewed in the interconnect fabric and the mechanisms used to route it to its destination make a significant difference in the latency seen by the parallel applications in the cluster. In the following section we briefly summarize the routing methodologies used by various cluster interconnects.

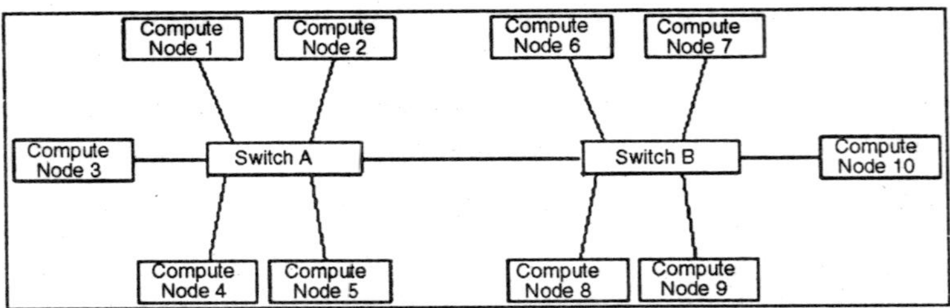

Fig: Cluster With two Switches Connected via an Uplink

Message Routing Through the Switches

There are two distinct ways on how interconnect fabrics transmit a message. *Packet switching (or store-and-forward switching)* transmits a message as a packet (or a sequence of packets), with each packet being solely present at either a cluster node or an intermediate switch. In describing network topologies, the switches and hubs in the network are sometimes referred to as *nodes*. We would avoid such usage to avoid confusion with *cluster nodes*. On the other hand *wormhole switching (or cut-through switching)* transmits a message as a *worm, i.e.* a continous stream of bits which make their way through the fabric, potentially spanning multiple cluster nodes and switches concurrently. Using wormhole based switches can significantly improve the latency characteristics of a cluster.Switches based on store-and-forward methodology wait for the whole packet to arrive before making the routing decision for next stop for the packet. There is some terminology ambiguity here as well. A technique where the routing decision of a packet is made before the whole packet arrives, but the packet is forwarded only if it is known that whole of it could be buffered at the next destination is called *virtual cut-through*. Wormhole switches do not have the overhead of storing whole packets before forwarding them to the next node or switch, and thus considerably decrease any latency overhead of passing through a switch.

Packet switching technology (using store-and-forward mechanism) used in many LAN/WAN switches can significantly detriment latency.

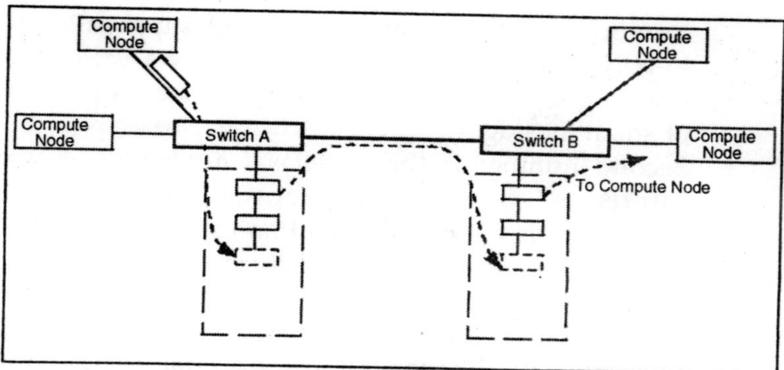

Fig: *Packet switching:* A switch Stores a Packet in its Queue until it can Forward the Packet to the next Switch or Node

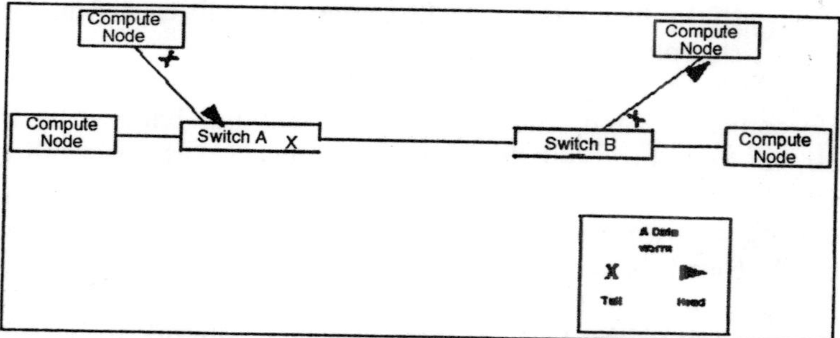

Fig: Wormhole Switching: A Worm Cuts through Various Switches to Reach its Destination

BANDWIDTH

Bandwidth refers to the amount of data that can flow through the interconnect fabric in a unit of time. As with latency, bandwidth should also be measured at the parallel API level, since the raw bandwidth of the physical network can be significantly higher than what the parallel application can actually realise.

There are two bandwidth numbers that need to be considered:

- First is the bandwidth of the network with a point-to-point link between two nodes in a cluster. Although in practice a cluster will rarely run in this configuration, this bandwidth number gives the best case scenario that a single port will support.Point-to-point bandwidth can be measured by a variant of the program 3.1, by sending large messages instead of small messages.

- Second number is the *bisectional bandwidth* of the interconnect fabric. Conceptually bisectional bandwidth is the rate of data that can be sent across an imaginary line dividing the cluster into two halves each with equal number of CPUs. Depending on how this imaginary line is drawn different bandwidth numbers can be obtained. The bisection bandwidth of the cluster is defined to be that offered by the worst case scenario. Bisectional bandwidth can get tricky to measure, in fact even difficult to define for complex network topologies.

If all the cluster compute nodes hook up to a single interconnect switch, then the cluster bisectional bandwidth is same as that of the switch. Say a switch has N ports (assuming N to be even). Now assume N/2 nodes in the cluster are sending a continuous stream of data, *i.e.* a very large packet, to the other N/2 nodes in the cluster.

These second set of N/2 nodes are also sending a continuos stream back to the first set (this assumes network to be full duplex). The amount of data that flows through the switch per unit time defines the bisectional bandwidth of the switch. This is the maximum network bandwidth a cluster can expect if the switch in above scenario is at the center of its fabric.

A non-blocking switch has the bisectional bandwidth equal to N times the point-to-point bandwidth. Bisectional bandwidth of an oversubscribed switch is less than the corresponding non-blocking switch with same number of ports. So, an oversubscribed switch may slow down a node from sending a message even if the link would allow higher bandwidth. In a cluster with very busy interconnect, with nodes having to send data out simultaneously at various times, use of a non-blocking switch may be essential. In a cluster where it is rare for nodes to be simultaneously pushing data out on the network, an oversubscribed switch may be a cost-effective choice. A critical number to note is the bisectional bandwidth per processor in the cluster. Again assuming all the nodes are connected to a single central switch, a non-blocking switch provides a constant bandwidth per processor as the number of nodes increase in the cluster. An oversubscribed switch, on the other hand, scales the bandwidth per processor upto a point after which the increase in number of nodes decreases the available bandwidth per processor.

Maintaining constant bandwidth per processor gets harder once the number of nodes in a cluster exceed the ports available in a single switch. For example, in fig 3.1 if there are no other connections between the nodes that connect to switch A and those connected to switch B, the wire connecting the two switches may become the bottleneck, limiting the total bisectional bandwidth of the cluster. One obvious way to avoid this is to use switches with higher count of ports.

This is sometimes impractical because it requires investing upfront in the capacity which may get used in the future. Furthermore for bigger clusters, switches may not exist to satisfy the port requirements for all the nodes. Another way to offset at least some of this bottleneck is to use switches with faster *uplinks*. For example if the two switches in fig 3.2 are both 8 port Fast Ethernet switches, and the link between the two is a Gigabit Ethernet connection (see section on Ethernet), this link will likely not be a choke point anymore.

If more than two switches are needed in the interconnect fabric, or if faster uplink is not an option, more complex topologies of inter-switch connections need to be used to reduce the worst case scenarios of multiple hops. The subject of optimal network topology under different conditions has been studied fairly extensively, especially in the MPP domain. A detailed exposition of this material is out of scope of this book. Nevertheless we provide some examples of key topologies used in the technology overview below and in the last part of this book. There are many parallel applications which put higher communication load on a few selected nodes, *i.e.* their communication load is not evenly balanced across the cluster. If a cluster is to be tuned for such applications, an irregular topology of network links could be use *e.g.* multiple links can be added to a single node. *E.g.* in fig 3.3 all nodes are one hop away from Node 1.

In this case the job scheduler will need to ensure that processes of applications are appropriately spawned to make use of such optimizations. In general we recommend using such irregular network topologies only in special cases where the cluster being deployed is going to run applications with communication skew for most of its deployment. Regular topologies result in ease of management, the allow use of well understood routing & job scheduling algorithms as well as are easy to administer.

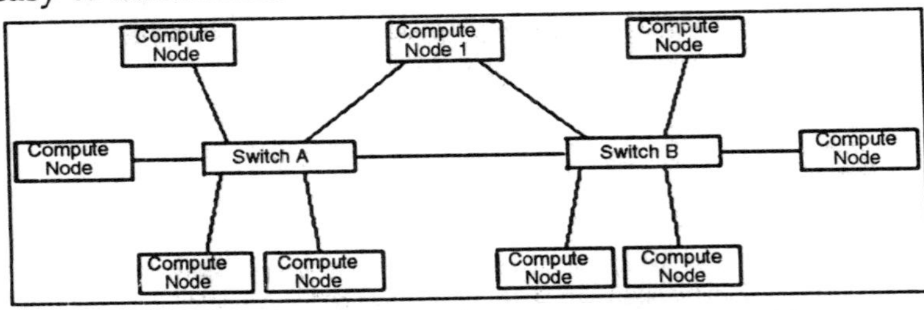

Fig: Cluster with a Designated node Optimized for Communication

CPU OVERHEAD

While analyzing how the application is going to perform on a cluster it is important to consider the affect of network activity on CPU performance. If bulk of the network processing is taking place in the host CPU, then this load will compete with the load of instructions within the application itself. Many intelligent NICs try to handle various pieces of network processing within themselves, thus freeing the CPU to do application work. For a very busy interconnect this could be a critical criteria, either the NICs would need to be intelligent, or the CPU power would be required to be higher to accommodate the network load. A low CPU overhead and careful overlaping of computation with communication, allows the application to do useful work in the CPU while processing is being done on the processor embedded in the NIC. Myrinet NIC is an example of such intelligent NICs. Myrinet NIC has a processor *embedded on the card, called the* Lanai *processor. The Lanai processor reduces the burden of the host CPU by taking over many of the network flow activities.*

Another significant optimization to reduce the CPU overhead is the use of light-weight protocols. These protocols are designed to specifically ship relatively small messages across a controlled network topology like that of a cluster. Traditional protocols such as TCP/IP are designed to run on very general purpose networks and hence must take care of many exceptions and errors which are not relevant to compute clusters. The protocols used in cluster interconnects can be much more optimistic and can make various assumptions as compared to general purpose protocols. Implementation of such protocols generally requires some level of intelligence from the underlying NIC. This could be either in the form of an embedded processor, like the Lanai processor in a Myrinet NIC, or it could be in form of special firmware in the NIC. In another chapter we go into details of some popular light-weight protocols.

MULTITHREADING

Multithreading refers to the ability of the network to transfer multiple messages concurrently as well as the ability of a node to use the fabric from different contexts. In a compute cluster using SMP nodes, *i.e.* nodes containing more than one processor, jobs may get scheduled in a way that independent applications on the same node want to use the interconnect for their message exchange. Certain NICs (and their corresponding drivers) are able to talk to multiple high level processes for message exchange, whereas some NICs are tied to a process until that process has completed its communication and relinquished the NIC.

COST

Various factors should be considered while calculating the cost of an interconnect. The base cost of the interconnect includes the cost of NICs, switches, cables and required software libraries. There are secondary cost considerations as well. Particular choice of NIC may require higher speed host processors thus adding to the cost. A non-standard network also requires training cost, which may not required if a more commonly used network such as Ethernet is used. Availability of good driver and API implementations on a specific vendor's network options may reduce the in-house development and tuning costs.

OTHER FACTORS

N In addition to above five key parameters, depending on particular cluster usage some other factors may also become key in choice. For example if the size of the problem, and hence the size of the cluster, is projected to grow in future it is critical to have a network infrastructure that scales gracefully. The latency and bandwidth as seen by a node in the cluster should stay as constant as possible as the cluster expands, otherwise the application performance can suffer significantly with expansion of the cluster. Certain application environments may put increased emphasis on reliability of the interconnect. This includes resiliency of individual software and hardware components as well as the ability to recover from faults while containing the impact of the fault as much as possible.

POPULAR INTERCONNECTS

This section describes the various interconnect choices currently (or soon) available in the marketplace, and various trade-offs along the lines of above parameters:

FAST ETHERNET AND GIGABIT ETHERNET

Various flavours of Ethernet running TCP/IP protocols form the core engine of Intranets and the Internet. Currently (Mid 2000) there are three popular flavours of Ethernet differing in their peak bandwidth: standard Ethernet (commanly referred to as just Ethernet), Fast Ethernet, and Gigabit Ethernet providing 10 Mbps, 100Mbps, and 1000Mbps of peak theoretical bandwidth respectively. Most desktops today (Mid 2000) connect to their local area networks using Ethernet. Fast Ethernet is catching up very fast, and is the dominant connectivity mechanism for the new backend servers. web servers, fileservers etc. Gigabit Ethernet is gaining rapid acceptance as the backbone network connecting switches together, as well as a connection into heavily accessed back end servers. The successive members of the Ethernet family benefit tremendously from the install base of previous generation. *E.g.* the Gigabit Ethernet over copper can use the same cable (CAT-5, using 1000Base-T) as being used for Fast Ethernet based networks.

Upgrading a server from Fast Ethernet to Gigabit Ethernet does not require a change in network topology. Organizations can leverage on their current infrastructure, network management tools, and personnel to add needed bandwidth at moderate upgrade costs. These factors have made Ethernet and Fast Ethernet very much commodity components, with Gigabit Ethernet heading that way as well. By one estimate more than 1.4 million Gigabet Ethernet switch ports were expected to ship in first half of year 2000 alone.

Omnipresence of various flavours of Ethernet and their relatively low cost makes Fast Ethernet and Gigabit Ethernet key contenders to be used as cluster interconnect fabric. Although Standard Ethernet is still a very popular port on desktops, it is fading away as a server networking option. Even most of the low end servers ship with a standard Fast Ethernet port. So, unless you are redeploying old PCs as cluster nodes, standard Ethernet need not be considered as an option.

From this point on we will use the term Ethernet to describe Fast Ethernet and Gigabit Ethernet networks. Among all the various interconnect options being discussed here, only Ethernet truly meets the Beowulf philosophy, in that it is a commodity hardware using standard protocols and is manufactured by multiple vendors. On the other hand the very omnipresence of Ethernet prevents it from being the most optimized interconnect fabric for a high performance compute cluster. In next few sections we go over some of these trade-offs.

Although Fast ethernet switches are coming down in price very aggressively, a repeater hub is still much cheaper than a switch. For clusters where bisectional bandwidth and scalability of the cluster are not of much concern, use of a hub can be considered. This is true for cases where the parallel application(s) running on the cluster make very infreqent and small exchanges of information, or if the cluster is being primarily run as a throughput cluster.

Others: SCI, Giganet, GSN, ATM as interconnect between clusters, *e.g.* in grid environment.

GAZING YOUR INTERCONNECT REQUIREMENTS

Latency is particularly important for a capability cluster, which is built for an application highly sensitive to speed of exchange of messages across cluster nodes. *E.g* FIND Example. Applications containing a lot of remote-reads or blocking remote-writes are usually latency sensitive. There are various programming techniques to hide the effect of latency on the application.

For a discussion of such techniques used in MPI based programs see section. Also note that bandwidth, at least to a limited extent, could be added to an interconnect by adding multiple paths, but reducing latency requires a change in techonology, either in the type of network hardware or in the software protocols being used.

For some clusters the application requirements may not dictate the highest bisectional bandwidth for the interconnect. In many cases most of the applications running on the cluster do not span all of the compute nodes present in the cluster. If a particular cluster installation has majority of its applications confined to a few compute nodes, and only very few non-critical applications requiring a vast span, the bandwidth of such a cluster need not be optimized for the weakest link in its interconnect.

As long as the job scheduler is intelligent enough to deploy the parallel applications such that all their processes run on nodes with close proximity (*e.g.* connected to the same switch), the cluster usage may prove to be optimal.

LINUX EMULATION

The NetBSD port for i386, alpha, mac68k, macppc, and many others can execute a great number of native Linux programs, using the Linux emulation layer. Generally, when you think about emulation you imagine something slow and inefficient because, often, emulations must reproduce hardware instructions and even architectures (usually from old machines) in software.

In the case of the Linux emulation this is radically different: it is only a thin software layer, mostly for system calls which are already very similar between the two systems. The application code itself is processed at the full speed of your CPU, so you don't get a degraded performance with the Linux emulation and the feeling is exactly the same as for native NetBSD applications.

This chapter explains how to configure the Linux emulation with an example: the installation of the well known Acrobat Reader version 7 program.

EMULATION SETUP

The installation of the Linux emulation is described in the compat_linux(8) man page; using the package system only two steps are needed.

1. Configuring the kernel.
2. Installing the Linux libraries.
3. Installing Linux applications like Acrobat Reader

Configuring the Kernel

If you use a GENERIC kernel you don't need to do anything because Linux compatibility is already enabled.

If you use a customised kernel, check that the following options are enabled:

- Option COMPAT_LINUX
- Option EXEC_ELF32

Or the following options if you are going to use 64-bit ELF binaries:

- Option COMPAT_LINUX
- Option EXEC_ELF64

when you have compiled a kernel with the previous options you can start installing the necessary software.

Installing the Linux Libraries

Usually, applications are linked against shared libraries, and for Linux applications, Linux shared libraries are needed. You can get the shared libraries from any Linux distribution, provided it's not too old, but the suggested method is to use the package system and install the libraries automatically (which uses SUSE libraries). When you install the libraries, the following happens:

- A *secondary root directory* is created which will be used for Linux programs. This directory is/emul/linux. The Linux programs in emulation mode will use this directory as their root directory and use files there. If a required file is not found, it will be searched with/ as root directory.

  For example, if a Linux application opens/etc/ ld.so.conf, it will first be searched in/emul/linux/etc/ ld.so.conf, and if not found there in/etc/ld.so.conf.
- The shared libraries for Linux are installed. Most applications are linked dynamically and expect to find the necessary libraries on the system. For example, forAcrobat Reader, if you go to the/usr/ pkgsrc/print/acroread7 and give the make depends command, pkgsrc will fetch and install all dependencies for Acrobat Reader.

Both operations will be handled automatically by the package system, without the need of manual intervention from the user (we suppose that, by now, you have already begun to love the package system...). Note that this section describes manual installation of the Linux libraries. To install the libraries, a program must be installed that handles the RPM format: it is rpm, which will be used to extract the SUSE libraries. Execute make and make install in the/usr/pkgsrc/ misc/rpm/directory to build and install rpm. Next the suse100_base package must be installed. The SUSE RPM files can be downloaded by the package system or, if you have a

SUSE CD, you can copy them in the/usr/pkgsrc/distfiles/ suse100 directory and then run make and make install after going to the/usr/pkgsrc/emulators/suse100_base directory. With the same method install suse100_compat and suse100_x11.

The final configuration is:

```
# pkg_info -a | grep suse
Suse_base-10.0nb3 Linux compatibility package
 suse_compat-10.0nb1 Linux compatibility package
with old shared libraries suse_x11-10.0nb2 Linux
compatibility package for X11 binaries
```

Installing Acrobat Reader

Now everything is ready for the installation of the Acrobat Reader program (or other Linux programs). Change to/usr/ pkgsrc/print/acroread7 and give the usual commands.

```
# make
# make install
```

Note: To download and install Acrobat Reader you need to add the line "ACCEPTABLE_LICENSES+=adobe-acrobat-license" to/etc/mk.conf to accept the Acrobat Reader license, simply follow the instructions given after make.

DIRECTORY STRUCTURE

If we examine the outcome of the installation of the Linux libraries and programs we find that/emul/linux is a symbolic link pointing to/usr/pkg/emul/linux, where the following directories have been created:

bin/
dev/
etc/
lib/
opt/
proc/
root/
sbin/
usr/
var/

Note: Please always refer to/emul/linux and not to/usr/pkg/emul/linux. The latter is an implementation detail and may change in the future. How much space is required for the Linux emulation software?.

On one system we got the following figure:

```
# cd/usr/pkg/emul
# du -k/emul/linux/
```

...

127804/emul/linux/

Acrobat Reader, the program, has been installed in the usual directory for package binaries:/usr/pkg/bin.

It can be run just as any other program:

```
$ acroread netbsd.pdf
```

EMULATING/PROC

Some Linux programs rely on a Linux-like/proc filesystem. The NetBSD procfs filesystem can emulate a/proc filesystem that contains Linux-specific pseudo-files.

To accomplish this you can mount the procfs with the "linux"-option:

```
# mount_procfs -o linux procfs/emul/linux/proc
```

In this example a Linux-like proc filesystem will be mounted to the/emul/linux/proc directory. You can also let NetBSD mount it automatically during the booting process of NetBSD, by adding the following line to/etc/fstab:

```
procfs/emul/linux/proc procfs ro,linux
```

USING LINUX BROWSER PLUGINS

Linux plugins for Mozilla-based browsers can be used on native NetBSD Firefox builds through nspluginwrapper, a wrapper that translates between the native browser and a foreign plugin. At the moment, nspluginwrapper only works reliably on Mozilla-based browsers that link against GTK2+ (GTK1+ is not supported).

Nspluginwrapper can be installed through pkgsrc:

```
# cd/usr/pkgsrc/www/nspluginwrapper
# make install
```

Plugins can then be installed in two steps: first, the plugin has to be installed on the system (*e.g.* through pkgsrc). After that the plugin should be registered with thenspluginwrapper by the users who want to use that plugin. In this short example we will have a look at installing the Macromedia Flash plugin.

We can fullfill the first step by installing the Flash plugin through pkgsrc:

```
# cd/usr/pkgsrc/multimedia/ns-flash
# make install
```

After that an unprivileged user can register the Flash plugin:

```
$ nspluginwrapper -i/usr/pkg/lib/netscape/plugins/
libflashplayer.so
```

The plugin should then be registered correctly. You can check this by using the *-l* option of nspluginwrapper (nspluginwrapper -l). If the plugin is listed, you can restart Firefox, and verify that the plugin was installed by entering *about:plugins* in the location bar.

4

The Sunset of Linux Hype

NO LONGER A ROCK STAR: LINUX COMPANIES STOCK CRASH

The Linux scene at the end of 2000 and the beginning of 2001 was much like the pop music scene, with faded stars littering the roadway. There's little question that the "Elvis days" of Linux are in the past. Dot-com crush changed the situation overnight. Although Linux in general and enterprise distributions in particular established itself as an important player in the OS market politically the situation changed dramatically. The first signs of coming shape-up appeared in spring 2000. As early as in May 2000 downturn of stock market forced TurboLinux to cut its staff by 52 people, about a sixth of its employees.

In the beginning of 2001 if one would collect Dotcom closing announcement he/she might get a Yellow Pages thick book. Expectations were low, particularly for the deeply troubled Linux business. And layoffs from almost all major Linux companies followed. For example SUSE cut its US office from 60 to 15 and then completely closed US office. Several smaller distributions (Corel Linux, Stampede, Stormix) disappeared from the face of the Earth.

Also the situation started to favour established players. IDS reported this that Red Hat managed to get nearly three-quarters of the $80 million in U.S. Linux sales in 2001. Most of the balance went to SuSE Linux AG, the report said. And that's the entire sum of Linux sales in the US. Interesting, is not it? When Bob Young in 1999 predicted that the server market (as in the money it generates) to decrease by an order of magnitude he was right. The only thing he got wrong was his Linux "gold rush" inspired hallucination that it will happen because of Linux. It happened sooner that he thought and not because of Linux, but with Linux market...

In April, 2001 S&P 500 returned to the level it was two years ago (on April 4, 2001 S&P 500 closed at 1100). On the same day the NASDAQ set a low not seen since Oct 98. Those Linux companies that got IPO money prior to the market correction acquired a huge competitive advantage over the smaller guys who need to operate on venture capital. Many Linux firms became, to say politely, less optimistic about their future. Here is what Red Hat wrote to in his early 2001 filing with the Securities and Exchange Commission and compare it with Bob Yong's self-congratulation book:

We have not demonstrated the success of our open source business model, which gives our customers the right to freely copy and distribute our software. No other company has built a successful open source business.

Later the loss of customers and hard economic times helped to evaporate the spirit of cooperation that was so often mentioned in good old days. In his (probably only) spring 2001 interview one of former Linux billionaires, now a modest multi-millionaire Bob Yong desperately wanted his company to become a Microsoft of a Linux world said:

Q. Where do you see Red Hat's position in a slumping technology market?

A: We see the market is really going back to the way it was. It values earnings, and it values quantifiable data as opposed to vision. In the last six years, people were buying into the vision. What's interesting is that some of those companies will in fact become the next International Business Machines Corp. or the next AT&T Corp. No one was arguing that all of them would.

The fact that some of them literally are going to disappear is not really a surprise. What it does do, in a perverse sort of way, is actually a good thing. Our competitors, who were being funded by these venture capitalists because of the vision, would give away the very same services. It was very difficult for us to expand our business to become more profitable. Cut-throat completion became norm among Linux companies.

And much like Microsoft Red Hat decided to leverage his market domination in Linux to enter other potentially lucrative areas. For example, Great Bridge, which tried to sell database software based on the open-source PostgreSQL project announced in early September, 2001 that they will go out of business. The companylowered its pricing scheme after Red Hat joined the fray, but it found difficult to compete with RH the company that essentially controls Linux OS market "We could not get customers to pay us big dollars for support contracts," Batten said. In their press release RH was not mentioned at all:

Since RH debut in August 1999 a dozen of Linux companies went public, a couple of them saw stock soared to several hundred dollar highs, and everyone wants Linus autograph. A couple years later, stock of these companies was trading close or below to their IPO price and that negatively affects the number of fans who sit to the end of Linus' speeches, especially fans who own stock of one or more Linux companies.

At the end of 2001, the stock of all Linux companies stock declined further. Call it collapse of the pyramid, investor backlash or a simple return to sanity after months of outrageous excess, but *whatever* you do, don't call it temporary. IPO dreams of several Linux companies were put on hold and layoffs became a common measure to keep companies afloat. "Surprised by wealth" Eric Raymond was the first to bless 25% layoff in VA Linux. Yes money change people. At this time the VA Linux founder Larry Augustin, who invited Eric Raymond to the board of directors lost his job. Still he managed to avoid jail.

To add insult to injury most stock analysts became openly negative. For example Pat Dorsey a senior stock analyst at Morningstar said in his December 13, 1999 Morningstar.com column Surprise! Linux Doesn't Cure Cancer: Let's get one thing straight: Neither VA Linux LNUX nor any of the other

Linux companies that have come onto the market lately are worth anything remotely close to their current valuations. Period.

And he was right. On Jan 12, 2001 Red Hat shares traded $8.67. It was better than it's 52 weeks low of $5, but far less then its 1998 high of more than $150 (adjusted for split). That means that shareholders lost approximately 23 billions to "make money fast" penguins. Here is a Jan 16, 2001 assessment of the Linux stock market situation:

Extremely important to revisit, reexamine and reevaluate one of the fair-haired segments of last year: companies touting various versions of the Linux operating system. Last year this sector had all the drama and glamour of a Hollywood flick, as Linus Torvalds, the Finnish native who helped create this free UNIX-based operating system, got almost as much press as Bill Gates.

Throughout the Linux world, where users soared past 15 million, the mantra was that Linux was well on its way to co-opting Microsoft's (MSFT) dominance. At the same time, shares in companies such as Red Hat (RHAT), VALinux soared as others Linux vendors like Caldera (CALD) and Linuxcare rushed to stake their claims in the open source gold rush.

Moreover, Red Hat and VALinux last year appeared to be trying to outdo one another as Red Hat shelled over about 400,000 of its shares from open source software company Hell's Kitchen Systems, while VALinux forked over $800 million and cash for Andover Net, a company owning several Linux Web sites. Certainly the euphoria surrounding Linux then, and today bolstered by numerous cult-like developers and users that embrace this operating system, made it as difficult then as it is now to cut to the chase about the system's real progress in the marketplace.

From the investor's point of view, the Linux picture has been nothing short of disastrous. Some Linux executive started to receive a death threats instead of interview invitations. As Red Herring reported in June 2001

Death threats have arrived at the doorsteps of some Wall Street analysts and CEOs. Class-action lawsuits are gobbling up the time and precious cash of technology companies, who are turning out to be the prime targets of late: more than half of investors' lawsuits targeted technology companies in 2000, up from 35 per cent in the 1990s. Meanwhile, investment banks are under fire from regulatory bodies for allegedly rigging the IPO process during the height of the Internet craze. No one is beyond suspicion; everyone is on edge.

"My kids' ages are off limits, because of security. We get death threats at work from dissatisfied shareholders," says Matthew Szulik, CEO of Red Hat(Nasdaq: RHAT), whose stock plummeted from a high of $143 in December 1999 to a low of $5 a year later, erasing $23 billion worth of market capitalization. "People bought in when the stock was hot and the movement was hot," Mr. Szulik groans, "and now they're pissed." With IBM Global Services deploying massive resources for Linux outsourcing, how can any start-up respond to that? They wanted a piece of service pie and it was eaten by bigger guys. IBM is a pretty daunting competition.

Access to venture capital in 2001 became a problem for many Linux startups. On Jan 12, 2001 Embedded Linux company Lineo scrapped IPO plan, a sign that investor pessimism has swept into the most optimistic part of the Linux landscape—imbedded market. The regular Linux market lost its luster:

"I think people are saying this is going to be a longer slog" than originally anticipated, said Booz-Allen & Hamilton analyst Barry Jaruzelski. "People are getting a little more sobre about expecting real revenue and real profits." Covert, too, acknowledged that investors are less patient with the general business strategy of IPO now, profitability later. Disgruntlement was most noticeable during last week's market bludgeoning.

I think a lot of the disgruntlement and anger over corporate Linux in spring 2001 were generated not only by layoffs, but also by the fact that volunteers were in essence participants, pawns and often victims of a new pyramid scheme, the pyramid that enriched a few Linux players that include Linus Torvalds and other members of so called "Linux cash community" (*i.e.* the portion of the Linux community which got substantial amount of shares and managed to sell some of them before the crash).

As Linus formulated this in one of his interviews:

- Q: How much of your stock have you sold?
- *A: Yes, I've sold the stocks. I'm not stupid.* I sold when the market was crazy. I said I'd rather have a house than worry about where the stock market is going.

If you look how owners of the companies sell their shares during initial, most difficult after-IPO year the impression is that none of them believed in the success and just wanted to jump from the sinking ship with as much money as possible. For example Yahoo! Insider Trades-VA LINUX SYSTEMS INC demonstrates that Larry Augustin really was determined to take as much gold from the sinking ship as possible. Full table also contains interesting information about other shareholders and top officers of VA Linux. It also helps to explain why VA Linux does not support AMD.

Actually fraudulent insider trading is especially tricky to prove with technology companies, because so many tech companies use stock and options as compensation. If an executive is selling, when does that activity allow you to infer that he knows that stock is going down in flames and "acted with conscious intent to defraud?" Otherwise you need to prove that the executive was engaged in the dissemination of materially false and misleading statements concerning, among other things, the company's deteriorating financial condition, the lack of demand for the company's products, its inability to control costs and maintain profit margins, and the effects these adverse undisclosed conditions would ultimately have on the company's operations, liquidity, and stock price.

The next logical step was Linux companies fighting with Linux piracy, which is pretty interesting because of GPL licensing. But Red Hat managed to do exactly this without any smiles. The Red Hat enterprise agreement was specifically designed in a way typical commercial license works or even worth. They essentially converted "free/open software" into one year agreements cash cow by withholding both the source and patches, from those who are unwilling or unable to pay the rent. They also reserved the right to audit customer each year for compliance. Here is the Red Hat subscription agreement in full glory:

This Subscription Agreement (the "Agreement") is between Red Hat, Inc. ("Red Hat") and any purchaser or user ("Customer") of Red Hat products and services that accepts the terms of this Agreement ("Customer").

Please Read This Agreement Carefully Before Purchasing Or Using Red Hat Products And Services. By Using Or Purchasing Red Hat Products Or Services, Customer Signifies Its Assent To This Agreement. If You Are Acting On Behalf Of An Entity, Then You Represent That You Have The Authority To Enter Into This Agreement On Behalf Of That Entity. If Customer Does Not Accept The Terms Of This Agreement, Then It Must Not Use Or Purchase Red Hat Products And Services.

The Effective Date of this Agreement is the earlier of the date that Customer accepts this Agreement or the date that Customer uses Red Hat's products or services.

GENERAL TERMS AND CONDITIONS

The term "Services" as used in this Agreement means, collectively, the Support Services provided under the purchased subscription and defined herein, RHN Services as defined herein, and any Learning Services purchased under this Agreement and defined herein. The term "Software" means the subscription for the family of software products purchased under this Agreement and defined herein, if any.

The term "Installed Systems" means the number of Systems on which Customer installs or executes the Software. The term "System" means any hardware on which the Software is installed, which may be, without limitation, a server, a work station, a virtual machine, a blade, a partition or an engine, as applicable.

The initial number of Installed Systems is the number of copies of the Software that Customer purchases. The parties agree that the terms of this Agreement will govern future purchases by

Customer of Red Hat's products and services unless otherwise agreed by the parties in writing.

TERM AND TERMINATION

Term

The term of this Agreement shall be for the duration of all Services provided under this Agreement. The initial term for Services shall commence on the Effective Date of this Agreement and shall continue for a period of one (1) year unless a different term is specified by the parties at the time of purchase. Thereafter, the term for Services shall renew for successive terms of one (1) year each unless a different term is agreed to by the parties at the time of renewal and unless either party gives written notice to the other of its intention not to renew at least sixty (60) days prior to the commencement of the next term; provided, however, Customer shall have the right to terminate this Agreement at any time after the first year by giving sixty (60) days prior written notice of termination to Red Hat. Customer shall remain obligated for all fees through the date of termination.

Termination for Breach

Red Hat may terminate this Agreement:

- In the event Customer fails to pay an invoice when due
- In the event Customer commits a material breach of this Agreement and fails to remedy that breach within thirty (30) days of receipt of written notice of material breach
- As otherwise provided in this Agreement.

Customer may terminate this Agreement in the event Red Hat commits a material breach of this Agreement and fails to remedy that breach within thirty (30) days of receipt of written notice of material breach.

PRICING, INVOICING AND TAXES

Customer agrees to provide Red Hat with accurate and

complete billing information (including legal name, address, telephone number, and billing or credit information). Customer will report to Red Hat all changes to this information within thirty (30) days of the change.

Red Hat reserves the right to suspend or cancel Services for non-payment. All fees are stated and must be paid in United States Dollars. If Customer is paying by credit card, then Customer authorizes Red Hat to bill Customer's credit card for the Services for the initial term and for the amount due at the time of renewal.

If Red Hat has approved Customer to be invoiced, then Red Hat will invoice Customer for the total fees at the time of execution of this Agreement, and payment shall be due within thirty (30) days of the invoice date and any additional fees shall be due within thirty (30) days of the invoice date.

All prices and rates quoted by Red Hat are exclusive of any foreign, federal, state, or local sales, excise, use, or similar taxes. Customer agrees to pay all such taxes, when applicable, regardless of whether such taxes are originally charged on Customer's credit card or appear on Red Hat's original invoice, or are later levied on Red Hat or Customer by a taxing authority, excluding any taxes levied solely on the net taxable income of Red Hat.

Any renewal of this Agreement will be at Red Hat's list prices in effect ninety (90) days prior to renewal; provided, however, the first such renewal shall be at the same price per Installed System paid during the initial term.

PAYMENT

Except in the case of breach of this Agreement by Red Hat or termination of this Agreement as provided in Section 1.1 hereof, any and all payments of amounts due under this Agreement are non-refundable.

In the event Customer fails to make payment to Red Hat in the manner provided by this Agreement, Red Hat's remedies include:

- Suspending Services until Red Hat receives full payment from Customer for all fees, including late fees and interest, due

- Terminating this Agreement without notice.

REPORTING AND AUDIT

If Customer wishes to increase the number of Installed System, then Customer will purchase from Red Hat additional Services for each additional Installed System. During the term of this Agreement and for one year thereafter, Customer expressly grants to Red Hat the right to audit Customer's facilities and records from time to time in order to verify Customer's compliance with the terms and conditions of this Agreement.

Any such audit shall only take place during Customer's normal business hours and upon no less than ten days prior written notice from Red Hat. Red Hat shall conduct no more than one such audit in any twelve-month period except for the express purpose of assuring compliance by Customer where non-compliance has been established in a prior audit. Red Hat shall give Customer written notice of any non-compliance, and if a payment deficiency exists, then Customer shall have fifteen days from the date of such notice to make payment to Red Hat for any payment deficiency. The amount of the payment deficiency will be determined by multiplying the number of underreported Installed Systems or Services by the annual fee for such item.

If Customer is found to have underreported the number of Installed Systems or amount of Services by more than five per cent (5%), Customer shall, in addition to the annual fee for such item, pay liquidated damages equal to twenty per cent (20%) of the underreported fees for loss of income and administration costs suffered by Red Hat as a result.

NON-TRANSFERABLE

This Agreement, and all Services provided by Red Hat pursuant to this Agreement, may not be transferred, assigned or distributed without the prior written consent of Red Hat. Any attempted transfer, assignment or distribution without Red Hat's prior written consent shall terminate this Agreement, and Red Hat shall have no further obligation hereunder. Even the leading Linux evangelist ESR well known for his economic determinism ("vulgar Marxism") was forced to depart from his CatB platform that Linux is a new and better method of producing software and being a new economic order magically can ensure business success of any startup that adopted it.

In June, 2001 VA Linux were he serves on the board of directors decided to fire 35% of staff as well as went out of hardware business (Linux-based servers). And VA Linux board member Eric "surprised by wealth" Raymond managed almost completely forget his CatB fairy tale commenting the event in Linux Today:

LT

On a broader level, what does this mean for Linux in general? A couple of years ago, it seemed as if the question many were asking wasn't so much whether Linux and open source software could get a piece of the pie: people seemed more convinced that there was a whole new pie to be carved up. Now there's been some culling and attrition, and companies are either specializing in order to cater to the needs of larger companies (like SuSE working so closely with IBM on high-end computing) or they're diversifying (Red Hat making big moves in embedded computing while introducing new services offerings and a database product).

In other words, it seems as if we've returned to a sense that there's really only one pie after all, and that the Linux market has a constrained piece of that pie. How much of the contraction we're seeing in Linux companies is a result of broader economic forces, and how much is a cooling of enthusiasm over Linux?

ESR

To quote some politician or other, *"It's the economy, stupid.":-)*

Don't take that personally, because you're asking an intelligent question that doesn't have a simple answer. Yes, *I think there has been some cooling of the initial enthusiasm for*

Linux—Wall Street's trendoids are notoriously fickle that way, always looking for the next buzzword.

But I think that has only been a minor factor in the recent troubles at VA and elsewhere. All the market surveys and projections still show Linux as a technology doing extremely well against its competition. The trouble is that capital spending is in collapse, hardware is commoditizing, *and it's getting increasingly hard to find decent profit margins anywhere you turn.*

It's tough all over, and Linux companies aren't the only or the worst affected. In a macroeconomic rainstorm like this, the best you can do is hunker down, minimize the burn rate, work on getting the close-to-profitable bits of the business really profitable, and hope the sun comes out soon. That's what VA is doing. We want to be there for our stockholders and stakeholders, with our skills still sharp and our commitment to open source still powerful, when the next expansion begins.

LT: On a related note, aren't the same forces that caused VA Linux to find itself in trouble on the hardware side similarly arrayed against it on the web content side? While no one's going to buy into a "ZD-Dot" or a "Fresh|Net," aren't the same risks of widespread acceptance present—the risk that a larger, better established player will just say "we're going to cover Linux and open source computing in general as another piece of the industry puzzle" and simply keep their existing reader base intact by saying, effectively, "we know you're interested in this 'new' technology, and we're covering it with n reporters?"

ESR: I'm not sure I ought to answer this one. Backing off from VA's business position a bit, I'll just observe that it's a lot harder to corral Web audiences than it is to boost hardware market share. Financial mass doesn't help in the same way; you can't buy audience share by lowering the margin you'll accept. Once a web community like eBay or Slashdot has reached a certain critical size, it's hard to lure people away from it to a competing service that's technically equivalent because most of the value to them is in *that particular community's* traditions and its trust network.

TRANSMETA IPO

George Orwell's barnyard parable of totalitarianism called Animal Farm, go out and buy yourself a copy; try not to be alarmed at how closely the farm is beginning to mirror our own society. In Animal Farm, a new order is established with lots of talk about freedom, but a certain species begins subjugating individual opinion and independent speech to the credo "All pigs are equal, but some pigs are more equal than others." If you are tempted to think that Orwell's gloomy story is nothing more than a fairy tale about a very naughty pig, read on. It is well applicable to penguins and it's funny that Linux Torvalds will do his best to help to enrich Microsoft founder Paul Allen. The rumors about Transmeta IPO started circulate in February 2000:

Transmeta appears to be taking its 'will they? won't they?' approach to chip announcements to the company's financial future. Speaking at a Banc of America Securities conference in San Francisco yesterday, Transmeta CEO Dave Ditzel told the assembled gathering of analysts that "it is possible we could do an IPO" during 2000. Or possibly not, he added, if circumstances change. For 'circumstances' read 'financial health of the company', and that depends on Transmeta winning sufficient customers for its x86-emulating CPU, Crusoe. The Crusoe launch was notably short on statements of support from computer and device manufacturers-- ie. there weren't any. Since then, the only significant announcement has come from S3, which has simply said it plans to ship a line of information appliances under its Diamond Multimedia brand, devices that will be based on the low-end Crusoe 3120. Ditzel said yesterday that notebooks based on the 700MHz Crusoe 5400 will appear by the end of the year.

And those rumors were actually true, so the next blow to the Torvalds' reputation came from the Transmeta IPO. Here is he supposed to he one of the key peddler of the shares of ultra closed, ultra secretive not profitable company: Like a number of start-ups, Transmeta is not profitable. In the first nine months of 2000, the company lost $71.1 million dollars and pulled in $3.8 million in revenue. In 1999, Transmeta lost

$41.1 million. Since it began in 1995, the company has lost approximately $147.5 million, according to documents filed with the Securities and Exchange Commission. Currently, more than half of the company's product revenue comes from a contract with Sony. Sony accounted for 50.2 per cent of Transmeta's product revenue, while sales to Fujitsu accounted for 20.3 per cent.

Before this year, the company's main revenue came from license fees from IBM and Toshiba. Both companies had licenses to manufacture Crusoe-like processors. Transmeta, however, later bought the rights by agreeing to pay IBM $38 million over four years and give 1.2 million shares of stock to Toshiba.

Currently, IBM is the sole manufacturer of Transmeta microprocessors, but starting next year, chips could be made by Taiwan Semiconductor Manufacturing Corp. (TSMC).

But who cares if the there is a smell of money in the air: In a sign of strong demand for its initial public offering, Transmeta Corp. (tmta) priced 13 million shares at $21, $3 above its range of $16 to $18. Shares trade Tuesday. As NYT noted in the article Transmeta's Stock Offering May Buck a Cooling Trend. That public stock offering is widely expected to get a blazing reception, despite a market far cooler to new technology offerings than last year's. After all, *the company is* backed by two prominent billionaire investors, the financier George Soros and Paul Allen, co-founder of Microsoft.

Its star employee is Linus Torvalds, the 30-year-old native of Finland who created the free Linux operating system and who is revered by many young programmers. And its Crusoe processors promise to be contenders in a rapidly growing market for laptops and mobile computing devices.

For some reason IBM was not completely happy, but Transmeta survived IBM torpedo (IBM announced just before IPO that power saving of Transmeta chips were not significant enough to justify creating of ThinkPad based on the chip): But IPO analysts have not given up on what they continually describe as a very strong offering. "This has taken a little polish off the apple, but it's still an apple," said John Fitzgibbon, IPO analysts with WorldFinanceNet.com. The deal, originally slated for the week of Nov. 6, had so much buzz that it was brought forward a week in anticipation of strong demand. But on Sunday, Oct. 29, it was unexpectedly moved back to the original week. Fitzgibbon said the pricing move was because the IBM announcement was coming down.

"They accelerated (the offering) because it was looking great," he said. "But if they had gone out this week they would have had a terrific first day, then the news would have hit and the stock would have fallen and they would have had to deal with a whole bunch of class actions."

Lead underwriters Morgan Stanley Dean Witter said they expect to price Transmeta's 13 million shares on Monday, Nov. 6, ready for trading the next day. The company hopes to raise about $156 million pricing between $11 and $13. Santa Clara, Calif.-based Transmeta will trade as "TMTA" on the Nasdaq

Due to Torvalds Transmeta has done an amazingly successful marketing pre-IPO push, overhyping the fact that Crusoe has low power consumption, while downplaying speed and stability concerns. Actually there was no quantum leap in battery performance and no laptops that would allow laptop computer batteries to last a full workday were produced to prove this. But the hype machine cranked up, leading to a successful multimillion IPO in November 7, 2000, at a time when technobubble burst already started to take a toll and most hardware startups and Linux related companies were crying out for a capital infusion from Wall Street. Companies like Hitachi, Casio, and Sony signed up to use the chip in computers, looking for a competitor to Intel that could provide processing power combined with frugal energy consumption. Here is CNET coverage of the event:

Transmeta, maker of the much-hyped Crusoe microprocessor, raised $273 million yesterday in its initial public offering. 13 million shares were bought at $21 each, easily beating Transmeta's $16-18 estimate set last Friday (which had been upped from the original $12 target). Shares are supposed to be trading to the public today—under the ticker TMTA—at around noon Eastern time.

Despite the fantastic IPO, Transmeta's future is under scrutiny. Since its founding in 1995, Transmeta has lost about US$147.5 million, including $71.1 million this year (through September) and $41.1 million last year, when the company first started getting media attention. These losses compare to only $3.8 million in revenue this year, over half of which comes from its contract with Sony (a further 20% comes from Fujitsu).

Sales of Crusoe chips in laptops were expected to begin boosting those revenue numbers, but recent processor benchmarks have shown less than stellar results for the Crusoe when compared to Intel chips (prompting noted Intel-defender Ashok Kumar of USB Piper Jaffray to question Transmeta's "lead" over Intel in power saving). IBM and Compaq were supposed to use Crusoe chips in some of their notebook computers, but IBM recently dropped plans to do that (despite being the only company currently producing Crusoe chips) and word this morning is that Compaq has also dropped the Crusoe from its Armada notebooks—despite the fact that Compaq is a Transmeta investor. Sony is still using Crusoes, however, and other product makers are as well. For much more information on the IPO and Transmeta's future, please CNET.

The next day shares went $46, which suggest good work by Morgan Stanley Dean Witter. But soon reality needed to be faced and savvy marketing did not solve the problems of fighting uphill battle with Intel and AMD. After Intel and AMD produced chips that consumed less power then Crusoe the game was over and Transmeta was left with a very narrow and not that profitable niche of ultra-portable notebooks, blades and wearable computers, if any. Most people was skeptical. For example on Linux Today forum bragging about getting Transmeta shares got comments like:

Even on Slashdot the news about Transmeta IPO generated a lot of criticism. There was much less friendly discussion that in the case of Red Hat IPO or VA Linux IPO. A lot of people questioned Linus Torvalds PR role in the ultra secretive company that rely on "on a combination of patents, copyrights, trademarks, trade secret laws and contractual obligations with employees and third parties to protect our proprietary rights."

As one Slashdot correspondent put it *"It probably means our fearless leader will soon be our *rich* fearless leader."* (He forgot that Linus Torvalds was already pretty rich person living in a multimillion house and driving BMW:-) There were several other unusually tough for Slashdot crowd (usually very favourable to anything connected with Linus Torvalds) posts from the same discussion:

Later things get really nasty for the Linus reputation and his Transmeta stock peddling to Linux enthusiasts became one of the worst parts of his biography. Not so power-stingy Crusoe-based notebooks materializing out of the pre IPO press release/trade show demo vapour demonstrated that like any real CPUs Crusoe chip has its problems. Accordingly Transmeta stock took a nosedive.

Some of the major laptop makers had been sending discouraging signals about their plans for Transmeta-processor-bearing products even before the IPO (IBM, Compaq). IBM complained that the Transmeta chip's power-saving gains have been overstated, and that these benefits fail to outweigh the research and development costs of rolling out a new processor in their product lines. Moreover much of what was available seemed to fall into the Asian-markets-only category. The other problem the Transmeta chip is connected with the performance hit that accompanies it. For the same frequency you get only 50-75% of the performance of the Pentium III CPU and Intel was not sleeping.

In Jan, 2001 Intel started to ship an "ultra-low-power" mobile Pentium III chip. With notebook sales going strong, especially compared with the current desktop market, Intel took steps to protect its mobile market share. The 500-MHz chip originally had been planned for introduction in the second half of the year but was moved up to Jan, 2001. The price was $200 which was better than Transmeta offerings. The new mobile Pentium III chip also had a better power consumption than Transmeta's current 5600 chip. Intel also introduced an ultra-low-power 500-MHz mobile Celeron chip for around

$100 which has much better price/performance ratio that any Transmeta offerings including 5800. Moreover Mobile Pentium III with SpeedStep won a prestigious Microprocessor Report Best PC Processor 2000 award in mobile category.

The Transmeta's stock price, which had been in the 50s, took a plunge and in April, 2001 was around $18. Later stock fall into a dollar range or approximately 50 times from its high. After the first Transmeta recall people start asking unpleasant questions and draw to unpleasant conclusions like in this message from ZDNet News Talkback Well, hello. I think everyone saw that the whole Transmeta thing was a giant ploy to get media attention. Hire Linus and expect everyone to buy your product, I think not.

And here the choice of Linus Torvalds looks really suspicious because from the point of view of architecture this chip can really benefit from VM (Virtual Machine) based OS, not from Linux monolithic kernel. And power saving alone is a pretty weak marketing tool, if they lead to substantial performance hits. News like recall also did not help: Transmeta Corp. confirmed Wednesday that it is working with Japanese computer maker NEC Corp. to recall notebook computers built with flawed versions of its power-saving Crusoe microprocessor.

Transmeta (stock: TMTA) said in a statement that the recall would take in "fewer than 300" NEC (stock: NIPNY) computers that are at risk of failing if the user reinstalled operating software. The company said that the recalled Crusoe chips came from a limited manufacturing batch, and it said any remaining inventory of the defective chips had been returned to Transmeta.

Transmeta said on Thursday that the flawed chips could have been used by computer makers other than NEC, but added that it was unlikely. "Right now, we have no clear evidence that any other customers are affected. Should we find evidence to the contrary, we will certainly deal with that," said James Chapman, Transmeta's senior vice president for sales and marketing. The Crusoe chips are also used in computers made by Sony Corp., Fujitsu Ltd. and Hitachi Ltd. Hitachi said in a statement it had found no problems with any of its computers that used the Crusoe chips.

Sony said on Thursday it had started to check its notebook computers which use the same Crusoe chip after seeing possible malfunctions, but had not decided whether to recall them.

Shares of Transmeta tumbled 15 per cent to close at $23 13/16 on Nasdaq Wednesday after a Japanese newspaper reported that NEC was considering a recall. In after-hours trade, Transmeta shares extended that slide, taking the cumulative loss on the day to nearly 25 per cent. The shares last traded on Instinet at $21.

The stock had surged to $50 on its first day of trading following its highly anticipated $273 million initial public offering on Nov. 7. On May 7, 2001 shares plummeted 23% ($3.40 from $11.17) in a single day after investors were freed from a restriction on selling stock. I suspect this day was not very good for Linus Torvalds as many people bought the stock due to the fact that he is employed at Transmeta. But this was just a start of troubles. Transmeta's Black Friday, when Linus needs to walk and tell his colleagues that they were laid off, was still a more than a year ahead... I also doubt that he might be too excited about commenting on Transmeta-IPO related investor lawsuits.

GREEDY LEADERS OF LINUX GOLD RUSH UNDER FIRE

In Jan 2001, long before real market decline, Red Hat shares traded around $8 and later declined to $5. The same is true for VA Linux, who managed to establish of the record for the first day stock gains: initial IPO price $30 rocketed the first day to $239.25. The stock closed at $8.94 on Jan 12, 2001 and was $3.95 in April, 2001—an almost 100 times decline. Instantly the question arise why stock flied so high and who is responsible for such a rapid decline. It looks like this disaster partially was provoked by actions by actions of the IPO underwriters and executives of those companies. There were allegation about direct manipulation of post IPO stock price.

The first suit against VA Linux Systems, Inc. was announced in Jan 2001 by Cauley Geller Bowman & Coates, LLP. In this Class Action Lawsuit they are seeking damages on behalf of shareholders. VA Linux Systems, whose shares had a record first-day run in December 1999, has been accused of deceiving investors. The suit, which also names the comp*any's lead underwriter, Credit Suisse First Boston, says* VA Linux failed to reveal in its prospectus that Credit Suisse promised shares in the stock offering to investors who pledged to buy more shares in the aftermarket at predetermined prices. "Such tie-in arrangements were designed to and did maintain, distort, and/or inflate the market price for Linux shares in the aftermarket," says the complaint, which was filed in federal court in New York.

The Law Firm of Cauley Geller Bowman & Coates, LLP announced today that it has filed a class action in the United States District Court for the Southern District of New York on behalf of all individuals and institutional investors who purchased the securities of VA Linux Systems, Inc. ("Linux" or the "Company") (Nasdaq: LNUX) between December 9, 1999 and December 6, 2000, inclusive (the "Class Period").

The complaint charges Linux and certain of its officers and directors with violations of the federal securities laws. On December 9, 1999, Linux completed an initial public offering of 4.4 million of its shares of common stock at an offering price of $30 per share (the "Linux IBO"). In connection therewith, Linux filed a registration statement, which incorporated a prospectus (the "Prospectus"), with the SEC.

The complaint further alleges that the Prospectus was materially false and misleading because it failed to disclose, among other things, that:

- Credit Suisse had solicited and received excessive and undisclosed commissions from certain investors in exchange for which Credit Suisse allocated to those investors material portions of the restricted number of Linux shares issued in connection with the Linux IBO; and
- Credit Suisse had entered into agreements with

customers whereby Credit Suisse agreed to allocate Linux shares to those customers in the Linux IBO in exchange for which the customers agreed to purchase additional Linux shares in the aftermarket at pre-determined prices.

In March, 2001 the number of federal lawsuits against VA Linux was close to 20. Most of them have been filed both against VA Linux and its lead underwriter, Credit Suisse First Boston. Other defendants charged in those suits read like a list who is who in investment banking: Salomon Smith Barney, Morgan Stanley Dean Witter, Merrill Lynch, Lehman Brothers, Goldman Sachs. A pretty interesting demonstration of the sexual appeal of Tux, the Penguin to the Wall Street;-)

Steven Schulman, a partner in the law firm Milberg Weiss Bershad Hynes & Lerach, which specializes in filing shareholder suits, and has sued VA Linux and CSFB over the VA Linux IBO said the VA Linux initial public offering is a prime example of market manipulation in an IPO by investment banks, their customers and the issuing firm. Because certain favoured customers of the investment banks agreed to buy shares in a new issue at inflated prices in the aftermarket (in return for getting an allocation of the shares at the initial offering price) the share prices to which the IBO eventually soared were actually driven by artificial market forces. Schulmansaid. "That is a manipulation and its purpose and effect, and it's illegal, is to cause a squeeze that pushes up the stock price very rapidly... It's an interrelated very lucrative set of arrangements that went on."

Red Hat also has been accused of violation of federal securities laws in a class-action lawsuit that alleges investors were misled about aspects of its initial public offering. The suit, filed in US District Court, Southern District of New York in April, 2001, charges the Linux distributor, its senior executives and securities houses of granting preferential share allocations during Red Hat's August 1999 IBO. These privileges were obtained, it is alleged, in exchange for "excessive commissions in transactions on other securities". Red Hat's shares were offered at $14 and almost quadrupled on the first day of trading, closing at $52 and the lawsuit rests on the argument that Red Hat made misleading statements in its prospectus and did not give smaller investors a fair slice of a lucrative pie. On April 4, 2001 the price was $4.74.

Law firm Milberg Weiss Bershad Hynes & Lerach has named Red Hat, and its executives Robert Young, Marc Ewing and Matthew Szulik in its action. Unspecified damages are also being sought from Goldman Sachs, the underwriters of the offer, and brokers Credit Suisse First Boston.

As previously reported, the Securities in Exchange Commission is investigating whether Wall Street firms made illegal payments in exchange for more shares in hot IPOs. The accusations made against Red Hat follows the pattern of charges against hardware firm VA Linux, which is accused of similar financial skulduggery in connection with its IBO.

Another Linux firm that was investigated was Linuxgruven, a controversial Linux tech support and training company Linuxgruven, which was launched in a blaze of glory in February 2000 and has offices in seven states. Investigation started in February 2001 was performed by the Missouri Attorney General's Office, local law enforcement and the Better Business Bureau. Linuxgruven, was allegedly involved in a scheme promising employment and then requiring prospective hires to pay several thousand dollars for training.

There are also charges of bounced checks, false advertising and unethical business practices. Linuxgruven was closed after several months of investigations. In the paper "Linux Training Pyramid Topples" Wired reported that job applicants were asked to pay $3,900 for the eight-week training course, and most said that they had the impression that they would be hired only if the fee was paid:

"Essentially they were selling training, but they found a novel way of doing that—they told you that you had a job, but then said you needed training to do that job properly," said Michael Browner, who applied for a job with Linuxgruven.

"Their interviewing process was a joke, essentially if you could keep from picking your nose at the interview, you got "hired," so long as you could write out a check for a few grand, that is," Browner said. Linuxgruven hasn't made an official announcement of its closure yet, but its phones are disconnected, and directory assistance has no current information for its St. Louis headquarters. The website is "being redesigned," but e-mails and calls to the site administrator were not answered.

"The company essentially hired anyone who walked in the door and coughed up $3,900 for training," said a former employee who requested anonymity because he is suing Linuxgruven for bounced paychecks and the promised reimbursement of his training fees.

"Their ads said that you needed two years minimum experience in programming or system administration or equivalent experience. To them, the 'equivalent experience' was you having $3,900 in the bank that you were willing to hand over. You could have been the most skilled systems guy in the world, but they still wanted you to cough up for their classes before they hired you," the source said.

Linuxgruven continued despite allegations that the company was nothing more than a scam. In March, company founder James Hibbits said Linuxgruven would continue to do business even after most of its top executives resigned. In an e-mail dated February 5, 2001, company founder James Hibbits said that Linuxgruven was not involved in any deceptive hiring practices.

"What we have done over the last year is amazing. We've actually introduced Linux to over 100,000 people who never even heard of it. We have offices in eight U.S. cities and will have 16 by (the) end of 2001," Hibbits said. Hibbits referred to Linuxgruven's practice of asking employees to pay for training as "a different business model.... Instead of raising a pile of cash and burning through it and hoping we're right, we had to make money from the beginning." But when Hibbits was arrested for a two-year-old fraud charge on April 19, the company disappeared.

Hibbits could not be reached by phone or e-mail after his arrest, but in previous e-mails he strongly refuted the charges that Linuxgruven had been accused of in posts on geek-site Slashdot. "A lot of those flames included false information and misrepresentation of what our company does and how we train and hire employees," Hibbits said.

Hibbits had claimed, in previous e-mails, that the company was training "roughly 200 people a month." Hibbits also noted that all the costs of Linuxgruven training were reimbursed to employees after a year's employment, a statement that Browner acknowledges was made to him during the interview.

But Browner questions how many people "hired with no qualifications to be a Linux tech besides a checkbook" would have managed to be employed for a full year. There's no way to tell, as the company had barely been in business for a year when it disappeared this week. "They planned to go ahead despite all the furor and problems, but when James (Hibbits) was arrested last week for an old insurance fraud charge, that was the straw that broke the camel's back," said a former employee of Linuxgruven, requesting anonymity since he is also involved in legal action against the company.

Hibbits has been accused of taking payments for car insurance but not providing the insurance coverage. He was served last week with a warrant for his arrest, and then released on a $10,000 dollar bond. A dozen or so former employees are suing Linuxgruven because of bounced paychecks in March. But some Linuxgruven employees said they were happy with the training they had received, and felt that the company's failure was due to the softening tech market.

"The classes were good, I was learning something, and I had no problems paying for that training. Linuxgruven offered me a chance that I probably won't get anywhere else. I am sorry to see them go out of business," said Michael Venders, a former employee. Others said that they had no qualms about paying for training, but were angered when their paychecks started bouncing, or when their classes were cancelled and no refunds were offered. "As soon as the CEO left I knew it was doomed. Matthew (Porter) was a great guy, and I think he got sucked into something he didn't fully understand with Linuxgruven," said a source, who also requested his name not be used because of pending legal actions against Linuxgruven. Matthew Porter, once a chairman of the St. Louis Linux Users Group, had replaced Hibbits as Linuxgruven's CEO in January 2001. Hibbits remained with the company as chairman of the board.

Porter resigned in March, and sources said he left when he realised the company would be unable to pay employees. "Matthew has said that he was disgusted by the fact that paychecks would bounce. He is a solid guy, and a true supporter of Linux, and he is sad over what happened here," said the source. Hibbits told the St. Louis Post-Dispatch on April 19 that all debts would be paid. "The company is going to go forward," he said. Hibbits was arrested on the insurance fraud charge by St. Louis police two hours after making that statement. This situation with greedy little yellow penguin presents a interesting parallel development to the Microsoft's legal troubles.

MAC OS X STOLE DESKTOP FROM LINUX

Linux is an Intel centric system. Yes, Alpha port does exist, as well as PowerPC and mainframe ports, but please remember than the only platform were Linux is relatively competitive is Intel platform. On less known platforms NetBSD is the king of the hill and Linux is not even close. And bloated kernels does not help Linux to enter markets were memory is a premium, or there is no alternative for the old machines that are no longer supported by manufacturer but still are nice and usable systems (like old Suns or HPs workstations).

Linus Torvalds was especially bad in dealing with Mac users and PowerPC platform. Historically he learned Alpha architecture because Alphas were his first freebies: he got free Alpha servers from DEC when just before Compaq acquisition DEC tried to play a Linux card for this very interesting CPU. But Intel platform grasped almost all his attention and situation even deteriorate after he joined Transmeta. As Linus controlled kernel development that means that outside Intel(and may be IBM mainframes) Linux does not have much sense. Not surprisingly Intel was early and major investor in the several Linux startups. And about the problems with Linux non-Intel ports you can get a lot of interesting information talking to any IBMer involved with running Linux in VM environment.

At the same time Linus not only ignored existence of Mac and Mac users but made a political blunder that converted some previous allies into enemies. With his careless remarks he created a problem that later became even worse: in March, 2001, Apple helped BSD accomplished what Linux has been promising for years: they put the power of Unix into a desktop system and made it available to the mass user. The launch of Mac OS X instantly turned Apple into the largest distributor of desktop Unix-like OS (neither Linux nor Mac OS cannot formally be called Unix because they never passes Open Consortium compliance tests).

"On March 24, Apple Computer, Inc. released its next-generation operating system, Mac OS X (the "X" is pronounced as "ten," for the version number of the operating system) to Mac addicts around the world. While this isn't such a big deal to some, others view it as a new beginning that could squash all thoughts of a desktop Linux for the general public.

What's this, "Apple out-maneuvering Linux?" you say? Well, maybe not as a server platform for the immediate future, but just think about this for a second: Would it be possible for Apple to deflate the hopes and dreams of developers worldwide of bringing Linux to the desktop? The short answer to this is yes, but it's more complicated than that.

At the core of Mac OS X is a kernel built on the Mach 3.0 kernel, BSD 4.4, and Darwin (Apple's open source kernel project), giving network and system administrators the ability to use Unix programs and add them to their Macs. When combined, these components offer a rock-solid operating system that's hard to beat. One of the advantages of Mac OS X is that it now offers Macintosh users with a command line on top of a slick, stable GUI, known as Aqua. With OS X's BSD core, Macintosh users will now be able to use GNU software. This means they will be able to run tools like Emacs, vi,

Apache, and even XFree86 andthe GIMP (something that Adobe Systems should fear). If you're looking for a place to download ports of GNU tools that run under Mac OS X, you should visit the GNU-Darwin Project on SourceForge.

So how does this make Mac OS X a threat to Linux? If you've given this any thought, the answer is quite clear. One of the challenges that the Linux community has been plagued with in recent years is the development of a stable and easy-to-use GUI. While some view X (or any GUI) as a hindrance to Linux's performance, a usable interface is a necessary evil if you want to convert users from Windows. And while the Linux kernel might be stable, the GUIs are, at times, buggy and less desirable for most people."

Now anyone with a desire to learn and run Unix can purchase it for about the same cost as a Microsoft operating system. For the regular user, it looks and acts just like a MacOS user would expect. However, all the powerful features that make it Unix are available for the Mac developers and power users who want to take the OS to its limits. That make Linux much less attractive as a desktop environment, especially in USA.

Linus reacted to this news in a pretty arrogant manner: he slammed OS X microkernel in his autobiography. As ZDnet reported in Torvalds rubbishes core of Apple's OS X: "The forthcoming autobiography from Linux Torvalds, creator of the Linux operating system and figurehead of the open source movement, Just For Fun, promises to cast a shadow over Apple's newly released OS X, which Torvalds describes in less than flattering terms."

"'Frankly, I think it's a piece of crap,' *Torvalds says of Mach, the microkernel on which Apple's new operating system is based.* 'It contains all the design mistakes you can make, and manages to even make up a few of its own.'" "Torvald's comments promise to upset not just Apple fanatics, but also some quarters of the free software movement. The Mach microkernel is also being used as the core of Hurd, a kernel project from the Free Software Foundation that will be an alternative to Linux as the heart of the GNU (Gnu's Not Unix) operating system, originally devised by free software advocate Richard Stallman."

That political blunder (may be not Linus own fault as autobiography was co-written (read written;-) with David Diamond) did not win him any friends in MAC crowd and for many MAC users saw this as an attempt to help Microsoft in their fight with Apple. As John Tachek put it in this column:

"It's also arrogance. So is the decision of the Linux god himself, Linus Torvalds, to ridicule the Mac OS X operating system. He's apparently ingested way too much of the Linux freedom fighters' fodder while forgetting that people just want their things to work." Even Linux zealots in Linux Today were mildly embarrassed. As one reader put it (Torvalds likes bananas! News at 11)

Please, enough of the Torvalds' preferences stories. His opinion is really only important in a narrow channel. This isn't one of them. By choosing to build Mac OS X on BSD Unix Apple opened up thousands of new applications to Mac owners--potentially expanding Apple's market share--and gave Unix developers (and especially BSD and System V applications developers) access to a lucrative new audience. The reason behind Unix developers' interest in Mac OS X is simple: it is the first desktop, Unix-based operating system to reach the mass market.

Apple has gone down the Unix road before. Steve Jobs created a very innovative Next computer with Next OS based on BSD. In the early 1990s, Apple sold A/UX, a version of Unix System V, designed to run on Apple's Macs and servers as an alternative to the Mac OS. But A/UX didn't easily run existing Mac applications and attracted few buyers. It was discontinued.

Mac OS X can also be thought of as NeXTStep 6.0. It's built upon many technologies and descendants of technologies from that innovative system. Technically I probably would have preferred a BeOS design. But, still it's a great OS -- the first truly usable Unix desktop. Some design decisions might have a bright future. I think DisplayPDF will be a boon to the DTP industry, and especially to Adobe, as workflow starts shifting towards PDF for creation, presentation, preview, proof, etc. It may also be the secret to resolution independent displays as displays get bigger and bigger (19" displaynow is normal, 21" looks like nothing special; it was gigantic five years ago).

Instantly OS X got important applications unavailable for Linux: Macromedia released FreeHand 10, Adobe Systems and Microsoft, promised to deliver software in six month. To facilitate Unix developer relations, Apple has entered a partnership with the O'Reilly Network. "Right now, there's definitely curiosity about Mac OS X" from Unix developers, said Derrick Story, managing editor for O'Reilly Network. "What they find when they begin poking around inside (Mac OS X) will have a lot to do with whether that interest is sustained or remains a curiosity. It's hard to say right now how that's going to go."

Apple's biggest inroad into the Unix community may not come from developers but from the education market. The education market offers two tremendous advantages: Apple is de-facto standard in USA K-12 schools. At the same time Unix is extremely popular in universities. Moreover education community in general, and university crowd in particular, firmly believes in open standards. And for the university community BSD Unix was and is the most appealing flavour of Unix. Now there is a possibility to have university graduates that can say "I learned on a BSD and I grew on the BSD," instead of a more typical current situation "I learned Mac at high school, moved to Windows and BSD at the university and went to Solaris at my first job." And the first operating system is very important almost life-defining experience for any computer professional.

David Coursey, Executive Editor of ZDNet AnchorDesk formulated this very clearly in on of his columns (ZDNet Story Hey, desktop Linux fans Buy a Mac... or just go away). I especially like "Like scientific socialism, it will go down as an idea that sounded good on paper but didn't work in the real world. If the proponents of desktop Linux are really honest, they will move to a Unix platform that has all the things Linux lacks: a great user interface, a large number of applications, support of a profitable major vendor, an industry guru who's taken extremely seriously, and even the cover of Time magazine." The only thing I disagree with Mr Coursey is that Linux has a bright future on the server. With all due respect I am inclined to see Linux place as a new free "superBIOS" and the best it can do is to became a workhorse for pilots and low to midrange departmental and small ISP servers. But here is a more complete version of David Coutney vews on the subject:

Let's get something straight right away. I don't mind Linux, and I certainly don't require an operating system to come from Redmond to be acceptable. Linux can be a great operating system when used for the server tasks that suit it best. Heck, I was even married to a Unix person, and Doug Michels, a Unix pioneer, is one of my best friends. But it would be just fine with me if the Linux-on-the-desktop people--at least the ones who leave TalkBack responses to my columns on seemingly any topic--would please go away. Read someone else's column.

Harass that person for a change:

- THESE DESKTOP LINUX people are just like the adherents to any concept that has failed in the marketplace of ideas: They don't know when to let go, and make fools of themselves as a result. The commercial Linux community, as represented by Red Hat Chairman Bob Young, has come to the conclusion that Linux on the desktop is a non-starter. Further, the controversy and distraction the issue creates takes attention from Linux as a server OS, where it really shines and provides a real alternative to Microsoft products. I encourage those of you who are willing to share my pain to check out the reaction to my Monday column, "Try a Mac? Why it won't hurt as much as you think." Reading between the lines of some of the TalkBacks, I see a five-letter word: CHEAP.
- YES, DESKTOP LINUX is almost free and doesn't require tithing to Microsoft. But soon the desktop Linux folks won't have the free StarOffice to throw

at me as proof of their platform's superiority and zero cost of entry. According to published reports, Sun Microsystems, which bought the German-built multiplatform productivity suite a few years ago, is going to start charging for versions adapted to non-Sun platforms. This means Sun has given up on the idea that giving away StarOffice would mess with sales of Microsoft Office. Sun now wants the program to pay its own way. StarOffice is a decent enough suite and is certainly worth the $50 to $100 Sun is expected to charge for it.

- BUT I WONDER how many desktop Linux zealots will be willing to pay for StarOffice? My guess: not many. My perception of these folks--and it's very likely I am describing only a vocal minority, so if this isn't you, I apologize--is that they don't want to spend a dime on software and consider themselves deserving and even superior because they possess the high level of technical skill required to make Linux work.

How you build a vibrant computing platform when nobody is willing to spend money on it escapes me. Running Linux on servers is different, mostly because the Linux that's available today is clearly capable of doing that job quite well. Server Linux is also becoming something the big systems companies seem to throw in as a way to sell expensive hardware, expensive server applications, and expensive services contracts.

MAKE NO MISTAKE

Linux servers are a cause for concern in Redmond and a source for happiness in data centers worldwide. Desktop Linux, on the other hand, is rapidly being assigned to the trash pile of computing history. Like scientific socialism, it will go down as an idea that sounded good on paper but didn't work in the real world.

If the proponents of desktop Linux are really honest, they will move to a Unix platform that has all the things Linux lacks:

a great user interface, a large number of applications, support of a profitable major vendor, an industry guru who's taken extremely seriously, and even the cover of Time magazine. I'm talking about buying a Macintosh, of course. But running OS X would actually cost these Linux geeks money, and that's something I am not sure any of them are willing to spend. Still, if these people hated all things Microsoft as much as many of them proclaim to, you'd think rallying around Unix-based OS X would be the best way to advance their cause.

But only if they're willing to put some money where their much-too-loud mouths are. As of the end of 2001 the ratio is approximately 3:1. According to Google Macs represent 4% of users, Linux-1% and all other non-Microsoft OSes-4%. And Apple's elegant user interface and the quality of the kernel does matter. Scientists at places like NASA are unplugging their old Sun workstations and replacing them with Macs, not with Linux.

The only problem with Mac is its cost: Linux is running on a more democratic hardware supported by two giants: Intel and Microsoft. In an interesting paper in Boston Globe Online the author aptly had shown why OS X represents a threat to Linux on desktop:

Linux, a cheap, highly compatible substitute for the advanced Unix operating system, has seized more than a quarter of the market for heavy-duty server computers. But at most, 2 per cent of desktop users are running the software, partly because it's notoriously difficult to use.

That makes Apple's Mac OS X operating system at least as much of a challenge to Linux as it is to Microsoft. Mac OS X is Unix, but with Apple's elegant user interface bolted on. Scientists at places like NASA are unplugging their old Unix workstations and replacing them with Macs. How long before Linux desktop loyalists abandon the digital wrestling match and switch to Apple as well?

The latest Linux release from market leader Red Hat Inc. should stave off a few defectors. While not exactly Mac-like in its ease of use, Red Hat 8 is far superior to earlier versions. It starts with setup. Linux installations can be hellish affairs.

There's the matter of laying out all the necessary hard drive partitions, for one thing. Then there's the question of compatibility-will your monitor, graphics card, mouse, CD-ROM drive all work? And even if they are compatible, how do you make sure Linux installs the correct driver?

In our test of Red Hat 8, none of this mattered. The disk partition process is automated now. As for compatibility, the software identified and self-installed all the vital peripherals on our test machine without incident. And there was none of this Microsoftian nonsense about software authentication. As a result, Red Hat is actually easier to install than Windows XP.

There's a new user interface called Bluecurve, a polished version of the Gnome interface that's familiar to Linux loyalists. Gnome's gaudier excesses have been tamped down a bit. The icons and menus have a more modest, graceful style, and a more consistent appearance. As always with Linux, there's a lot of useful software built into Red Hat 8. The Web browser is Mozilla, the open source version of Netscape Navigator. While Microsoft Internet Explorer remains, for better or worse, the best browser out there, Mozilla holds its own for run-of-the-mill surfing purposes.

There's Sun Microsystems' OpenOffice, with a spreadsheet, presentation graphics program, and a word processor good enough to use in writing this article. Boston's own Ximian Inc. has contributed Evolution, a personal information manager that does a fair imitation of Microsoft Outlook. In short, a PC loaded with Red Hat 8 can handle about 95 per cent of the average user's needs. This much software from Microsoft would cost about $400. But Red Hat 8 can be downloaded from the Internet for free. To get service and support, you have to pay for the software, but only $39.95 for the basic desktop version.

However, cheap is not enough. Red Hat 8 is still a ragbag of code, written by amateurs and part-timers and jumbled all together. And it shows. For instance, the feature for allowing you to share information with a Handspring handheld computer didn't work properly. A Red Hat engineer admitted that he wasn't sure of the reason, because the underlying software was written by somebody outside the company and he knew little about it. Corporate users pay for Microsoft products largely because they get a decent level of support from the company. Because Linux isn't controlled by Red Hat or any other company, delivering the same level of service is far harder. But it'll have to be done.

There are other off-putting problems. The Bluecurve interface still has its share of kinks. For instance, sometimes open windows are too large to fit onto the screen. Certain functions still assume the user is a software engineer. Dialing onto the Internet, for instance, requires clicking "Network Device Control." Now there's the first place the average guy would look. Indeed, the menu is crammed with programs that'll mean nothing to the typical user. The Red Hat designers should hide them to avoid confusing the newbies.

Still, Red Hat 8 is a major advance, and at just the right moment. Microsoft's new software licensing scheme has driven up the price of its software for thousands of its corporate customers. One survey from the research firm Giga found 36 per cent of corporate software buyers were getting mad enough to consider switching to another supplier. Moving to Mac would require installing a lot of new computers, while Linux will run on any late-model PC. Which means that, in the elephantine struggle between PC and Mac, Linux still has a fighting chance.

The author cites reasons that Linux is not ready for everyone. Linux trails both MS-Windows and Mac OS X in terms of third-party vendor support; more people are familiar with those OSes than Linux; those other OSes have significant advantages in implementation of high-level integration between applications. Linux ismaking progress, not is pretty small while the enthusiasts continue to show signs of an Amiga Persecution Complex.

DECLINE AND FALL OF VA LINUX

VA Linux was undermined by warring internal factions, out-of-control spending and a management team hell-bent capitalizing on their IPO shares. The result: VA Linux's ship took too much water and surviving executives had found themselves desperately scrambling to keep the company afloat. *I remember how Eric Raymond said about Linuxcare (sited from News Can Linuxcare stay afloat):*

"Linuxcare's management screwed up big-time," said Eric Raymond, open-source luminary and a member of VA Linux Systems' board of directors. "They had a lot of good people at the line level, too. This was definitely a case of top-down incompetence." Now it's time to apply this harsh words to Eric Raymond himself as well as to Larry Augustin and other members of VA Linux Systems' board of directors.

In June 27, 2001 VA Linux too a drastic measure; it decided to exit hardware market. Afer reading this news I got the feeling that this is the last desperate measure, doomed to be a failure. Much like Michael Cowpland's "new vision" for Corel last year. And we know how this move affect Corel as a company and Michael Cowpland as a CEO... On August 24, 2001 VA Linux stock felt below $2. And many analysts predict that the days of the company are numbered. Morningstar has given them just five more quarters.

5

Linux Security

INTRODUCTION TO LINUX SECURITY

Up until now, this book has been primarily concerned with the variations of Windows and how to secure information on a computer running windows. Windows, however, is not the only game in town. There is a small but growing number of people who choose Linux as their operating system, because it is an open source operating system that is freely available to change by its users.

"Open source" is all the buzz these days in the way of the Linux operating system, because anyone can view the source code and examine it, modify it, and suggest and make changes to it. Thousands of programmers are constantly improving Linux, and when a bug or security exploit is found, these open source programmers fix it immediately. Open source software has been around for a very long time, although perhaps not exactly as we all know it today.

The very first software ever developed was open source, and all software remained this way for many years. Licensing was not an issue at the time, the concept of software as product wasn't even a fully developed thought and the commercial aspect of computing appeared to rely purely on hardware sales and production. UNIX was the operating system of choice by the mid 70's. Although developed mostly by Bell Labs, it was a prime example of an open source software project. Developers from universities and institutions around the world have made countless contributions to the project as the operating system grew and changed.

SOME LINUX SECURITY PRECAUTIONS

In many ways, securing Linux is a much less difficult than securing Windows, simply because most attackers and hackers write their code specifically to attack Windows and Window's users. However, just because there are fewer worms, viruses, etc., out their waiting to attack the Linux operating system does not mean that people who run Linux should not also take security precautions. Many of the same principles apply to both users, such as creating solid passwords and keeping those passwords secure.

For those of you using Linux, what follows is a list of things to do in order to secure your computer.

- Re-install the system. There is absolutely no point in securing a system that has already been broken in to, or for which backdoors have already been created. If you are in the least bit unsure if this has been the case, then just go on ahead and reinstall the system.
- Configure iptables, if you have the technical know-how. Iptables work much like a firewall on a system running windows, keeping packets of information from leaving or entering your computer. The Linux kernel needs configured correctly, and then installed correctly. You may want to review the Linux Kernel HOWTO, and practice a few times before trying to configure iptables. There are also step-by-step instruction guides available on the web, this google search offers several. Also, here is the Linux Firewall and Proxy Server HOWTO which gives details on setting up both a filtering and proxy firewall on a Linux based system.
- Install LIDS. LIDS stands for Linux intrusion detection system. LIDS consist of a patch for the Linux kernel and two user space utilities. This system increases the level of security on your computer by restricting access to files and processes. LIDS also alert you when someone or something attempts to access the protected files and processes. When it's in effect, no one (including root) can change the

protected files or directories and their sub-directories. You have to reboot the system with a security=1 LILO setting to modify secure files.

- Maintain the security. You can maintain security on your Linux system by running chkrootkit every week or so. This script detects well known root-kits. Most people running Linux will know that a rootkit is a set of tools that a hacker or attacker can use to hide his/her tracks. Running chkrootkit keeps you aware if anyone has been using your system, and if they have, you can then basically kick them out.

As you can see, Linux can be very easy to secure indeed with a little aptitude for computers. This is not a problem since most Linux users pride themselves on having aptitude with computers and leave Windows to the rest of us.

WHEN YOUR LINUX SYSTEM HAS ALREADY BEEN COMPROMISED

Every program on every computer has, at one time or another had a bug. If the program is the operating system itself, having a bug is a serious problem because the bug can be exploited by a person with questionable morals, allowing him to gain access to everything on the computer. Operating system security exploits are discovered all the time, and they are exploited by crackers who have sophisticated channels of communication, who share their exploits with others of their type, and who pass along their method of gaining access to countless others with questionable moral intent.

The result is that, when an operating system exploit is found, all machines using that operating system are also vulnerable to a similar attack. What do you do if the system has already been compromised? Well, I already hinted at what the solution is at the beginning of this chapter. You must re-install. But there is more you must do to figure out what went wrong and how not to do that again.

Here are a couple of things to do if your system is ever compromised:

- Go to the Coroners Tool Kit and install this tool.

There are how-to guides for installation on the bottom of the page. It is highly recommended that you go through the tutorial several times before attempting the real thing. After installing it successfully, you can watch the programs and files that have been compromised come up on your screen.

- Learn more by going to the Honey Net Project. On this site you can learn much more about computer security. Their mission is to teach and inform about computer security. They also do forensic research on violated computers in the hopes of coming up with better ways to protect your Linux system.

LINUX OPERATING SYSTEM SECURITY

Ever since the start of the security wars, with crackers being their usual destructive selves and hackers trying to prevent them from breaking into systems, Linux has been considered to be the most secure solution of an Operating System. Its free source code and its millions of users and programmers around the world strived to make it more secure both by auditing the freely available code of the OS and its utilities as well as by writing tools to help non-gurus secure it.

KERNEL SECURITY

As it is known, the Linux Kernel is the most important part of the Linux Operating system. In fact Linux is basically the kernel, the rest of the components are programs under the GNU license. The person who created the Linux Kernel was Linus Torvalds, a student in the University of Finland. When the first kernel was created it was around 24KB, growing in size as the years passed, and is now around 25MB.

Being the most important part of the Linux Operating System, the Kernel needs to be secured so as to avoid anybody altering it in order to bring it down or take control of it. This process is called Kernel Hardening. Kernel Hardening therefore is defined as enabling additional kernel-level security mechanisms to improve the security of the system, while keeping system close to traditional Linux. One approach to secure the Linux kernel is to compile it with no module support, which is what most rootkits (programs that are designed to take control of the kernel by exploiting the weaknesses inherent in various kernel modules) aim for, as well as some security-related kernel options turned on.

LIDS (Linux Intrusion Detection System)

LIDS was written by Xie Huagang and Philippe Biondi. LIDS is a patch that provides Mandatory Access Control (MAC) to the kernel. MAC enables higher levels of security than standard UNIX Discretionary Access Control (DAC) since it allows more fine-grained access control and protection of files from owner and superuser (who lose a lot of power in a MAC-enabled system). LIDSs philosophy views the system as a set of subjects (programs) and objects (files), with the subjects being given the right to access objects and perform some operations.

Those rights can be restricted by time, and there is also a set of global capabilities. LIDS can also protect and hide files and processes, grant access privileges on an individual basis, and give programs special rights called capabilities. It also works in the kernel, disallowing malicious kernel modules from loading and has a kernel-based port-scan detector.

Medusa DS9

The Medusa project was born in the summer of 1997, when the first version of the kernel patch was released. Incidentally, all the Medusa kernel patches got their second initials from the Star Trek terminology (DS9 being Deep Space 9, and the previous version being NG, Next Generation). The Medusa DS9 is a package that improves the overall security of the Linux OS by extending the standard Linux security architecture while preserving backward compatibility. The tool implements the ZP Security Framework, which is intended to be a framework for implementation of any security model. The project consists of two major parts; the VS monitor which works in the kernel of the OS and the SDC (Security Decision Center), which works as a user-space daemon.

The VS model (Virtual Spaces model) replaces the access control matrix. The objects and subjects are separated into the finite number of domains, named virtual spaces. Each object is assigned a set of abilities (a set of virtual terminals), one for each access type. Access is granted when the object and the subject share at least one common virtual space for the given access type.

The Security Decision Center is responsible for the dynamic changes of a security model in time. Before the execution of certain operations, the kernel asks the authorization server for confirmation. The authorization server then permits or forbids the operation. The authorization server can also affect the way an operation is executed in some cases.

Communication between the SDC (called Constable) and the kernel goes through the special device "/dev/medusa" as this makes it faster and more flexible. When the kernel needs confirmation, it writes data to this device which makes the current process sleep and wakes up Constable. Constable reads the data from/dev/medusa, chooses a response, and sends it back to the kernel and then sleeps.

The kernel gets the data, wakes up the process and determines the result of the operation. The security daemon has to use a specific communication protocol defined in kernel, so it is possible to implement a full-featured authorization server by only knowing this protocol and knowing that the kernel supports it without worrying what's really happening in the kernel.

Saint Jude LKM

Saint Jude is a model for the detection of unauthorized or improper root transitions. It detects remote compromises of protected daemons via the Override directive, thus averting attacks in the form of Internet worms and direct attacks using unpublished exploit code. It also protects itself as well as core components of the system with the addition of features that block the removal of the immutable flags on ext2 and ext3 (the old and new version of the file system in Linux), which make the system read-only by inhibiting the OS from modifying the protected file system object.

Lomac

LOMAC is a security enhancement for Linux that uses Low Water-Mark Mandatory Access Control to protect the integrity of processes and data from viruses, Trojan Horses, malicious remote users, and compromised root daemons. LOMAC is implemented as a kernel module and, although it is still not complete, still provides some useful integrity protection. It operates on single-CPU machines and utilizes the Linux kernel version 2.2. Once loaded, LOMAC divides the system into two levels of integrity, high and low.

The high side contains all process and files that should be protected from malicious code. The low side contains the processes that interact with remote users and the files they download from the net. During run-time, LOMAC protects high files and processes by preventing low processes from modifying or signaling them. Lomac makes decisions based solely on integrity levels and not user identity and its permission checking is done in addition to the current Linux protection mechanisms.

LINUX FILE SYSTEM SECURITY

The Linux file system is basically a network file system where each user has different privileges from another user in the system, thus being able to keep their files private from all other users except root. And this last bit about the root having access to just about anything is the problem and the thing most coveted by any malicious attacker wishing to break into the system. A malicious attacker, when gaining access to the system (in the form of a simple user) will first try to obtain the status of the root, either by exploiting their way via one of the attacks mentioned in the Kernel Security or by finding and cracking the root password. Once they have root access, the first thing they will do is disable any logging features the OS has in place and destroy any logs of the attack to erase their tracks and make sure no tracks of their activities inside the system exist.

Permissions

One way to check the permissions and scan for existing SUIDs and new SUIDS and GIDS in a system is to use the find command, by entering:

```
#find/-perm -4000
```

This will give you all the files that have the SUID bit set. The problem with this command, of course, is that okay, it will give you all the SUID/SGID files but you will need to run it daily/monthly and manually figure out which files have been given SUID/SGID since the last check, which is a very long and tedious process.

Passwords

Passwords are the first line of defense in just about any system there is. To enter the Linux OS, a user needs to type in his username and password. If the username and password combination is correct then the user is admitted and a login prompt appears, if not the user has to re-type the username and password. Passwords are created using the crypt() program, which has traditionally been used in UNIX systems. Crypt was based on the enigma encryption algorithm but was considerably trivialized. Recently, a new encryption program is used for password creation and encryption.

Mcrypt, created by Nikos Mavrogyanopoulos, has replaced crypt and supports multiple encryption algorithms, such as Blowfish, DES, 3-DES etc. The problem with passwords is that they can also be guessed if the/etc/passwd and/etc/shadow files fall in the hands of a malignant user or an attacker. If such a person gets their hands on these two files, they can use a program such as crack or John the Ripper to decode the password file and gather up all the passwords of all the users.

Logging

Logs are very important for any administrator of a system

to read, as they are the reporting mechanisms for all actions the system takes, from login information to intruder detection. Their detailed reporting, though, is also the problem as not a lot of administrators have the time necessary to shift through pages and pages of system logs, so they conveniently ignore them. Below are some log-watching programs that are used to glean useful information from all these logs.

Syslog-ng

Syslog-ng ("syslog new generation") is an attempt to increase syslog's flexibility by adding better message filtering, better forwarding, and eventually message integrity and encryption. Syslog-ng is able to filter messages based on the contents of messages in addition to the priority/facility pair. Another design principle was to make log forwarding between firewalled segments easier: long hostname format, which makes it easy to find the originating and chain of forwarding hosts even if a log message traverses several computers.

And last principle was a clean and powerful configuration file format. In addition, Syslog-ng supports remote logging over both the TCP and UDP protocols. Furthermore, Syslog-ng can be used in conjunction with TCP tunneling tools such as stunnel and ssh to authenticate or encrypt log messages sent to remote hosts.

Swatch

Swatch was a perl program written by E. Todd Atkins and was originally written to actively monitor messages as they are written to a log file via the syslog utility and notify the administrator when interesting events occur. Swatch monitors the log files for specific triggers, when those triggers are matched it notifies you in a pre-determined manner.

You can run swatch in either batch mode, where you examine a log file's contents and then exit, or in monitor mode, where swatch continually monitors the log files evaluating each new record.

It provides a variety of notification options and offers great ease of configuration as well as a very easy installation script that will copy all the libraries, manpages and perl files to their proper directories.

PERIMETER SECURITY IN LINUX

Perimeter Security is defined as the process and tools involved in securing the outside points of contact of a Linux system.

Points of contact include web and ftp services, remote access to the system and resistance to outside attacks. Usually, the attacker will first run a portscan tool to determine the open ports of a system and the services running on them, and in the case of a specific tool called nmap, the system and kernel running on it as well as the owner of each of the processes.

Then, the attacker will try to find a way to exploit one or more of the services so as to either gain a simple user account of the system, or grab the passwd file or spawn a root shell. There are many ways to exploit each of the services running on a system, depending on which ones are running at the time the attack commences, the skill of the attacker and the current bugs of each of the services running on the machine.

Most dangerous services to be running on a system are usually the web-server, the ftp server, all the R utilities (as they are called) which include portmap, rhosts and rsh, the X server, the nfs services such as exported filesystems and the remote access services (telnet) as well as the mail servers. These services are dangerous from a security standpoint because of the lack of proper authentication mechanisms.

SECURITY TOOLS

TCP Wrapper

The TCP wrapper is a simple but effective tool for monitoring and controlling network activity.

It was written by Wietse Venema when his university was under attack from a malicious user and has been expanded and updated ever since, with millions all over the world using it for their systems and major Linux distributions including it in their structures.

Some of its features include:

- No need to modify configuration files or existing software.
- Ease of installation, as it is installed without any need of further configuration.
- No impact on the legal users of the system.
- There is no exchange of data with the network client or server process, eliminating the risk of software bugs.
- Suitable for both TCP and UDP services.
- Protection against name server spoofing.
- Optional access-control facility, shielding off open systems.

With TCP wrapper, the system launches the wrapper for inetd connections, logs all attempts and then verifies the attempt against an access control list. If the connection is permitted, the wrapper hands over the connection to the relevant binary. If the connection is rejected by the acl, then the connection is dropped.

Rpcbind

This is yet another TCP wrapper-style tool, this time for the rpcbind daemon, and it provides a simple mechanism to stop remote access to the NIS (YP), NFS and other rpc services from malicious intruders.

It features host access control on IP addresses, forwarding through an unprivileged port of requests that are forwarded by the rpcbind process, refusal of REMOTE requests sent to high-numbered UDP ports.

However, there is no protection against IP address spoofing attacks, but it does provide the system with another early-warning mechanism.

Portmapper

Another of Wietse Venema's tools, this time as a replacement for the portmapper daemon, implementing protection against theft of NIS passwd files, forcing ypset to bind hosts to a rogue NIS server, and theft of NFS file handles.

Secure Sockets Host

Secure shell was created in 1995, to first replace the R commands, but later became an entire suite of tools used for securely accessing servers. Secure Shell is a protocol that provides authentication, encryption and data integrity to secure network communication. Implementations of Secure Shell offer a secure command shell, secure file transfer and remote access to various applications through a secure tunnel.

Secure shell basically offers three main capabilities, which are Secure-command shell, to replace telnet, secure file transfer to replace ftp, and port forwarding. In the case of the secure-command shell, one can access the remote host as they would by issuing the telnet command. However, while the telnet command allows for clear-text communication and data interchange (such as usernames and passwords and other sensitive communication), SSH adds a variety of encryption standards in the communications interchange, thus achieving encryption capabilities with little to no speed variations.

Currently, there are two SSH standards available. This happened when the normal SSH's license was turned into a closed source one, thus limiting the open access to its source code. That prompted the development of an open source version of SSH, called OpenSSH, primarily used in OpenBSD and then ported to Linux and other flavours of UNIX.

Secure Sockets Layer (SSL)

The Secure Sockets Layer was designed and implemented by Netscape Communications, which claims the protocol to have been created to protect any higher-level protocol built on sockets. Therefore, it ignores the details of higher-level protocols and what they carry. SSL provides encryption of a session, authentication of a server and message authentication. Both the Handshake and the Application protocols in SSL operate on top of the SSL Record Protocol, a means of encapsulating authentication information.

The authentication of the session takes from 5 to 8 messages and it relies on the existence of a key certification mechanism to authenticate the server. A great deal of ciphers and security hashes are supported. As SSL too is closed source, though, an open version of it has been created. OpenSSL is the open standard for SSL communication, created using SSLeay as a predecessor, and accomplishes the same functionality as the proprietarycounterpart. OpenSSL too was first created for OpenBSD and then ported to other operating systems, Linux included.

Postfix

Created by Wietse Venema, Postfix is an MTA (Mail Transport Agent) that attempts to replace sendmail, the widely-known MTA used in Linux and the UNIX environment. It is considered to be fast, easy to administer and much more secure than sendmail is, in the same time being as compatible as possible to the sendmail way of doing things so as to make the transition easier. Postfix is designed to behave rationally under stress. When the local system runs out of disk space or memory, the Postfix software backs off, instead of making the problem worse. By design, no Postfix program keeps growing as the number of messages etc. increases.

Postfix is designed to stay in control. The MTA is built from over a dozen little programs that each performs only one specific task: receive a message via SMTP, deliver a message via SMTP, deliver a message locally, rewrite an address, and so on. Sites with specific requirements can replace one or more little programs by alternative versions. And it is easy to disable functionality, too: firewalls and client workstations don't need local delivery at all. Security-wise, Postfix uses multiple layers of defence to protect the local system against attackers.

Just about every daemon can run in a chroot jail with fixed low privileges. There is no direct path from the network to the security-sensitive local delivery programs. Postfix does not even trust the contents of its own queue files, or the contents of its own IPC messages. It filters sender-provided information before exporting it via environment variables.

Qmail

Qmail, created by Dan Bernstein, is a secure, reliable, very efficient and very simple MTA. Built as a replacement of sendmail it supports host and user masquerading, full host hiding, virtual domains, relay control, etc., up to the point of including a sendmail wrapper to be transparent to the clients. Security-wise, it features clear separation between addresses, files, and programs, minimization of setuid code (qmail-queue), minimization of root code (qmail-start, qmail-lspawn), five-way trust partitioning and optional logging of one-way hashes, entire contents, etc. Qmail also supports all UNIX variants and adapts itself easily to just about any UNIX and Linux version/distribution.

NETWORK VULNERABILITY SCANNERS

Network Vulnerability Scanners are kind of ambiguous tools. Their use stands somewhere between good and malicious usage. It is true, a great deal of Vulnerability Scanners are used by attackers to map out the system before an attack, so they can be dangerous. However, the same great deal of scanners is also used by prudent administrators who wish to check their networks for vulnerabilities and bugs, which makes their use legal.

One thing is for certain, though, when a system is scanned by such tools, the logs fill up extremely fast, which can be used as an early-warning system, especially if a tool is constructed that will detect sudden changes in the log file created by increased alert activity.

NESSUS

The Nessus project is a very fast, reliable security scanner, with a modular architecture that is free and up-to-date. It features a plug in architecture, allowing one to add their own tests apart from the ones in the package using the scanner's own test writing language, NASL (Nessus Attack Scripting Language). It has an up-to-date vulnerability database for recent security holes which is updated on a daily basis, a client-server architecture, the server running as the attacker and the client serving as a front-end and concurrency in its scanning procedures, which allows it check multiple hosts at the same time. Its mart service recognition and multiples scanning identify services that run on customised ports and services that run in more than one instance and it has the ability to test SSL-aware services. Furthermore, it will not only tell you what security problems it finds on your system but also give out a solution as to a possible fix.

SECURITY AUDITOR'S RESEARCH ASSISTANT (SARA)

SARA is a third generation Unix-based security analysis tool written by Bob Todd, based on the early work and model of Farmer's and Venema's SATAN (Security Administrator's Tool for Analyzing Networks). The program works by remotely probing the system and storing its findings in a database. The results can be viewed with any web browser that supports the http protocol. It supports and is fully compliant with the FBI/SANS Top 20 Consensus, which is a list of security vulnerabilities the SANS institute has published, and it is SANS/ISTS Certified. It features standalone or server mode, it is updated twice a month and supports third-party plug-ins and remote self-scan and API.

It also interfaces with Nmap and SAMBA for operating system fingerprinting and SMB security analysis. SARA can also generate reports of hosts by type, service, and vulnerability and by trust relationship. In addition it offers tutorials that explain the nature of the vulnerabilities and how they can be eliminated.

SAINT

SAINT (Security Administrator's Integrated Toolkit) supports two scanning modes, a simple one and an exploratory one. In the first one, it gathers as much information about remote hosts and networks as possible by examining the services on the host(s) it is searching, gathering such things as the presence of potential security flaws, well-known bugs, and poor policy decisions. Reporting and using a simple rule-based system to search for potential security flaws is then initialized, as per user specification.

In the second one, it will examine the trust and dependency relationships between hosts on the network but also over secondary hosts, allowing the user to also examine the entire network and services from the point of trust and its implications in the general network security policy.

SAINT first uses fping to test if the servers are up when a firewall does not exist. If a firewall does exist, it uses tcp_scan probing of common ports to achieve the same result. It then passes the results to a data collection engine, which correlates the data and runs tests and probes as per the probe level that is set.

The record that results contains the host, the tests run and the results found, if any. The user interface, which is basically an HTML page, links the data together to form a coherent description of the system that the user can understand.

LINUX FIREWALLS

Shorewall

The Shoreline Firewall, more commonly known as "Shorewall", is a Netfilter (iptables) based firewall that can be used on a dedicated firewall system, a multi-function gateway/router/server or on a standalone Linux system.

Its features include stateful packet filtering, integration with Webmin to provide a graphical user interface, flexible address management and routing support, blacklisting of individual and sub networks of IP addresses. It also has VPN support, support for Traffic control and shaping and Media Access control verification.

Firewall Builder

Firewall Builder is multi-platform firewall configuration and management tool. It basically consists of a graphical user interface and set of policy compilers designed for many different platforms. It uses an object-oriented approach, helping the administrator maintain a database of network objects and allows the editing of policy models using simple drag-and-drop operations. Firewall Builder can generate configuration files for any supported target firewall platform using the policies created by the graphical user interface, thus providing both a consistent policy management and possible migration paths.

Firewall Builder allows the system administrator to maintain multiple firewalls using the same network object database.

Any change made to an object is immediately enforced in the policy of all firewalls under this object. The only thing the administrator needs to do is recompile and install the policies on the actual firewall machines.

Administrator works with an abstraction of firewall policy and NAT rules. That means that software effectively "hides" specifics of particular target firewall platform, helping the administrator to focus on the implementation of the security policy.

Policy compilers can deduct many parameters of policy rules using the information available through network and service objects therefore generating fairly complex code for the target firewall, resulting in relieving the administrator remembering all its details and limitations. They can also run sanity checks on firewall rules to make sure errors are caught before the deployment of the policy.

PORTSCAN DETECTION TOOLS

A portscan is broadly defined as sending packets of data to all the ports defined in/etc/services and, by waiting for a reply of any kind from them, determining what services are running on a system. Portscanning has been used by both attackers and system administrators to check what ports a system has open to the outside world. The former use this method to locate services, which might be susceptible to one form of attack or another and in the same time profile the system they are about to attack. The latter use it for things ranging from making sure the services they have opened or closed have indeed been so, up to verifying the state of those ports after a firewall has been installed and filtering rules have been applied.

THE SCANLOG DAEMON

The scanlogd daemon is a TCP port scan detection tool, originally designed to illustrate various attacks an IDS developer has to deal with. It is designed to use either libnids or libcap or a combination of both libraries as well as its raw socket. The portscan detection tool is basically designed to be totally safe, as it does not use user privileges. Instead it uses its own user id and group id, a user/group called scanlogd. When it detects a portscan in progress it sends all alerts of it in the syslog reporting process.

THE SCANLOG DAEMON

The scanlogd daemon is a TCP port scan detection tool, originally designed to illustrate various attacks an IDS developer has to deal with. It is designed to use either libnids or libcap or a combination of both libraries as well as its raw socket. The portscan detection tool is basically designed to be totally safe, as it does not use user privileges. Instead it uses its own user id and group id, a user/group called scanlogd. When it detects a portscan in progress it sends all alerts of it in the syslog reporting process.

PSIONIC PORTSENTRY

Psionic's PortSentry portscan detector was previously a part of the Abacus set of tools, along with HostSentry and LogSentry, but at some stage they split up into individual tools, however keeping their coverage of each other's techniques combined when all three are in action. Portscan is designed to detect SYN/half-open, FIN, NULL, X-MAS and oddball packet stealth scans.

PortSentry can be used in three ways:

- In classic portscanning mode, utilizing a set of predefined ports, which can be customised from bare bones logging to a very analytical logging.
- In its stealth portscan detection mode (also known as stealth mode), it does not bind to anything. An attacker still has to hit a tripwired port to activate the sensor though. To prevent other issues, this scan

mode will not react if the ACK flag of the TCP packet is set. This prevents causing alarms on "established" connections that happen to take one of your high ports temporarily.

For some protocols such as FTP the client actually opens up ports in the ephemeral range (1024-65535) and the server then connects *back* to you. This would normally cause the port scanner to activate.

- In its advanced portscan detection mode, PortSentry will look at the incoming connection and determine if it is destined for one of these "temporary" bindings. If it is, then the connection is ignored for that one time. As soon as the connection is torn down the window closes and full protection is back again.

Once a portscanning process is detected, the program will block the host in real-time by using an ipfwadm/ipchains/ iptables rule and/or adding the offender's IP in hosts.deny, and/or add a rejection route in the system's routing table for the offender's IP address, making the system turn into a black hole and disappearing from the attacker.

GENERAL SECURITY TIPS

BIOS SECURITY

Always set a password on BIOS to disallow booting from floppy by changing the BIOS settings. This will block undesired people from trying to boot your Linux system with a special boot disk and will protect you from people trying to change BIOS feature like allowing boot from floppy drive or booting the server without password prompt.

DISABLE ALL SPECIAL ACCOUNTS

You should delete all default users and group accounts that you don't use on your system like lp, sync, shutdown, halt, news, uucp, operator, games, gopher etc

CHOOSE A RIGHT PASSWORD

You should follow the following guidelines before choosing the right password.

The password Length: The minimum acceptable password length by default when you install your Linux system is 5. This is not enough and must be 8.

To do this you have to edit the login.defs file (vi/etc/login.defs) and change the line that read:

- PASS_MIN_LEN 5
- To read:
- PASS_MIN_LEN 8

The "login.defs" is the configuration file for the login program.

ENABLE SHADOW PASSWORD SUPPORT

You should enable the shadow password feature. You can use the "/usr/sbin/authconfig" utility to enable the shadow password feature on your system. If you want to convert the existing passwords and group on your system to shadow passwords and groups then you can use the commands pwconv, grpconv respectively.

LINUX SECURITY GLOSSARY

Authentication [SH

] The process of knowing that the data received is the same as the data that was sent, and that the claimed sender is in fact the actual sender.

Bastion Host

A computer system that must be highly secured because it is vulnerable to attack, usually because it is exposed to the Internet and is a main point of contact for users of internal networks. It gets its name from the highly fortified projects on the outer walls of medieval castles. Bastions overlook critical areas of defence, usually having strong walls, room for extra troops, and the occasional useful tub of boiling hot oil for discouraging attackers.

BUFFER OVERFLOW

Common coding style is to never allocate large enough

buffers, and to not check for overflows. When such buffers overflow, the executing program (daemon or set-uid program) can be tricked in doing some other things. Generally this works by overwriting a function's return address on the stack to point to another location.

Denial of Service

- An attack that consumes the resources on your computer for things it was not intended to be doing, thus preventing normal use of your network resources for legitimate purposes.

Dual-Homed Host

- A general-purpose computer system that has at least two network interfaces.

Firewall

- A component or set of components that restricts access between a protected network and the Internet, or between other sets of networks.

Host

- A computer system attached to a network

IP Spoofing

- IP Spoofing is a complex technical attack that is made up of several components. It is a security exploit that works by tricking computers in a trust relationship into thinking that you are someone that you really aren't.

Non-Repudiation

- The property of a receiver being able to prove that the sender of some data did in fact send the data even though the sender might later deny ever having sent it.

Packet

- The fundamental unit of communication on the Internet.

Packet FiltEring

- The action a device takes to selectively control the flow of data to and from a network. Packet filters allow or block packets, usually while routing them from one network to another (most often from the Internet to an internal network, and vice-versa). To accomplish packet filtering, you set up rules that specify what types of packets (those to or from a particular IP address or port) are to be allowed and what types are to be blocked.

Perimeter Network

- A network added between a protected network and an external network, in order to provide an additional layer of security. A perimeter network is sometimes called a DMZ.

Proxy Server

- A program that deals with external servers on behalf of internal clients. Proxy clients talk to proxy servers, which relay approved client requests to real servers, and relay answers back to clients.

PAPERCUT NG ON LINUX

THE INSTALLATION PROCESS

The Linux version of PaperCut NG is supplied as a pre-compiled self-installing application. The installation process is designed to work with all major Linux distributions. Due to the varied nature of some installations and administrator preferences, often some manual configuration is required. This section describes the installation process in detail as well as some additional options available to system administrators.

Manual Extraction

The Linux version of PaperCut NG is supplied in a self-extracting, self-installing archive. The archive is simply a tar archive compressed with gzip, and headed with a shell script to facilitate self-extracting. After extraction is complete, the installation script named install is executed to begin the install process.

Some system administrators may like to inspect the contents of the archive, and possibly the installation process itself prior to the actual install. The self-extracting installer takes a number of command line arguments. The -e argument will extract the archive into the current working directory ready for inspection. Further options and documentation is available via the —help option.

```
Usage: pcng-setup.sh [-e|-i|-l] [-v] [-n]
[list...]
  -e Extract the files and then exit without
     installing.
  -i Install after extracting the files (default).
-l List the contents of the archive and exit
    without
    extracting.
-v Verbose. Print the names of the files as
   they are
   extracted.
   list The list of files to extract."
```

The Install Process

Even though the majority of the installation process is completed under the identity of the non-privileged user account called papercut, most administrators would like to know what the install process does. The main steps are outlined below:

EXTRACTION

The first stage in the install process extracts the archive to/tmp or a location as defined by an environment variable TMPDIR. The command-line programs tar and gunzip are used during this phase.

INSTALLATION

After extraction is complete the installation script is called.

The install script, called install, will present the EULA and request acceptance. The script then determines the install location.

This is the papercut user's home directory. The home directory is determined by the HOMEenvironment variable, or if not set, the result of a call to getpwnam().

Files are then copied into the papercut user's home directory. Care is taken not to overwrite any existing data or configuration files if this is an install-over-the-top upgrade.

FIREWALL

The PaperCut NG *Application Server* (pc-app process) listens on port 9191. This port is used for browser based administration access, for client access, and other services. Ensure that any firewall or local IP filtering software such as iptables is set to allow local network traffic access to this port.

ROOT LEVEL TASKS

A small part of the install process needs to run as the root account. The tasks conducted as root include:

- Setting the authpam binary as setuid-root. This binary is used for password verification.
- Installing a CUPS backend. This is done by placing a symlink in the CUPS lib/backend directory.
- Setting up SYSV style start scripts if the system uses this boot process.

This is done by placing symlinks in the:

```
/etc/init.d/
/etc/rc3.d/
/etc/rc5.d/
 and so on...
```

If the administrator decides not to run the root-level tasks during the install process, the tasks can be run again post-install by executing the shell scripts:

```
~/server/bin/linux-*/roottasks
~/providers/print/linux-*/roottasks
```

Alternatively the administrator can view the scripts and make the required changes by hand.

Linux Print Queue Integration

PaperCut NG is able to integrate with and monitor CUPS, Samba and Novell iPrint based print queues. The configuration and an explanation of the integration methods follows:

CUPS CONFIGURATION OVERVIEW

If the print queues are managed and controlled via CUPS, the Device URI on each printer should be modified so the papercut backend is incorporated into the print process.

This can be done automatically by running the configure-cups script as root (the simplest option):

`~/providers/print/linux-*/configure-cups`

and following the interactive instructions.

Alternatively, it can be done manually via the CUPS web admin interface or by editing the CUPSprinters.conf file:

- Open printers.conf (*e.g.*/etc/cups/printers.conf)
- Prefix the DeviceURL for each printers with "papercut:". For example:
- DeviceURI socket://192.168.1.200:9100
  Would become:
  DeviceURI papercut:socket://192.168.1.200:9100
- Restart cupsd so the new configuration is detected (*e.g.*/etc/init.d/cupsd reload)

CUPS INTEGRATION EXPLAINED

CUPS, the Common UNIX Printing System, is a popular system for managing printers on Linux servers. CUPS uses a chain-of-commands concept where filters and backends combine together to form a process steam-a workflow. PaperCut NG hooks into this workflow at the backend level, intercepting the job before it's passed on to physical printer hardware.

The interception is done by wrapping or proxying the real CUPS backend. CUPS calls the PaperCut NG backend which processes the job. If the job is approved, it passes the document onto the real backend. If the job is denied, it is deleted and proceeds no further. The PaperCut NG backend is usually set up and installed by default during the standard installation.

Setting up the PaperCut NG CUPS backend proxy is a relatively simple task. All the administrator needs to do is prefix the existing DeviceURIwith papercut:.

For example the entry:

```
DeviceURI socket://192.168.1.200:9100
```

would become:

```
DeviceURI papercut:socket://192.168.1.200:9100
```

The printer will register itself with PaperCut NG on the first print event.

Paper Cut NG CUPS Architecture

The PaperCut NG CUPS backend is a native compiled binary. In PaperCut NG documentation it is referred to it as a Print Provider-a component that provides print event information to the Application Server.

It's responsible for analyzing the print job and then communicating this information to the Application Server component.

Communication is via an XML-RPC based Web Services call. This means that the backend does not even need to be on the same server as the system hosting the Application Server component.

SAMBA CONFIGURATION OVERVIEW

If the print queues are exposed to network workstations using Samba, and a print system other than CUPS is used (*e.g.* BSD, LPRNG, SYSV, etc.) the smb.conf needs some additional configuration.

The "print command" needs to be replaced with a PaperCut NG command.

- Open the smb.conf (*e.g.*/etc/samba/smb.conf)
- Under the [global] section insert the line:
- Print command=/home/papercut/providers/print/linux-i686/samba-print-provider
- -u "%u" -J "%J" -h "%h" -m "%m" -p "%p" -s "%s"
- -a "[standard print command]" &

(IMPORTANT: The above information should appear all on a single line. Note the use of the & (ampersand) on the end

of the line.) where [standard print command] is the command that would normally called for printing.

Typical examples of commands usually used for printer are listed below:

```
BSD, AIX, QNX, LPRNG or PLP
lpr -r -P%p %s
SYSV or HPUX
lp -c -d%p %s; rm %s
```

More information on standard print commands is available under the Samba documentation installed on your system (see man smb.conf).

SAMBA INTEGRATION EXPLAINED

Samba is used to provide file and print sharing to Windows systems and is a popular solution. One of the main reasons for its popularity is that it avoids the need for expensive Microsoft Windows server licenses!

Samba exposes the locally set up Linux/Unix printers as network shared Windows printers. It does this by wrapping the underlying print system-usually CUPS or LPR/LPD. In the case of LPR, Samba calls the standard lp command line programs to perform printing. PaperCut NG works by wrapping or proxying the "print command". More information on how Samba interacts with the underlying print system is available in the Samba documentation.

A typical entry in the Samba configuration file smb.conf defining the PaperCut NG print command wrapper would be:

```
print command =/home/papercut/providers/print/
linux-i686/samba-print-provider
-u "%u" -J "%J" -h "%h" -m "%m" -p "%p" -s "%s"
-a "[standard print command]" &
IMPORTANT: The above information should appear
all on the one line.
Note the use of the & (ampersand) on the end of
the line.)
```

where [standard print command] is the command that would normally be called for printing. The %u, %p, etc., are Samba substitution variables. These are replaced with content such as the username, printer name, etc. and are used by PaperCut NG in the reporting and logging. The printer will register itself with the PaperCut NG web interface after the first print is received.

Paper Cut NG Samba Architecture

The PaperCut NG Samba print command wrapper is a native compiled executable. The PaperCut NG documentation refers to it as a Print Provider. It's responsible for analyzing the print job and then communicating this information to the Application Server component. Communication is via an XML-RPC based Web Services call. This means that the command does not even need to be on the same server as the system hosting the Application Server component.

NOVELL IPRINT CONFIGURATION

PaperCut NG works by directly integrating with the Novell iPrint Print Manager. The configuration process is detailed in the section called "Step 5-Printer/iPrint Configuration". The development team at PaperCut Software has worked with the Novell iPrint engineers during 2008 to ensure an iPrint API was avaliable that allow iPrint users to have access to the same feature set as seen on Windows, Mac and Linux CUPS. PaperCut NG uses this API set to intercept and account for jobs as they pass into the iPrint queue.

6

An Introduction to Device Drivers

INTRODUCTION

One of the many advantages of free operating systems, as typified by Linux, is that their internals are open for all to view. The operating system, once a dark and mysterious area whose code was restricted to a small number of programmers, can now be readily examined, understood, and modified by anybody with the requisite skills. Linux has helped to democratize operating systems. The Linux kernel remains a large and complex body of code, however, and would-be kernel hackers need an entry point where they can approach the code without being overwhelmed by complexity. Often, device drivers provide that gateway.

Device drivers take on a special role in the Linux kernel. They are distinct "black boxes" that make a particular piece of hardware respond to a well-defined internal programming interface; they hide completely the details of how the device works. User activities are performed by means of a set of standardized calls that are independent of the specific driver; mapping those calls to device-specific operations that act on real hardware is then the role of the device driver. This programming interface is such that drivers can be built separately from the rest of the kernel and "plugged in" at runtime when needed. This modularity makes Linux drivers easy to write, to the point that there are now hundreds of them available.

There are a number of reasons to be interested in the writing of Linux device drivers. The rate at which new hardware becomes available (and obsolete!) alone guarantees that driver writers will be busy for the foreseeable future. Individuals may need to know about drivers in order to gain access to a particular device that is of interest to them. Hardware vendors, by making a Linux driver available for their products, can add the large and growing Linux user base to their potential markets. And the open source nature of the Linux system means that if the driver writer wishes, the source to a driver can be quickly disseminated to millions of users.

This book teaches you how to write your own drivers and how to hack around in related parts of the kernel. We have taken a device-independent approach; the programming techniques and interfaces are presented, whenever possible, without being tied to any specific device. Each driver is different; as a driver writer, you need to understand your specific device well. But most of the principles and basic techniques are the same for all drivers. This book cannot teach you about your device, but it gives you a handle on the background you need to make your device work.

As you learn to write drivers, you find out a lot about the Linux kernel in general; this may help you understand how your machine works and why things aren't always as fast as you expect or don't do quite what you want. We introduce new ideas gradually, starting off with very simple drivers and building on them; every new concept is accompanied by sample code that doesn't need special hardware to be tested.

This chapter doesn't actually get into writing code. However, we introduce some background concepts about the Linux kernel that you'll be glad you know later, when we do launch into

THE ROLE OF THE DEVICE DRIVER

As a programmer, you are able to make your own choices about your driver, and choose an acceptable trade-off between the programming time required and the flexibility of the result. Though it may appear strange to say that a driver is "flexible," we like this word because it emphasizes that the role of a device driver is providing *mechanism*, not *policy*.

The distinction between mechanism and policy is one of the best ideas behind the Unix design. Most programming problems can indeed be split into two parts: "what capabilities are to be provided" (the mechanism) and "how those capabilities can be used" (the policy). If the two issues are addressed by different parts of the program, or even by different programs altogether, the software package is much easier to develop and to adapt to particular needs.

For example, Unix management of the graphic display is split between the X server, which knows the hardware and offers a unified interface to user programs, and the window and session managers, which implement a particular policy without knowing anything about the hardware. People can use the same window manager on different hardware, and different users can run different configurations on the same workstation. Even completely different desktop environments, such as KDE and GNOME, can coexist on the same system.

Another example is the layered structure of TCP/IP networking: the operating system offers the socket abstraction, which implements no policy regarding the data to be transferred, while different servers are in charge of the services (and their associated policies). Moreover, a server like *ftpd* provides the file transfer mechanism, while users can use whatever client they prefer; both command-line and graphic clients exist, and anyone can write a new user interface to transfer files.

Where drivers are concerned, the same separation of mechanism and policy applies. The floppy driver is policy free its role is only to show the diskette as a continuous array of data blocks. Higher levels of the system provide policies, such as who may access the floppy drive, whether the drive is accessed directly or via a filesystem, and whether users may mount filesystems on the drive. Since different environments usually need to use hardware in different ways, it's important to be as policy free as possible.

When writing drivers, a programmer should pay particular attention to this fundamental concept: write kernel code to access the hardware, but don't force particular policies on the user, since different users have different needs. The driver should deal with making the hardware available, leaving all the issues about *how* to use the hardware to the applications. A driver, then, is flexible if it offers access to the hardware capabilities without adding constraints. Sometimes, however, some policy decisions must be made. For example, a digital I/O driver may only offer byte-wide access to the hardware in order to avoid the extra code needed to handle individual bits.

You can also look at your driver from a different perspective: it is a software layer that lies between the applications and the actual device. This privileged role of the driver allows the driver programmer to choose exactly how the device should appear: different drivers can offer different capabilities, even for the same device. The actual driver design should be a balance between many different considerations. For instance, a single device may be used concurrently by different programs, and the driver programmer has complete freedom to determine how to handle concurrency. You could implement memory mapping on the device independently of its hardware capabilities, or you could provide a user library to help application programmers implement new policies on top of the available primitives, and so forth.

One major consideration is the trade-off between the desire to present the user with as many options as possible and the time you have to write the driver, as well as the need to keep things simple so that errors don't creep in.

Policy-free drivers have a number of typical characteristics. These include support for both synchronous and asynchronous operation, the ability to be opened multiple times, the ability to exploit the full capabilities of the hardware, and the lack of software layers to "simplify things" or provide policy-related operations.

Drivers of this sort not only work better for their end users, but also turn out to be easier to write and maintain as well. Being policy-free is actually a common target for software designers. Many device drivers, indeed, are released together with user programs to help with configuration and access to the target device. Those programs can range from simple utilities to complete graphical applications. Examples include the *tunelp* program, which adjusts how the parallel port printer driver operates, and the graphical *cardctl* utility that is part of the PCMCIA driver package. Often a client library is provided as well, which provides capabilities that do not need to be implemented as part of the driver itself.

The scope of this book is the kernel, so we try not to deal with policy issues or with application programs or support libraries.

Sometimes we talk about different policies and how to support them, but we won't go into much detail about programs using the device or the policies they enforce. You should understand, however, that user programs are an integral part of a software package and that even policy-free packages are distributed with configuration files that apply a default behaviour to the underlying mechanisms.

SPLITTING THE KERNEL

In a Unix system, several concurrent *processes* attend to different tasks. Each process asks for system resources, be it computing power, memory, network connectivity, or some other resource. The *kernel* is the big chunk of executable code in charge of handling all such requests. Although the distinction between the different kernel tasks isn't always clearly marked, the kernel's role can be split

Process Mmanagement

The kernel is in charge of creating and destroying processes and handling their connection to the outside world (input and output). Communication among different processes (through signals, pipes, or interprocess communication primitives) is basic to the overall system functionality and is also handled by the kernel. In addition, the scheduler, which controls how processes share the CPU, is part of process management. More generally, the kernel's process management activity implements the abstraction of several processes on top of a single CPU or a few of them.

Memory Management

The computer's memory is a major resource, and the policy used to deal with it is a critical one for system performance. The kernel builds up a virtual addressing space for any and all processes on top of the limited available resources. The different parts of the kernel interact with the memory-management subsystem through a set of function calls, ranging from the simple *malloc/free* pair to much more complex functionalities.

File Systems

Unix is heavily based on the filesystem concept; almost everything in Unix can be treated as a file. The kernel builds a structured filesystem on top of unstructured hardware, and the resulting file abstraction is heavily used throughout the whole system. In addition, Linux supports multiple filesystem types, that is, different ways of organizing data on the physical medium. For example, disks may be formatted with the Linux-standard ext3 filesystem, the commonly used FAT filesystem or several others.

Device Control

Almost every system operation eventually maps to a physical device. With the exception of the processor, memory, and a very few other entities, any and all device control operations are performed by code that is specific to the device being addressed. That code is called a *device driver*. The kernel must have embedded in it a device driver for every peripheral present on a system, from the hard drive to the keyboard and the tape drive. This aspect of the kernel's functions is our primary interest in this book.

Networking

Networking must be managed by the operating system, because most network operations are not specific to a process: incoming packets are asynchronous events. The packets must be collected, identified, and dispatched before a process takes care of them. The system is in charge of delivering data packets across program and network interfaces, and it must control the execution of programs according to their network activity. Additionally, all the routing and address resolution issues are implemented within the kernel.

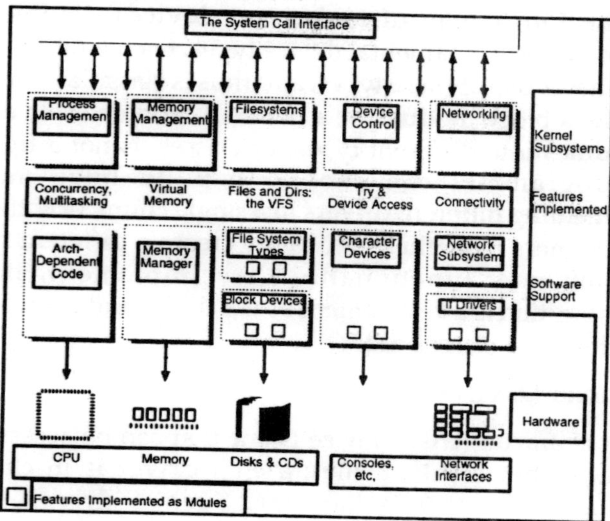

Fig: A split view of the kernel

Loadable Modules

One of the good features of Linux is the ability to extend at runtime the set of features offered by the kernel. This means that you can add functionality to the kernel (and remove functionality as well) while the system is up and running.

Each piece of code that can be added to the kernel at runtime is called a *module*. The Linux kernel offers support for quite a few different types (or classes) of modules, including, but not limited to, device drivers. Each module is made up of object code (not linked into a complete executable) that can be dynamically linked to the running kernel by the *insmod* program and can be unlinked by the *rmmod* program.

Figure identifies different classes of modules in charge of specific tasks a module is said to belong to a specific class according to the functionality it offers. The placement of modules in Figure covers the most important classes, but is far from complete because more and more functionality in Linux is being modularized.

CLASSES OF DEVICES AND MODULES

The Linux way of looking at devices distinguishes between three fundamental device types. Each module usually implements one of these types, and thus is classifiable as a char module, a block module, or a network module. This division of modules into different types, or classes, is not a rigid one; the programmer can choose to build huge modules implementing different drivers in a single chunk of code. Good programmers, nonetheless, usually create a different module for each new functionality they implement, because decomposition is a key element of scalability and extendability.

The three classes are:

Character Devices

A character (char) device is one that can be accessed as a stream of bytes (like a file); a char driver is in charge of implementing this behaviour. Such a driver usually implements at least the *open, close, read,* and *write* system calls. The text console (*/dev/console*) and the serial ports (*/dev/ttyS0* and friends) are examples of char devices, as they are well represented by the stream abstraction. Char devices are accessed by means of filesystem nodes, such as*/dev/tty1* and*/dev/lp0*.

The only relevant difference between a char device and a regular file is that you can always move back and forth in the regular file, whereas most char devices are just data channels, which you can only access sequentially. There exist, nonetheless, char devices that look like data areas, and you can move back and forth in them; for instance, this usually applies to frame grabbers, where the applications can access the whole acquired image using *mmap* or *lseek*.

Block Devices

Like char devices, block devices are accessed by filesystem nodes in the*/dev* directory. A block device is a device (*e.g.*, a disk) that can host a filesystem. In most Unix systems, a block device can only handle I/O operations that transfer one or more whole blocks, which are usually 512 bytes (or a larger power of two) bytes in length. Linux, instead, allows the application to read and write a block device like a char device it permits the transfer of any number of bytes at a time.

As a result, block and char devices differ only in the way data is managed internally by the kernel, and thus in the kernel/driver software interface. Like a char device, each block device is accessed through a filesystem node, and the difference between them is transparent to the user. Block drivers have a completely different interface to the kernel than char drivers.

Network Interfaces

Any network transaction is made through an interface, that is, a device that is able to exchange data with other hosts. Usually, an*interface* is a hardware device, but it might also be a pure software device, like the loopback interface. A network interface is in charge of sending and receiving data packets, driven by the network subsystem of the kernel, without knowing how individual transactions map to the actual packets being transmitted. Many network connections (especially those using TCP) are stream-oriented, but network devices are, usually, designed around the transmission and receipt of packets. A network driver knows nothing about individual connections; it only handles packets.

Not being a stream-oriented device, a network interface isn't easily mapped to a node in the filesystem, as/dev/tty1 is. The Unix way to provide access to interfaces is still by assigning a unique name to them (such as eth0), but that name doesn't have a corresponding entry in the filesystem. Communication between the kernel and a network device driver is completely different from that used with char and block drivers. Instead of read and write, the kernel calls functions related to packet transmission.

There are other ways of classifying driver modules that are orthogonal to the above device types. In general, some types of drivers work with additional layers of kernel support functions for a given type of device. For example, one can talk of universal serial bus (USB) modules, serial modules, SCSI modules, and so on. Every USB device is driven by a USB module that works with the USB subsystem, but the device itself shows up in the system as a char device (a USB serial port, say), a block device (a USB memory card reader), or a network device (a USB Ethernet interface).

Other classes of device drivers have been added to the kernel in recent times, including FireWire drivers and I2O drivers. In the same way that they handled USB and SCSI drivers, kernel developers collected class-wide features and exported them to driver implementers to avoid duplicating work and bugs, thus simplifying and strengthening the process of writing such drivers.

In addition to device drivers, other functionalities, both hardware and software, are modularized in the kernel. One common example is filesystems. A filesystem type determines how information is organized on a block device in order to represent a tree of directories and files. Such an entity is not a device driver, in that there's no explicit device associated with the way the information is laid down; the filesystem type is instead a software driver, because it maps the low-level data structures to high-level data structures.

It is the filesystem that determines how long a filename can be and what information about each file is stored in a directory entry. The filesystem module must implement the lowest level of the system calls that access directories and files, by mapping filenames and paths (as well as other information, such as access modes) to data structures stored in data blocks. Such an interface is completely independent of the actual data transfer to and from the disk (or other medium), which is accomplished by a block device driver.

If you think of how strongly a Unix system depends on the underlying filesystem, you'll realise that such a software concept is vital to system operation. The ability to decode filesystem information stays at the lowest level of the kernel hierarchy and is of utmost importance; even if you write a block driver for your new CD-ROM, it is useless if you are not able to run ls or cp on the data it hosts. Linux supports the concept of a filesystem module, whose software interface declares the different operations that can be performed on a filesystem inode, directory, file, and superblock. It's quite unusual for a programmer to actually need to write a filesystem module, because the official kernel already includes code for the most important filesystem types.

SECURITY ISSUES

Security is an increasingly important concern in modern times. We will discuss security-related issues as they come up throughout the book. There are a few general concepts, however, that are worth mentioning now.

Any security check in the system is enforced by kernel code. If the kernel has security holes, then the system as a whole has holes. In the official kernel distribution, only an authorized user can load modules; the system call init_module checks if the invoking process is authorized to load a module into the kernel.

Thus, when running an official kernel, only the superuser, or an intruder who has succeeded in becoming privileged, can exploit the power of privileged code.

When possible, driver writers should avoid encoding security policy in their code. Security is a policy issue that is often best handled at higher levels within the kernel, under the control of the system administrator. There are always exceptions, however. As a device driver writer, you should be aware of situations in which some types of device access could adversely affect the system as a whole and should provide adequate controls. For example, device operations that affect global resources (such as setting an interrupt line), which could damage the hardware (loading firmware, for example), or that could affect other users (such as setting a default block size on a tape drive), are usually only available to sufficiently privileged users, and this check must be made in the driver itself.

Driver writers must also be careful, of course, to avoid

introducing security bugs. The C programming language makes it easy to make several types of errors. Many current security problems are created, for example, by buffer overrun errors, in which the programmer forgets to check how much data is written to a buffer, and data ends up written beyond the end of the buffer, thus overwriting unrelated data. Such errors can compromise the entire system and must be avoided. Fortunately, avoiding these errors is usually relatively easy in the device driver context, in which the interface to the user is narrowly defined and highly controlled.

Some other general security ideas are worth keeping in mind. Any input received from user processes should be treated with great suspicion; never trust it unless you can verify it. Be careful with uninitialized memory; any memory obtained from the kernel should be zeroed or otherwise initialized before being made available to a user process or device. Otherwise, information leakage (disclosure of data, passwords, etc.) could result. If your device interprets data sent to it, be sure the user cannot send anything that could compromise the system. Finally, think about the possible effect of device operations; if there are specific operations (*e.g.*, reloading the firmware on an adapter board or formatting a disk) that could affect the system, those operations should almost certainly be restricted to privileged users.

Be careful, also, when receiving software from third parties, especially when the kernel is concerned: because everybody has access to the source code, everybody can break and recompile things. Although you can usually trust precompiled kernels found in your distribution, you should avoid running kernels compiled by an untrusted friend if you wouldn't run a precompiled binary as root, then you'd better not run a precompiled kernel. For example, a maliciously modified kernel could allow anyone to load a module, thus opening an unexpected back door via init_module.

Note that the Linux kernel can be compiled to have no module support whatsoever, thus closing any module-related security holes. In this case, of course, all needed drivers must be built directly into the kernel itself. It is also possible, with

2.2 and later kernels, to disable the loading of kernel modules after system boot via the capability mechanism.

VERSION NUMBERING

Before digging into programming, we should comment on the version numbering scheme used in Linux and which versions are covered by this book. First of all, note that every software package used in a Linux system has its own release number, and there are often interdependencies across them: you need a particular version of one package to run a particular version of another package. The creators of Linux distributions usually handle the messy problem of matching packages, and the user who installs from a prepackaged distribution doesn't need to deal with version numbers. Those who replace and upgrade system software, on the other hand, are on their own in this regard. Fortunately, almost all modern distributions support the upgrade of single packages by checking interpackage dependencies; the distribution's package manager generally does not allow an upgrade until the dependencies are satisfied.

To run the examples we introduce during the discussion, you won't need particular versions of any tool beyond what the 2.6 kernel requires; any recent Linux distribution can be used to run our examples. We won't detail specific requirements, because the fileDocumentation/Changes in your kernel sources is the best source of such information if you experience any problems.

As far as the kernel is concerned, the even-numbered kernel versions (*i.e.*, 2.6.x) are the stable ones that are intended for general distribution. The odd versions (such as 2.7.x), on the contrary, are development snapshots and are quite ephemeral; the latest of them represents the current status of development, but becomes obsolete in a few days or so.

This book covers Version 2.6 of the kernel. Our focus has been to show all the features available to device driver writers in 2.6.10, the current version at the time we are writing. This edition of the book does not cover prior versions of the kernel. For those of you who are interested, the second edition covered

Versions 2.0 through 2.4 in detail. Kernel programmers should be aware that the development process changed with 2.6. The 2.6 series is now accepting changes that previously would have been considered too large for a "stable" kernel. Among other things, that means that internal kernel programming interfaces can change, thus potentially obsoleting parts of this book; for this reason, the sample code accompanying the text is known to work with 2.6.10, but some modules don't compile under earlier versions.

Programmers wanting to keep up with kernel programming changes are encouraged to join the mailing lists and to make use of the web sites listed in the bibliography. There is also a web page maintained, which contains information about API changes that have happened since this book was published.

This text doesn't talk specifically about odd-numbered kernel versions. General users never have a reason to run development kernels. Developers experimenting with new features, however, want to be running the latest development release. They usually keep upgrading to the most recent version to pick up bug fixes and new implementations of features. Note, however, that there's no guarantee on experimental kernels, and nobody helps you if you have problems due to a bug in a noncurrent odd-numbered kernel. Those who run odd-numbered versions of the kernel are usually skilled enough to dig in the code without the need for a textbook, which is another reason why we don't

Note that there's no guarantee on even-numbered kernels as well, unless you rely on a commercial provider that grants its own warranty. Another feature of Linux is that it is a platform-independent operating system, not just "a Unix clone for PC clones" anymore: it currently supports some 20 architectures. This book is platform independent as far as possible, and all the code samples have been tested on at least the x86 and x86-64 platforms. Because the code has been tested on both 32-bit and 64-bit processors, it should compile and run on all other platforms. As you might expect, the code samples that rely on particular hardware don't work on all the supported platforms, but this is always stated in the source code.

LICENSE TERMS

Linux is licensed under Version 2 of the GNU General Public License (GPL), a document devised for the GNU project by the Free Software Foundation. The GPL allows anybody to redistribute, and even sell, a product covered by the GPL, as long as the recipient has access to the source and is able to exercise the same rights. Additionally, any software product derived from a product covered by the GPL must, if it is redistributed at all, be released under the GPL.

The main goal of such a license is to allow the growth of knowledge by permitting everybody to modify programs at will; at the same time, people selling software to the public can still do their job. Despite this simple objective, there's a never-ending discussion about the GPL and its use. If you want to read the license, you can find it in several places in your system, including the top directory of your kernel source tree in the *COPYING* file.

Vendors often ask whether they can distribute kernel modules in binary form only. The answer to that question has been deliberately left ambiguous. Distribution of binary modules as long as they adhere to the published kernel interface has been tolerated so far. But the copyrights on the kernel are held by many developers, and not all of them agree that kernel modules are not derived products. If you or your employer wish to distribute kernel modules under a nonfree license, you really need to discuss the situation with your legal counsel. Please note also that the kernel developers have no qualms against breaking binary modules between kernel releases, even in the middle of a stable kernel series. If it is at all possible, both you and your users are better off if you release your module as free software.

If you want your code to go into the mainline kernel, or if your code requires patches to the kernel, you *must* use a GPL-compatible license as soon as you release the code. Although personal use of your changes doesn't force the GPL on you, if you distribute your code, you must include the source code in the distribution people acquiring your package must be allowed to rebuild the binary at will.

As far as this book is concerned, most of the code is freely redistributable, either in source or binary form, and neither we nor O'Reilly retain any right on any derived works.

JOINING THE KERNEL DEVELOPMENT COMMUNITY

As you begin writing modules for the Linux kernel, you become part of a larger community of developers. Within that community, you can find not only people engaged in similar work, but also a group of highly committed engineers working towards making Linux a better system. These people can be a source of help, ideas, and critical review as well they will be the first people you will likely turn to when you are looking for testers for a new driver.

The central gathering point for Linux kernel developers is the linux-kernel mailing list. All major kernel developers, from Linus Torvalds on down, subscribe to this list. Please note that the list is not for the faint of heart: traffic as of this writing can run up to 200 messages per day or more. Nonetheless, following this list is essential for those who are interested in kernel development; it also can be a top-quality resource for those in need of kernel development help.

To join the linux-kernel list, follow the instructions found in the linux-kernel mailing list FAQ: http://www.tux.org/lkml. Read the rest of the FAQ while you are at it; there is a great deal of useful information there. Linux kernel developers are busy people, and they are much more inclined to help people who have clearly done their homework first.

BUILDING AND RUNNING MODULES

It's almost time to begin programming. This chapter introduces all the essential concepts about modules and kernel programming. In these few pages, we build and run a complete (if relatively useless) module, and look at some of the basic code shared by all modules. Developing such expertise is an essential foundation for any kind of modularized driver. To avoid throwing in too many concepts at once, this chapter talks only about modules, without referring to any specific device class.

SETTING UP YOUR TEST SYSTEM

Starting with this chapter, we present example modules to demonstrate programming concepts. (All of these examples are available on O'Reilly's FTP site, as explained in Chapter 1.) Building, loading, and modifying these examples are a good way to improve your understanding of how drivers work and interact with the kernel.

The example modules should work with almost any 2.6.x kernel, including those provided by distribution vendors. However, we recommend that you obtain a "mainline" kernel directly from the kernel.org mirror network, and install it on your system. Vendor kernels can be heavily patched and divergent from the mainline; at times, vendor patches can change the kernel API as seen by device drivers. If you are writing a driver that must work on a particular distribution, you will certainly want to build and test against the relevant kernels. But, for the purpose of learning about driver writing, a standard kernel is best.

Regardless of the origin of your kernel, building modules for 2.6.x requires that you have a configured and built kernel tree on your system. This requirement is a change from previous versions of the kernel, where a current set of header files was sufficient. 2.6 modules are linked against object files found in the kernel source tree; the result is a more robust module loader, but also the requirement that those object files be available. So your first order of business is to come up with a kernel source tree (either from the kernel.org network or your distributor's kernel source package), build a new kernel, and install it on your system.

For reasons we'll see later, life is generally easiest if you are actually running the target kernel when you build your modules, though this is not required. So, if you do not yet have a suitable system with a configured and built kernel source tree on disk, now would be a good time to set that up. We'll wait. Once that task is taken care of, you'll be ready to start playing with kernel modules.

THE HELLO WORLD MODULE

Many programming books begin with a "hello world" example as a way of showing the simplest possible program. This book deals in kernel modules rather than programs; so, for the impatient reader, the following code is a complete "hello world" module:

```
#include <linux/init.h>
#include <linux/module.h>
MODULE_LICENSE("Dual BSD/GPL");
static int hello_init(void)
{
printk(KERN_ALERT "Hello, world\n");
return 0;
}
static void hello_exit(void)
{
printk(KERN_ALERT "Goodbye, cruel world\n");
}
module_init(hello_init);
module_exit(hello_exit);
```

This module defines two functions, one to be invoked when the module is loaded into the kernel (*hello_init*) and one for when the module is removed (*hello_exit*). The *module_init* and *module_exit* lines use special kernel macros to indicate the role of these two functions. Another special macro (*MODULE_LICENSE*) is used to tell the kernel that this module bears a free license; without such a declaration, the kernel complains when the module is loaded.

The *printk* function is defined in the Linux kernel and made available to modules; it behaves similarly to the standard C library function *printf*. The kernel needs its own printing function because it runs by itself, without the help of the C library. The module can call *printk* because, after *insmod* has loaded it, the module is linked to the kernel and can access the kernel's public symbols (functions and variables, as detailed in the next section). The string KERN_ALERT is the priority of the message.[1] We've specified a high priority in this module, because a message with the default priority might not show up anywhere useful, depending on the kernel version you are running. The priority is just a string, such as <1>, which is prepended to the *printk* format string. Note the lack of a comma afterKERN_ALERT; adding a comma there is a common and annoying typo (which, fortunately, is caught by the compiler).

You can test the module with the *insmod* and *rmmod* utilities, as shown below. Note that only the superuser can load and unload a module.

```
% make
make[1]: Entering directory '/usr/src/linux-
2.6.10'
CC [M]/home/ldd3/src/misc-modules/hello.o
Building modules, stage 2.
MODPOST
CC/home/ldd3/src/misc-modules/hello.mod.o
LD [M]/home/ldd3/src/misc-modules/hello.ko
make[1]: Leaving directory '/usr/src/linux-2.6.10'
% su
root# insmod./hello.ko
Hello, world
root# rmmod hello
Goodbye cruel world
root#
```

Please note once again that, for the above sequence of commands to work, you must have a properly configured and built kernel tree in a place where the makefile is able to find it (*/usr/src/linux-2.6.10* in the example shown). We get into the details of how modules According to the mechanism your system uses to deliver the message lines, your output may be different. In particular, the previous screen dump was taken from a text console; if you are running *insmod* and *rmmod* from a terminal emulator running under the window system, you won't see anything on your screen.

The message goes to one of the system log files, such as/

var/log/messages (the name of the actual file varies between Linux distributions). The mechanism used to deliver kernel messages is described. As you can see, writing a module is not as difficult as you might expect at least, as long as the module is not required to do anything worthwhile. The hard part is understanding your device and how to maximize performance. We go deeper into modularization throughout this chapter and leave device-specific issues for later chapters.

KERNEL MODULES VERSUS APPLICATIONS

Before we go further, it's worth underlining the various differences between a kernel module and an application.

While most small and medium-sized applications perform a single task from beginning to end, every kernel module just registers itself in order to serve future requests, and its initialization function terminates immediately. In other words, the task of the module's initialization function is to prepare for later invocation of the module's functions; it's as though the module were saying, "Here I am, and this is what I can do." The module's exit function (*hello_exit* in the example) gets invoked just before the module is unloaded.

It should tell the kernel, "I'm not there anymore; don't ask me to do anything else." This kind of approach to programming is similar to event-driven programming, but while not all applications are event-driven, each and every kernel module is. Another major difference between event-driven applications and kernel code is in the exit function: whereas an application that terminates can be lazy in releasing resources or avoids clean up altogether, the exit function of a module must carefully undo everything the *init* function built up, or the pieces remain around until the system is rebooted.

Incidentally, the ability to unload a module is one of the features of modularization that you'll most appreciate, because it helps cut down development time; you can test successive versions of your new driver without going through the lengthy shutdown/reboot cycle each time. As a programmer, you know that an application can call functions it doesn't define: the linking stage resolves external references using the appropriate library of functions. *printf* is one of those callable functions and is defined in *libc*.

A module, on the other hand, is linked only to the kernel, and the only functions it can call are the ones exported by the kernel; there are no libraries to link to. The *printk* function used in *hello.c* earlier, for example, is the version of *printf* defined within the kernel and exported to modules. It behaves similarly to the original function, with a few minor differences, the main one being lack of floating-point support.

Figure shows how function calls and function pointers are used in a module to add new functionality to a running kernel.

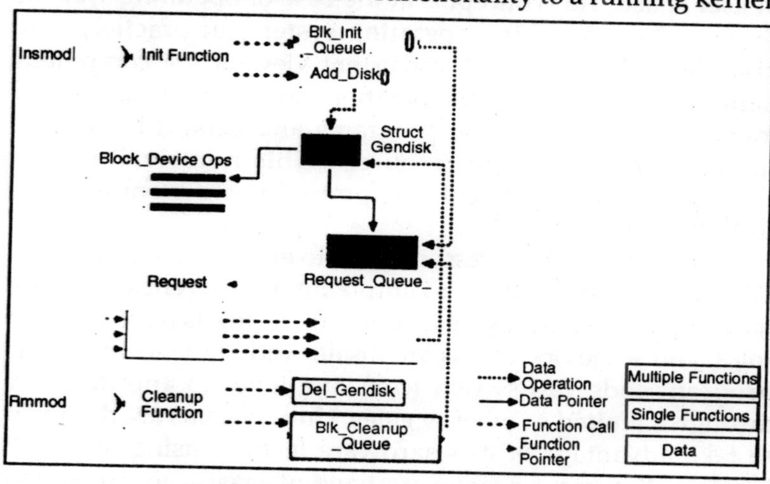

Fig: Linking a Module to the Kernel

Because no library is linked to modules, source files should never include the usual header files, *<stdarg.h>* and very special situations being the only exceptions. Only functions that are actually part of the kernel itself may be used in kernel modules. Anything related to the kernel is declared in headers found in the kernel source tree you have set up and configured; most of the relevant headers live in *include/linux* and *include/asm*, but other subdirectories of *include* have been added to host material associated to specific kernel subsystems.

The role of individual kernel headers is introduced throughout the book as each of them is needed.

Another important difference between kernel programming and application programming is in how each environment handles faults: whereas a segmentation fault is harmless during application development and a debugger can always be used to trace the error to the problem in the source code, a kernel fault kills the current process at least, if not the whole system.

User Space and Kernel Space

A module runs in kernel space, whereas applications run in user space. This concept is at the base of operating systems theory. The role of the operating system, in practice, is to provide programs with a consistent view of the computer's hardware. In addition, the operating system must account for independent operation of programs and protection against unauthorized access to resources. This nontrivial task is possible only if the CPU enforces protection of system software from the applications.

Every modern processor is able to enforce this behaviour. The chosen approach is to implement different operating modalities (or levels) in the CPU itself. The levels have different roles, and some operations are disallowed at the lower levels; program code can switch from one level to another only through a limited number of gates. Unix systems are designed to take advantage of this hardware feature, using two such levels. All current processors have at least two protection levels, and some, like the x86 family, have more levels; when several levels exist, the highest and lowest levels are used. Under Unix, the kernel executes in the highest level (also called supervisor mode), where everything is allowed, whereas applications execute in the lowest level (the so-called user mode), where the processor regulates direct access to hardware and unauthorized access to memory.

We usually refer to the execution modes as kernel space and user space. These terms encompass not only the different privilege levels inherent in the two modes, but also the fact that each mode can have its own memory mapping its own address space as well.

Unix transfers execution from user space to kernel space whenever an application issues a system call or is suspended by a hardware interrupt. Kernel code executing a system call is working in the context of a process it operates on behalf of the calling process and is able to access data in the process's address space. Code that handles interrupts, on the other hand, is asynchronous with respect to processes and is not related to any particular process.

The role of a module is to extend kernel functionality; modularized code runs in kernel space. Usually a driver performs both the tasks outlined previously: some functions in the module are executed as part of system calls, and some are in charge of interrupt handling.

Concurrency in the Kernel

One way in which kernel programming differs greatly from conventional application programming is the issue of concurrency. Most applications, with the notable exception of multithreading applications, typically run sequentially, from the beginning to the end, without any need to worry about what else might be happening to change their environment. Kernel code does not run in such a simple world, and even the simplest kernel modules must be written with the idea that many things can be happening at once.

There are a few sources of concurrency in kernel programming. Naturally, Linux systems run multiple processes, more than one of which can be trying to use your driver at the same time. Most devices are capable of interrupting the processor; interrupt handlers run asynchronously and can be invoked at the same time that your driver is trying to do something else.

Several software abstractions (such as kernel timers, introduced in run asynchronously as well. Moreover, of course, Linux can run on symmetric multiprocessor (SMP) systems, with the result that your driver could be executing concurrently on more than one CPU. Finally, in 2.6, kernel code has been made preemptible; this change causes even uniprocessor systems to have many of the same concurrency issues as multiprocessor systems. As a result, Linux kernel code, including driver code, must be *reentrant* it must be capable of running in more than one context at the same time. Data structures must be carefully designed to keep multiple threads of execution separate, and the code must take care to access shared data in ways that prevent corruption of the data. Writing code that handles concurrency and avoids race conditions (situations in which an unfortunate order of execution causes undesirable behaviour) requires thought and can be tricky.

Proper management of concurrency is required to write correct kernel code; for that reason, every sample driver in this book has been written with concurrency in mind. The techniques used are explained as we come to them; also been dedicated to this issue and the kernel primitives available for concurrency management.

A common mistake made by driver programmers is to assume that concurrency is not a problem as long as a particular segment of code does not go to sleep (or "block"). Even in previous kernels (which were not preemptive), this assumption was not valid on multiprocessor systems. In 2.6, kernel code can (almost) never assume that it can hold the processor over a given stretch of code. If you do not write your code with concurrency in mind, it will be subject to catastrophic failures that can be exceedingly difficult to debug.

The Current Process

Although kernel modules don't execute sequentially as applications do, most actions performed by the kernel are done on behalf of a specific process. Kernel code can refer to the current process by accessing the global itemcurrent, defined in *<asm/current.h>*, which yields a pointer to struct task_struct, defined by *<linux/sched.h>*. The current pointer refers to the process that is currently executing. During the execution of a system call, such as *open* or *read*, the current process is the one that invoked the call. Kernel code can use process-specific information by using current, if it needs to do so. Actually, current is not truly a global variable. The need to support SMP systems forced the kernel developers to develop a mechanism that finds the current process on the relevant CPU. This mechanism must also be fast, since references to current happen frequently. The result is an architecture-dependent mechanism that, usually, hides a pointer to the task_struct structure on the kernel stack. The details of the implementation remain hidden to other kernel subsystems though, and a device driver can just include *<linux/sched.h>* and refer to the currentprocess. For example, the following statement prints the process ID and the command name of the current process by accessing certain fields in struct task_struct:

```
printk(KERN_INFO "The process is \"%s\" (pid
%i)\n",
current->comm, current->pid);
```

The command name stored in current->comm is the base name of the program file (trimmed to 15 characters if need be) that is being executed by the current process.

A Few Other Details

Kernel programming differs from user-space programming in many ways. We'll point things out as we get to them over the course of the book, but there are a few fundamental issues which, while not warranting a section of their own, are worth a mention. So, as you dig into the kernel, the following issues should be kept in mind.

Applications are laid out in virtual memory with a very large stack area. The stack, of course, is used to hold the function call history and all automatic variables created by currently active functions. The kernel, instead, has a very small stack; it can be as small as a single, 4096-byte page. Your functions must share that stack with the entire kernel-space call chain. Thus, it is never a good idea to declare large automatic variables; if you need larger structures, you should allocate them dynamically at call time.

Often, as you look at the kernel API, you will encounter function names starting with a double underscore (_ _). Functions so marked are generally a low-level component of the interface and should be used with caution. Essentially, the double underscore says to the programmer: "If you call this function, be sure you know what you are doing."

Kernel code cannot do floating point arithmetic. Enabling floating point would require that the kernel save and restore the floating point processor's state on each entry to, and exit from, kernel spaceat least, on some architectures. Given that there really is no need for floating point in kernel code, the extra overhead is not worthwhile.

COMPILING AND LOADING

The "hello world" example at the beginning of this chapter included a brief demonstration of building a module and loading it into the system. There is, of course, a lot more to that whole process than we have seen so far. This section provides more detail on how a module author turns source code into an executing subsystem within the kernel.

Compiling Modules

As the first step, we need to look a bit at how modules must be built. The build process for modules differs significantly from that used for user-space applications; the kernel is a large, standalone program with detailed and explicit requirements on how its pieces are put together. The build process also differs from how things were done with previous versions of the kernel; the new build system is simpler to use and produces more correct results, but it looks very different from what came before. The kernel build system is a complex beast, and we just look at a tiny piece of it. The files found in the Documentation/kbuild directory in the kernel source are required reading for anybody wanting to understand all that is really going on beneath the surface.

There are some prerequisites that you must get out of the way before you can build kernel modules. The first is to ensure that you have sufficiently current versions of the compiler, module utilities, and other necessary tools. The file Documentation/Changes in the kernel documentation directory always lists the required tool versions; you should consult it before going any further. Trying to build a kernel (and its modules) with the wrong tool versions can lead to no end of subtle, difficult problems. Note that, occasionally, a version of the compiler that is too new can be just as problematic as one that is too old; the kernel source makes a great many assumptions about the compiler, and new releases can sometimes break things for a while.

If you still do not have a kernel tree handy, or have not yet configured and built that kernel, now is the time to go do it. You cannot build loadable modules for a 2.6 kernel without this tree on your filesystem. It is also helpful (though not required) to be actually running the kernel that you are building for. Once you have everything set up, creating a makefile for your module is straightforward. In fact, for the "hello world" example shown earlier in this chapter, a single line will suffice:

```
obj-m:= hello.o
```

Readers who are familiar with *make*, but not with the 2.6 kernel build system, are likely to be wondering how this makefile works. The above line is not how a traditional makefile looks, after all. The answer, of course, is that the kernel build system handles the rest. The assignment above (which takes advantage of the extended syntax provided by GNU *make*) states that there is one module to be built from the object file *hello.o*. The resulting module is named *hello.ko* after being built from the object file.

If, instead, you have a module called *module.ko* that is generated from two source files (called, say, *file1.c* and*file2.c*), the correct incantation would be:

```
obj-m:= module.o
module-objs:= file1.o file2.o
```

For a makefile like those shown above to work, it must be invoked within the context of the larger kernel build system. If your kernel source tree is located in, say, your *~/kernel-2.6* directory, the *make* command required to build your module (typed in the directory containing the module source and makefile) would be:

```
make -C ~/kernel-2.6 M='pwd' modules
```

This command starts by changing its directory to the one

provided with the -C option (that is, your kernel source directory). There it finds the kernel's top-level makefile. The M= option causes that makefile to move back into your module source directory before trying to build the modules target. This target, in turn, refers to the list of modules found in the obj-m variable, which we've set to *module.o* in our examples.

Typing the previous *make* command can get tiresome after a while, so the kernel developers have developed a sort of makefile idiom, which makes life easier for those building modules outside of the kernel tree.

The trick is to write your makefile as follows:

```
# If KERNELRELEASE is defined, we've been invoked
from the
# kernel build system and can use its language.
ifneq ($(KERNELRELEASE),)
obj-m:= hello.o
# Otherwise we were called directly from the
command
# line; invoke the kernel build system.
else
KERNELDIR ?=/lib/modules/$(shell uname -r)/build
PWD:= $(shell pwd)
default:
$(MAKE) -C $(KERNELDIR) M=$(PWD) modules
endif
```

Once again, we are seeing the extended GNU make syntax in action. This makefile is read twice on a typical build. When the makefile is invoked from the command line, it notices that the KERNELRELEASE variable has not been set. It locates the kernel source directory by taking advantage of the fact that the symbolic link build in the installed modules directory points back at the kernel build tree. If you are not actually running the kernel that you are building for, you can supply a KERNELDIR= option on the command line, set the KERNELDIR environment variable, or rewrite the line that sets KERNELDIR in the makefile. Once the kernel source tree has been found, the makefile invokes the default: target, which runs a second make command (parameterized in the makefile as$(MAKE)) to invoke the kernel build system as described previously. On the second reading, the makefile setsobj-m, and the kernel makefiles take care of actually building the module.

This mechanism for building modules may strike you as a bit unwieldy and obscure. Once you get used to it, however, you will likely appreciate the capabilities that have been programmed into the kernel build system. Do note that the above is not a complete makefile; a real makefile includes the usual sort of targets for cleaning up unneeded files, installing modules, etc. See the makefiles in the example source directory for a complete example.

LOADING AND UNLOADING MODULES

After the module is built, the next step is loading it into the kernel. As we've already pointed out, insmod does the job for you. The program loads the module code and data into the kernel, which, in turn, performs a function similar to that of ld, in that it links any unresolved symbol in the module to the symbol table of the kernel. Unlike the linker, however, the kernel doesn't modify the module's disk file, but rather an in-memory copy. insmod accepts a number of command-line options (for details, see the manpage), and it can assign values to parameters in your module before linking it to the current kernel. Thus, if a module is correctly designed, it can be configured at load time; load-time configuration gives the user more flexibility than compile-time configuration, which is still used sometimes. Load-time configuration is explained in later in this chapter.

Interested readers may want to look at how the kernel supports insmod: it relies on a system call defined inkernel/ module.c. The function sys_init_module allocates kernel memory to hold a module (this memory is allocated with vmalloc; it then copies the module text into that memory region, resolves kernel references in the module via the kernel symbol table, and calls the module's initialization function to get everything going.

If you actually look in the kernel source, you'll find that the names of the system calls are prefixed with sys_. This is true for all system calls and no other functions; it's useful to keep this in mind when grepping for the system calls in the sources. The modprobe utility is worth a quick mention. modprobe, like insmod, loads a module into the kernel. It differs in that it will look at the module to be loaded to see whether it references any symbols that are not currently defined in the kernel. If any such references are found, modprobe looks for other modules in the current module search path that define the relevant symbols. When modprobe finds those modules (which are needed by the module being loaded), it loads them into the kernel as well. If you use insmod in this situation instead, the command fails with an "unresolved symbols" message left in the system logfile.

As mentioned before, modules may be removed from the kernel with the rmmod utility. Note that module removal fails if the kernel believes that the module is still in use (*e.g.*, a program still has an open file for a device exported by the modules), or if the kernel has been configured to disallow module removal. It is possible to configure the kernel to allow "forced" removal of modules, even when they appear to be busy. If you reach a point where you are considering using this option, however, things are likely to have gone wrong badly enough that a reboot may well be the better course of action.

The lsmod program produces a list of the modules currently loaded in the kernel. Some other information, such as any other modules making use of a specific module, is also provided. lsmod works by reading the/proc/modulesvirtual file. Information on currently loaded modules can also be found in the sysfs virtual filesystem under/sys/module.

Version Dependency

Bear in mind that your module's code has to be recompiled for each version of the kernel that it is linked toâ€"at least, in the absence of modversions, not covered here as they are more for distribution makers than developers. Modules are strongly tied to the data structures and function prototypes defined in a particular kernel version; the interface seen by a module can change significantly from one kernel version to the next. This is especially true of development kernels, of course.

The kernel does not just assume that a given module has been built against the proper kernel version. One of the steps in the build process is to link your module against a file (called *vermagic.o*) from the current kernel tree; this object contains a fair amount of information about the kernel the module was built for, including the target kernel version, compiler version, and the settings of a number of important configuration variables. When an attempt is made to load a module, this information can be tested for compatibility with the running kernel. If things don't match, the module is not loaded; instead, you see something like:

```
# insmod hello.ko
Error inserting './hello.ko': -1 Invalid module
format
```

A look in the system log file (*/var/log/messages* or whatever your system is configured to use) will reveal thespecific problem that caused the module to fail to load.

If you need to compile a module for a specific kernel version, you will need to use the build system and source tree for that particular version. A simple change to the KERNELDIR variable in the example makefile shown previously does the trick.

Kernel interfaces often change between releases. If you are writing a module that is intended to work with multiple versions of the kernel (especially if it must work across major releases), you likely have to make use of macros and #ifdef constructs to make your code build properly. This edition of this book only concerns itself with one major version of the kernel, so you do not often see version tests in our example code. But the need for them does occasionally arise. In such cases, you want to make use of the definitions found in *linux/version.h*.

This header file, automatically included by linux/module.h, defines the following macros:

UTS_RELEASE

This macro expands to a string describing the version of this kernel tree. For example, "2.6.10".

`LINUX_VERSION_CODE`

This macro expands to the binary representation of the kernel version, one byte for each part of the version release number. For example, the code for 2.6.10 is 132618 (*i.e.*, 0x02060a).[2] With this information, you can (almost) easily determine what version of the kernel you are dealing with.

[2] This allows up to 256 development versions between stable versions.

`KERNEL_VERSION(major,minor,release)`

This is the macro used to build an integer version code from the individual numbers that build up a version number. For example, KERNEL_VERSION(2,6,10) expands to 132618. This macro is very useful when you need to compare the current version and a known checkpoint.

Most dependencies based on the kernel version can be worked around with preprocessor conditionals by exploiting KERNEL_VERSION and LINUX_VERSION_CODE. Version dependency should, however, not clutter driver code with hairy #ifdef conditionals; the best way to deal with incompatibilities is by confining them to a specific header file. As a general rule, code which is explicitly version (or platform) dependent should be hidden behind a low-level macro or function. High-level code can then just call those functions without concern for the low-level details. Code written in this way tends to be easier to read and more robust.

Platform Dependency

Each computer platform has its peculiarities, and kernel designers are free to exploit all the peculiarities to achieve better performance in the target object file. Unlike application developers, who must link their code with precompiled libraries and stick to conventions on parameter passing, kernel developers can dedicate some processor registers to specific roles, and they have done so. Moreover, kernel code can be optimized for a specific processor in a CPU family to get the best from the target platform: unlike applications that are often distributed in binary format, a custom compilation of the kernel can be optimized for a specific computer set.

For example, the IA32 (x86) architecture has been subdivided into several different processor types. The old 80386 processor is still supported (for now), even though its instruction set is, by modern standards, quite limited. The more modern processors in this architecture have introduced a number of new capabilities, including faster instructions for entering the kernel, interprocessor locking, copying data, etc.

Newer processors can also, when operated in the correct mode, employ 36-bit (or larger) physical addresses, allowing them to address more than 4 GB of physical memory. Other processor families have seen similar improvements. The kernel, depending on various configuration options, can be built to make use of these additional features. Clearly, if a module is to work with a given kernel, it must be built with the same understanding of the target processor as that kernel was. Once again, the *vermagic.o* object comes in to play. When a module is loaded, the kernel checks the processor-specific configuration options for the module and makes sure they match the running kernel. If the module was compiled with different options, it is not loaded.

If you are planning to write a driver for general distribution, you may well be wondering just how you can possibly support all these different variations. The best answer, of course, is to release your driver under a GPL-compatible license and contribute it to the mainline kernel. Failing that, distributing your driver in source form and a set of scripts to compile it on the user's system may be the best answer.

Some vendors have released tools to make this task easier. If you must distribute your driver in binary form, you need to look at the different kernels provided by your target distributions, and provide a version of the module for each. Be sure to take into account any errata kernels that may have been released since the distribution was produced. Then, there are licensing issues to be considered, as we discussed. As a general rule, distributing things in source form is an easier way to make your way in the world.

THE KERNEL SYMBOL TABLE

We've seen how *insmod* resolves undefined symbols against the table of public kernel symbols. The table contains the addresses of global kernel itemsâ€"functions and variablesâ€"that are needed to implement modularized drivers. When a module is loaded, any symbol exported by the module becomes part of the kernel symbol table. In the usual case, a module implements its own functionality without the need to export any symbols at all. You need to export symbols, however, whenever other modules may benefit from using them.

New modules can use symbols exported by your module, and you can stack new modules on top of other modules. Module stacking is implemented in the mainstream kernel sources as well: the *msdos* filesystem relies on symbols exported by the *fat* module, and each input USB device module stacks on the *usbcore* and *input*modules.

Module stacking is useful in complex projects. If a new abstraction is implemented in the form of a device driver, it might offer a plug for hardware-specific implementations. For example, the video-for-linux set of drivers is split into a generic module that exports symbols used by lower-level device drivers for specific hardware. According to your setup, you load the generic video module and the specific module for your installed hardware.

Support for parallel ports and the wide variety of attachable devices is handled in the same way, as is the USB kernel subsystem. Stacking in the parallel port subsystem is shown in Figure; the arrows show the communications between the modules and with the kernel programming interface.

When using stacked modules, it is helpful to be aware of the *modprobe* utility. As we described earlier, *modprobe* functions in much the same way as *insmod*, but it also loads any other modules that are required by the module you want to load. Thus, one *modprobe* command can sometimes replace several invocations of*insmod* (although you'll still need *insmod* when loading your own modules from the current directory, because*modprobe* looks only in the standard installed module directories).

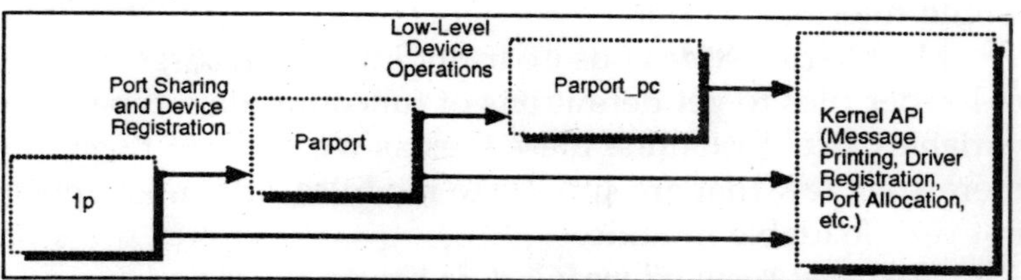

Fig: Stacking of Parallel Port Driver Modules

Using stacking to split modules into multiple layers can help reduce development time by simplifying each layer. This is similar to the separation between mechanism and policy that we discussed. The Linux kernel header files provide a convenient way to manage the visibility of your symbols, thus reducing namespace pollution (filling the namespace with names that may conflict with those defined elsewhere in the kernel) and promoting proper information hiding. If your module needs to export symbols for other modules to use, the following macros should be used.

```
EXPORT_SYMBOL(name);
EXPORT_SYMBOL_GPL(name);
```

Either of the above macros makes the given symbol available outside the module. The _GPL version makes the symbol available to GPL-licensed modules only. Symbols must be exported in the global part of the module's file, outside of any function, because the macros expand to the declaration of a special-purpose variable that is expected to be accessible globally. This variable is stored in a special part of the module executible (an "ELF section") that is used by the kernel at load time to find the variables exported by the module. (Interested readers can look at *<linux/module.h>* for the details, even though the details are not needed to make things work.)

PRELIMINARIES

We are getting closer to looking at some actual module code. But first, we need to look at some other things that need to appear in your module source files. The kernel is a unique environment, and it imposes its own requirements on code that would interface with it.

Most kernel code ends up including a fairly large number of header files to get definitions of functions, data types, and variables. We'll examine these files as we come to them, but there are a few that are specific to modules, and must appear in every loadable module.

Thus, just about all module code has the following:

```
#include <linux/module.h>
#include <linux/init.h>
```

module.h contains a great many definitions of symbols and functions needed by loadable modules. You need*init.h* to specify your initialization and cleanup functions, as we saw in the "hello world" example above, and which we revisit in the next section. Most modules also include *moduleparam.h* to enable the passing of parameters to the module at load time; we will get to that shortly. It is not strictly necessary, but your module really should specify which license applies to its code. Doing so is just a matter of including a MODULE_LICENSE line:

```
MODULE_LICENSE("GPL");
```

The specific licenses recognized by the kernel are "GPL" (for any version of the GNU General Public License), "GPL v2" (for GPL version two only), "GPL and additional rights," "Dual BSD/GPL," "Dual MPL/GPL," and "Proprietary." Unless your module is explicitly marked as being under a free license recognized by the kernel, it is assumed to be proprietary, and the kernel is "tainted" when the module is loaded. As we mentioned in kernel developers tend to be unenthusiastic about helping users who experience problems after loading proprietary modules.

Other descriptive definitions that can be contained within a module include MODULE_AUTHOR (stating who wrote the module), MODULE_DESCRIPTION (a human-readable statement of what the module does), MODULE_VERSION (for a code revision number; see the comments in *<linux/module.h>* for the conventions to use in creating version strings),

MODULE_ALIAS (another name by which this module can be known), and MODULE_DEVICE_TABLE (to tell user space about which devices the module supports).

The various MODULE_ declarations can appear anywhere within your source file outside of a function. A relatively recent convention in kernel code, however, is to put these declarations at the end of the file.

INITIALIZATION AND SHUTDOWN

As already mentioned, the module initialization function registers any facility offered by the module. By *facility*, we mean a new functionality, be it a whole driver or a new software abstraction, that can be accessed by an application.

The actual definition of the initialization function always looks like:

```
static int _ _init initialization_function(void)
{
/* Initialization code here */
}
module_init(initialization_function);
```

Initialization functions should be declared static, since they are not meant to be visible outside the specific file; there is no hard rule about this, though, as no function is exported to the rest of the kernel unless explicitly requested. The _ _init token in the definition may look a little strange; it is a hint to the kernel that the given function is used only at initialization time. The module loader drops the initialization function after the module is loaded, making its memory available for other uses. There is a similar tag (_ _initdata) for data used only during initialization. Use of _ _init and _ _initdata is optional, but it is worth the trouble. Just be sure not to use them for any function (or data structure) you will be using after initialization completes. You may also encounter _ _devinit and _ _devinitdata in the kernel source; these translate to _ _init and _ _initdata only if the kernel has not been configured for hotpluggable devices. We will look at hotplug support.

The use of *module_init* is mandatory. This macro adds a special section to the module's object code stating where the module's initialization function is to be found. Without this definition, your initialization function is never called.

Modules can register many different types of facilities, including different kinds of devices, filesystems, cryptographic transforms, and more.

For each facility, there is a specific kernel function that accomplishes this registration. The arguments passed to the kernel registration functions are usually pointers to data structures describing the new facility and the name of the facility being registered. The data structure usually contains pointers to module functions, which is how functions in the module body get called.

The items that can be registered go beyond the list of device types mentioned. They include, among others, serial ports, miscellaneous devices, sysfs entries,/*proc* files, executable domains, and line disciplines. Many of those registrable items support functions that aren't directly related to hardware but remain in the "software abstractions" field. Those items can be registered, because they are integrated into the driver's functionality anyway (like/*proc* files and line disciplines for example).

There are other facilities that can be registered as add-ons for certain drivers, but their use is so specific that it's not worth talking about them; they use the stacking technique, as described. If you want to probe further, you can grep for EXPORT_SYMBOL in the kernel sources, and find the entry points offered by different drivers. Most registration functions are prefixed with register_, so another possible way to find them is to grep forregister_ in the kernel source.

The Cleanup Function

Every nontrivial module also requires a cleanup function, which unregisters interfaces and returns all resources to the system before the module is removed.

This function is defined as:

```
static void _ _exit cleanup_function(void)
{
/* Cleanup code here */
```

```
}
module_exit(cleanup_function);
```

The cleanup function has no value to return, so it is declared void. The _ _exit modifier marks the code as being for module unload only (by causing the compiler to place it in a special ELF section). If your module is built directly into the kernel, or if your kernel is configured to disallow the unloading of modules, functions marked _ _exit are simply discarded. For this reason, a function marked _ _exit can be called *only* at module unload or system shutdown time; any other use is an error. Once again, the *module_exit* declaration is necessary to enable to kernel to find your cleanup function. If your module does not define a cleanup function, the kernel does not allow it to be unloaded.

Error Handling During Initialization

One thing you must always bear in mind when registering facilities with the kernel is that the registration could fail. Even the simplest action often requires memory allocation, and the required memory may not be available. So module code must always check return values, and be sure that the requested operations have actually succeeded.

If any errors occur when you register utilities, the first order of business is to decide whether the module can continue initializing itself anyway. Often, the module can continue to operate after a registration failure, with degraded functionality if necessary. Whenever possible, your module should press forward and provide what capabilities it can after things fail.

If it turns out that your module simply cannot load after a particular type of failure, you must undo any registration activities performed before the failure. Linux doesn't keep a per-module registry of facilities that have been registered, so the module must back out of everything itself if initialization fails at some point. If you ever fail to unregister what you obtained, the kernel is left in an unstable state; it contains internal pointers to code that no longer exists. In such situations, the only recourse, usually, is to reboot the system. You really do want to take care to do the right thing when an initialization error occurs. Error recovery is sometimes best handled with the goto statement. We normally hate to use goto, but in our opinion, this is one situation where it is useful. Careful use of goto in error situations can eliminate a great deal of complicated, highly-indented, "structured" logic. Thus, in the kernel, goto is often used as shown here to deal with errors.

The following sample code (using fictitious registration and unregistration functions) behaves correctly if initialization fails at any point:

```
int __init my_init_function(void)
{
int err;
/* registration takes a pointer and a name */
err = register_this(ptr1, "skull");
if (err) goto fail_this;
err = register_that(ptr2, "skull");
if (err) goto fail_that;
err = register_those(ptr3, "skull");
if (err) goto fail_those;
return 0;/* success */
fail_those: unregister_that(ptr2, "skull");
fail_that: unregister_this(ptr1, "skull");
fail_this: return err;/* propagate the error */
}
```

This code attempts to register three (fictitious) facilities. The goto statement is used in case of failure to cause the unregistration of only the facilities that had been successfully registered before things went bad.

Another option, requiring no hairy goto statements, is keeping track of what has been successfully registered and calling your module's cleanup function in case of any error. The cleanup function unrolls only the steps that have been successfully accomplished. This alternative, however, requires more code and more CPU time, so in fast paths you still resort to goto as the best error-recovery tool.

The return value of *my_init_function*, err, is an error code. In the Linux kernel, error codes are negative numbers belonging to the set defined in *<linux/errno.h>*. If you want to generate your own error codes instead of returning what you get from other functions, you should include *<linux/errno.h>* in order to use symbolic values such as -ENODEV, -ENOMEM, and so on. It is always good practice to return appropriate error codes, because user programs can turn them to meaningful strings using *perror* or similar means.

Obviously, the module cleanup function must undo any registration performed by the initialization function, and it is customary (but not usually mandatory) to unregister facilities in the reverse order used to register them:

```
void _ _exit my_cleanup_function(void)
{
unregister_those(ptr3, "skull");
unregister_that(ptr2, "skull");
unregister_this(ptr1, "skull");
return;
}
```

If your initialization and cleanup are more complex than dealing with a few items, the goto approach may become difficult to manage, because all the cleanup code must be repeated within the initialization function, with several labels intermixed. Sometimes, therefore, a different layout of the code proves more successful.

What you'd do to minimize code duplication and keep everything streamlined is to call the cleanup function from within the initialization whenever an error occurs. The cleanup function then must check the status of each item before undoing its registration.

In its simplest form, the code looks like the following:

```
struct something *item1;
struct somethingelse *item2;
int stuff_ok;
void my_cleanup(void)
{
if (item1)
release_thing(item1);
if (item2)
```

```
release_thing2(item2);
if (stuff_ok)
unregister_stuff();
return;
}
int _ _init my_init(void)
{
int err = -ENOMEM;
item1 = allocate_thing(arguments);
item2 = allocate_thing2(arguments2);
if (!item2 || !item2)
goto fail;
err = register_stuff(item1, item2);
if (!err)
stuff_ok = 1;
else
goto fail;
return 0;/* success */
fail:
my_cleanup();
return err;
}
```

As shown in this code, you may or may not need external flags to mark success of the initialization step, depending on the semantics of the registration/allocation function you call. Whether or not flags are needed, this kind of initialization scales well to a large number of items and is often better than the technique shown earlier. Note, however, that the cleanup function cannot be marked _ _exit when it is called by nonexit code, as in the previous example.

Module-Loading Races

Thus far, our discussion has skated over an important aspect of module loading: race conditions. If you are not careful in how you write your initialization function, you can create situations that can compromise the stability of the system as a whole. We will discuss race conditions later in this book; for now, a couple of quick points will have to suffice.

The first is that you should always remember that some other part of the kernel can make use of any facility you register immediately after that registration has completed. It is entirely possible, in other words, that the kernel will make calls into your module while your initialization function is still running. So your code must be prepared to be called as soon as it completes its first registration. Do not register any facility until all of your internal initialization needed to support that facility has been completed.

You must also consider what happens if your initialization function decides to fail, but some part of the kernel is already making use of a facility your module has registered. If this situation is possible for your module, you should seriously consider not failing the initialization at all. After all, the module has clearly succeeded in exporting something useful. If initialization must fail, it must carefully step around any possible operations going on elsewhere in the kernel until those operations have completed.

MODULE PARAMETERS

Several parameters that a driver needs to know can change from system to system. These can vary from the device number to use (as we'll see in the next chapter) to numerous aspects of how the driver should operate. For example, drivers for SCSI adapters often have options controlling the use of tagged command queuing, and the Integrated Device Electronics (IDE) drivers allow user control of DMA operations. If your driver controls older hardware, it may also need to be told explicitly where to find that hardware's I/O ports or I/O memory addresses. The kernel supports these needs by making it possible for a driver to designate parameters that may be changed when the driver's module is loaded.

These parameter values can be assigned at load time by *insmod* or *modprobe*; the latter can also read parameter assignment from its configuration file (*/etc/modprobe.conf*). The commands accept the specification of several types of values on the command line. As a way of demonstrating this capability, imagine a much-needed enhancement to the "hello world" module (called *hellop*) shown at the beginning of this chapter. We add two parameters: an integer value called howmany and a character string called whom. Our vastly more functional module then, at load time, greets whom not just once, but howmany times.

Such a module could then be loaded with a command line such as:

```
insmod hellop howmany=10 whom="Mom"
```

Upon being loaded that way, *hellop* would say "Hello, Mom" 10 times. However, before *insmod* can change module parameters, the module must make them available. Parameters are declared with the module_param macro, which is defined in *moduleparam.h*. module_param takes three parameters: the name of the variable, its type, and a permissions mask to be used for an accompanying sysfs entry. The macro should be placed outside of any function and is typically found near the head of the source file.

So hellop would declare its parameters and make them available to insmod as follows:

```
static char *whom = "world";
static int howmany = 1;
module_param(howmany, int, S_IRUGO);
module_param(whom, charp, S_IRUGO);
```

Numerous types are supported for module parameters:

bool

invbool

A boolean (true or false) value (the associated variable should be of type int). The invbool type inverts the value, so that true values become false and vice versa.

charp

A char pointer value. Memory is allocated for user-provided strings, and the pointer is set accordingly.

int

long

short

uint

ulong

ushort

Basic integer values of various lengths. The versions starting with u are for unsigned values. Array parameters, where the values are supplied as a comma-separated list, are also supported by the module loader.

To declare an array parameter, use:

module_param_array(name,type,num,perm);

Where name is the name of your array (and of the parameter), type is the type of the array elements, num is an integer variable, and perm is the usual permissions value. If the array parameter is set at load time, num is set to the number of values supplied. The module loader refuses to accept more values than will fit in the array. If you really need a type that does not appear in the list above, there are hooks in the module code that allow you to define them; see *moduleparam.h* for details on how to do that. All module parameters should be given a default value; *insmod* changes the value only if explicitly told to by the user. The module can check for explicit parameters by testing parameters against their default values. The final *module_param* field is a permission value; you should use the definitions found in *<linux/stat.h>*. This value controls who can access the representation of the module parameter in sysfs. If perm is set to 0, there is no sysfs entry at all; otherwise, it appears under*/sys/module*[3] with the given set of permissions. Use S_IRUGO for a parameter that can be read by the world but cannot be changed; S_IRUGO | S_IWUSR allows root to change the parameter. Note that if a parameter is changed by sysfs, the value of that parameter as seen by your module changes, but your module is not notified in any other way. You should probably not make module parameters writable, unless you are prepared to detect the change and react accordingly.

DOING IT IN USER SPACE

A Unix programmer who's addressing kernel issues for the first time might be nervous about writing a module. Writing a user program that reads and writes directly to the device ports may be easier. Indeed, there are some arguments in favour of user-space programming, and sometimes writing a so-called user-space device driver is a wise alternative to kernel hacking. In this section, we discuss some of the reasons why you might write a driver in user space. This book is about kernel-space drivers, however, so we do not go beyond this introductory discussion.

The advantages of user-space drivers are:

- The full C library can be linked in. The driver can perform many exotic tasks without resorting to external programs (the utility programs implementing usage policies that are usually distributed along with the driver itself).
- The programmer can run a conventional debugger on the driver code without having to go through contortions to debug a running kernel.
- If a user-space driver hangs, you can simply kill it. Problems with the driver are unlikely to hang the entire system, unless the hardware being controlled is *really* misbehaving.
- User memory is swappable, unlike kernel memory. An infrequently used device with a huge driver won't occupy RAM that other programs could be using, except when it is actually in use.
- A well-designed driver program can still, like kernel-space drivers, allow concurrent access to a device.
- If you must write a closed-source driver, the user-space option makes it easier for you to avoid ambiguous licensing situations and problems with changing kernel interfaces.

For example, USB drivers can be written for user space; see the (still young) libusb project at libusb.sourceforge.net and "gadgetfs" in the kernel source. Another example is the X server: it knows exactly what the hardware can do and what it can't, and it offers the graphic resources to all X clients. Note, however, that there is a slow but steady drift towards frame-buffer-based graphics environments, where the X server acts only as a server based on a real kernel-space device driver for actual graphic manipulation. Usually, the writer of a user-space driver implements a server process, taking over from the kernel the task of being the single agent in charge of hardware control. Client applications can then connect to the server to perform actual communication with the device; therefore, a smart driver process can allow concurrent access to the device. This is exactly how the X server works.

But the user-space approach to device driving has a number of drawbacks.

The most important are:

- Interrupts are not available in user space. There are workarounds for this limitation on some platforms, such as the *vm86* system call on the IA32 architecture.
- Direct access to memory is possible only by *mmapping/dev/mem,* and only a privileged user can do that.
- Access to I/O ports is available only after calling *ioperm* or *iopl.* Moreover, not all platforms support these system calls, and access to*/dev/port* can be too slow to be effective. Both the system calls and the device file are reserved to a privileged user.
- Response time is slower, because a context switch is required to transfer information or actions between the client and the hardware.
- Worse yet, if the driver has been swapped to disk, response time is unacceptably long. Using the *mlock*system call might help, but usually you'll need to lock many memory pages, because a user-space program depends on a lot of library code. *mlock,* too, is limited to privileged users.
- The most important devices can't be handled in user space, including, but not limited to, network interfaces and block devices.

As you see, user-space drivers can't do that much after all. Interesting applications nonetheless exist: for example, support for SCSI scanner devices (implemented by the *SANE* package) and CD writers (implemented by*cdrecord* and other tools). In both cases, user-level device drivers rely on the "SCSI generic" kernel driver, which exports low-level SCSI functionality to user-space programs so they can drive their own hardware. One case in which working in user space might make sense is when you are beginning to deal with new and unusual hardware. This way you can learn to manage your hardware without the risk of hanging the whole system. Once you've done that, encapsulating the software in a kernel module should be a painless operation.

QUICK REFERENCE

This section summarizes the kernel functions, variables, macros, and/*proc* files that we've touched on in this chapter. It is meant to act as a reference. Each item is listed after the relevant header file, if any. A similar section appears at the end of almost every chapter from here on, summarizing the new symbols introduced in the chapter.

Entries in this section generally appear in the same order in which they were introduced in the chapter:

- insmod
- modprobe
- rmmod

User-space utilities that load modules into the running kernels and remove them.

`#include <linux/init.h>`
`module_init(init_function);`
`module_exit(cleanup_function);`

Macros that designate a module's initialization and cleanup functions.

`_ _init`
`_ _initdata`
`_ _exit`
`_ _exitdata`

Markers for functions (_ _init and _ _exit) and data (_ _initdata and _ _exitdata) that are only used at module initialization or cleanup time. Items marked for initialization may be discarded once initialization completes; the exit items may be discarded if module unloading has not been configured into the kernel. These markers work by causing the relevant objects to be placed in a special ELF section in the executable file.

#include <linux/sched.h>

One of the most important header files. This file contains definitions of much of the kernel API used by the driver, including functions for sleeping and numerous variable declarations.

struct task_struct *current;

The current process.

current->pid

current->comm

The process ID and command name for the current process.

obj-m

A makefile symbol used by the kernel build system to determine which modules should be built in the current directory.

/sys/module

/proc/modules

/sys/module is a sysfs directory hierarchy containing information on currently-loaded modules.*/proc/modules* is the older, single-file version of that information. Entries contain the module name, the amount of memory each module occupies, and the usage count. Extra strings are appended to each line to specify flags that are currently active for the module.

vermagic.o

An object file from the kernel source directory that describes the environment a module was built for.

#include <linux/module.h>

Required header. It must be included by a module source.

#include <linux/version.h>

A header file containing information on the version of the kernel being built.

LINUX_VERSION_CODE

Integer macro, useful to #ifdef version dependencies.

EXPORT_SYMBOL (symbol);

EXPORT_SYMBOL_GPL (symbol);

Macro used to export a symbol to the kernel. The second form exports without using versioning information, and the third limits the export to GPL-licensed modules.

```
MODULE_AUTHOR(author);
MODULE_DESCRIPTION(description);
MODULE_VERSION(version_string);
MODULE_DEVICE_TABLE(table_info);
MODULE_ALIAS(alternate_name);
```

Place documentation on the module in the object file.

```
module_init(init_function);
module_exit(exit_function);
```

Macros that declare a module's initialization and cleanup functions.

```
#include <linux/moduleparam.h>
module_param(variable, type, perm);
```

Macro that creates a module parameter that can be adjusted by the user when the module is loaded (or at boot time for built-in code). The type can be one of bool, charp, int, invbool, long, short, ushort, uint,ulong, or intarray.

```
#include <linux/kernel.h>
int printk(const char * fmt...);
```

The analogue of *printf* for kernel code.

CHAR DRIVERS

The goal of this chapter is to write a complete char device driver. We develop a character driver because this class is suitable for most simple hardware devices. Char drivers are also easier to understand than block drivers or network drivers (which we get to in later chapters). Our ultimate aim is to write a *modularized* char driver, but we won't talk about modularization issues in this chapter.

Throughout the chapter, we present code fragments extracted from a real device driver: *scull* (Simple Character Utility for Loading Localities). *scull* is a char driver that acts on a memory area as though it were a device. In this chapter, because of that peculiarity of *scull*, we use the word *device* interchangeably with "the memory area used by*scull*."

The advantage of *scull* is that it isn't hardware dependent. *scull* just acts on some memory, allocated from the kernel. Anyone can compile and run *scull*, and *scull* is portable across the computer architectures on which Linux runs. On the other hand, the device doesn't do anything "useful" other than demonstrate the interface between the kernel and char drivers and allow the user to run some tests.

THE DESIGN OF SCULL

The first step of driver writing is defining the capabilities (the mechanism) the driver will offer to user programs. Since our "device" is part of the computer's memory, we're free to do what we want with it. It can be a sequential or random-access device, one device or many, and so on.

To make *scull* useful as a template for writing real drivers for real devices, we'll show you how to implement several device abstractions on top of the computer memory, each with a different personality. The *scull* source implements the following devices. Each kind of device implemented by the module is referred to as a *type*.

Scull0 to Scull3

Four devices, each consisting of a memory area that is both global and persistent. Global means that if the device is opened multiple times, the data contained within the device is shared by all the file descriptors that opened it. Persistent means that if the device is closed and reopened, data isn't lost. This device can be fun to work with, because it can be accessed and tested using conventional commands, such as *cp*, *cat*, and shell I/O redirection.

Scullpipe0 to Scullpipe3

Four FIFO (first-in-first-out) devices, which act like pipes. One process reads what another process writes. If multiple processes read the same device, they contend for data. The internals of *scullpipe* will show how blocking and nonblocking *read* and *write* can be implemented without having to resort to interrupts.

Although real drivers synchronize with their devices using hardware interrupts, the topic of blocking and nonblocking operations is an important one and is separate from interrupt handling.

scullsingle
scullpriv
sculluid
scullwuid

These devices are similar to scull0 but with some limitations on when an open is permitted. The first (scullsingle) allows only one process at a time to use the driver, whereas scullpriv is private to each virtual console (or X terminal session), because processes on each console/terminal get different memory areas.sculluid and scullwuid can be opened multiple times, but only by one user at a time; the former returns an error of "Device Busy" if another user is locking the device, whereas the latter implements blocking open. These variations of scull would appear to be confusing policy and mechanism, but they are worth looking at, because some real-life devices require this sort of management.

Each of the scull devices demonstrates different features of a driver and presents different difficulties. This chapter covers the internals of scull0 to scull3; the more advanced devices are covered. scullpipe is described in others are described

MAJOR AND MINOR NUMBERS

Char devices are accessed through names in the filesystem. Those names are called special files or device files or simply nodes of the filesystem tree; they are conventionally located in the/dev directory.

Special files for char drivers are identified by a "c" in the first column of the output of ls -l. Block devices appear in/dev as well, but they are identified by a "b." The focus of this chapter is on char devices, but much of the following information applies to block devices as well.

If you issue the ls -l command, you'll see two numbers (separated by a comma) in the device file entries before the date of the last modification, where the file length normally appears. These numbers are the major and minor device number for the particular device. The following listing shows a few devices as they appear on a typical system. Their major numbers are 1, 4, 7, and 10, while the minors are 1, 3, 5, 64, 65, and 129.

```
crw-rw-rw- 1 root root 1, 3 Apr 11 2002 null
crw------- 1 root root 10, 1 Apr 11 2002 psaux
crw------- 1 root root 4, 1 Oct 28 03:04 tty1
crw-rw-rw- 1 root tty 4, 64 Apr 11 2002 ttys0
crw-rw---- 1 root uucp 4, 65 Apr 11 2002 ttyS1
crw--w---- 1 vcsa tty 7, 1 Apr 11 2002 vcs1
crw--w---- 1 vcsa tty 7, 129 Apr 11 2002 vcsa1
crw-rw-rw- 1 root root 1, 5 Apr 11 2002 zero
```

Traditionally, the major number identifies the driver associated with the device. For example,*/dev/null* and*/dev/zero* are both managed by driver 1, whereas virtual consoles and serial terminals are managed by driver 4; similarly, both *vcs1* and *vcsa1* devices are managed by driver 7. Modern Linux kernels allow multiple drivers to share major numbers, but most devices that you will see are still organized on the one-major-one-driver principle.

The minor number is used by the kernel to determine exactly which device is being referred to. Depending on how your driver is written (as we will see below), you can either get a direct pointer to your device from the kernel, or you can use the minor number yourself as an index into a local array of devices. Either way, the kernel itself knows almost nothing about minor numbers beyond the fact that they refer to devices implemented by your driver.

The Internal Representation of Device Numbers

Within the kernel, the dev_t type (defined in *<linux/types.h>*) is used to hold device numbers both the major and minor parts. As of Version 2.6.0 of the kernel, dev_t is a 32-bit quantity with 12 bits set aside for the major number and 20 for the minor number. Your code should, of course, never make any assumptions about the internal organization of device numbers; it should, instead, make use of a set of macros found in*<linux/kdev_t.h>*.

To obtain the major or minor parts of a dev_t, use:

```
MAJOR(dev_t dev);
```

```
MINOR(dev_t dev);
```

If, instead, you have the major and minor numbers and need to turn them into a dev_t, use:

```
MKDEV(int major, int minor);
```

Note that the 2.6 kernel can accommodate a vast number of devices, while previous kernel versions were limited to 255 major and 255 minor numbers. One assumes that the wider range will be sufficient for quite some time, but the computing field is littered with erroneous assumptions of that nature. So you should expect that the format ofdev_t could change again in the future; if you write your drivers carefully, however, these changes will not be a problem.

ALLOCATING AND FREEING DEVICE NUMBERS

One of the first things your driver will need to do when setting up a char device is to obtain one or more device numbers to work with. The necessary function for this task is *register_chrdev_region*, which is declared in*<linux/fs.h>*:

```
int register_chrdev_region(dev_t first, unsigned
int count,
char *name);
```

Here, first is the beginning device number of the range you would like to allocate. The minor number portion offirst is often 0, but there is no requirement to that effect. count is the total number of contiguous device numbers you are requesting. Note that, if count is large, the range you request could spill over to the next major number; but everything will still work properly as long as the number range you request is available. Finally, name is the name of the device that should be associated with this number range; it will appear in*/proc/devices* and sysfs.

As with most kernel functions, the return value from *register_chrdev_region* will be 0 if the allocation was successfully performed. In case of error, a negative error code will be returned, and you will not have access to the requested region.

register_chrdev_region works well if you know ahead of time exactly which device numbers you want. Often, however, you will not know which major numbers your device will use;

there is a constant effort within the Linux kernel development community to move over to the use of dynamicly-allocated device numbers. The kernel will happily allocate a major number for you on the fly, but you must request this allocation by using a different function:

```
int alloc_chrdev_region(dev_t *dev, unsigned int
firstminor,
unsigned int count, char *name);
```

With this function, dev is an output-only parameter that will, on successful completion, hold the first number in your allocated range. firstminor should be the requested first minor number to use; it is usually 0. The count and nameparameters work like those given to *request_chrdev_region.*

Regardless of how you allocate your device numbers, you should free them when they are no longer in use.

Device numbers are freed with:

```
void unregister_chrdev_region(dev_t first,
unsigned int count);
```

The usual place to call *unregister_chrdev_region* would be in your module's cleanup function. The above functions allocate device numbers for your driver's use, but they do not tell the kernel anything about what you will actually do with those numbers. Before a user-space program can access one of those device numbers, your driver needs to connect them to its internal functions that implement the device's operations. We will describe how this connection is accomplished shortly, but there are a couple of necessary digressions to take care of first.

Dynamic Allocation of Major Numbers

Some major device numbers are statically assigned to the most common devices. A list of those devices can be found in *Documentation/devices.txt* within the kernel source tree. The chances of a static number having already been assigned for the use of your new driver are small, however, and new numbers are not being assigned. So, as a driver writer, you have a choice: you can simply pick a number that appears to be unused, or you can allocate major numbers in a dynamic manner. Picking a number may work as long as the only user of your driver is you; once your driver is more widely deployed, a randomly picked major number will lead to conflicts and trouble.

Thus, for new drivers, we strongly suggest that you use dynamic allocation to obtain your major device number, rather than choosing a number randomly from the ones that are currently free. In other words, your drivers should almost certainly be using *alloc_chrdev_region* rather than *register_chrdev_region*.

The disadvantage of dynamic assignment is that you can't create the device nodes in advance, because the major number assigned to your module will vary. For normal use of the driver, this is hardly a problem, because once the number has been assigned, you can read it from/*proc/devices*.

[1] Even better device information can usually be obtained from sysfs, generally mounted on/*sys* on 2.6-based systems. Getting *scull* to export information via sysfs is beyond the scope of this chapter, however; we'll return to this topic.

To load a driver using a dynamic major number, therefore, the invocation of *insmod* can be replaced by a simple script that, after calling *insmod*, reads/*proc/devices* in order to create the special file(s).

A typical/proc/devices file looks like the following:

- *Character Devices:*

```
1 mem
2 pty
3 ttyp
4 ttyS
6 lp
7 vcs
10 misc
13 input
14 sound
21 sg
180 usb
```

- *Block Devices:*

```
2 fd
```

```
8 sd
11 sr
65 sd
66 sd
```

The script to load a module that has been assigned a dynamic number can, therefore, be written using a tool such as *awk* to retrieve information from*/proc/devices* in order to create the files in*/dev*.

The following script, *scull_load*, is part of the *scull* distribution. The user of a driver that is distributed in the form of a module can invoke such a script from the system's *rc.local* file or call it manually whenever the module is needed.

```
#!/bin/sh
module="scull"
device="scull"
mode="664"
# invoke insmod with all arguments we got
# and use a pathname, as newer modutils don't
look in. by default
/sbin/insmod./$module.ko $* || exit 1
# remove stale nodes
rm -f/dev/${device}[0-3]
major=$(awk "\\$2= =\"$module\" {print \\$1}"/
proc/devices)
mknod/dev/${device}0 c $major 0
mknod/dev/${device}1 c $major 1
mknod/dev/${device}2 c $major 2
mknod/dev/${device}3 c $major 3
# give appropriate group/permissions, and change
the group.
# Not all distributions have staff, some have
"wheel" instead.
group="staff"
grep -q '^staff:'/etc/group || group="wheel"
chgrp $group/dev/${device}[0-3]
chmod $mode/dev/${device}[0-3]
```

The script can be adapted for another driver by redefining the variables and adjusting the *mknod* lines. The script just shown creates four devices because four is the default in the *scull* sources.

The last few lines of the script may seem obscure: why change the group and mode of a device? The reason is that the script must be run by the superuser, so newly created special files are owned by root. The permission bits default so that only root has write access, while anyone can get read access. Normally, a device node requires a different access policy, so in some way or another access rights must be changed. The default in our script is to give access to a group of users, but your needs may vary. Code for *sculluid*demonstrates how the driver can enforce its own kind of authorization for device access.

A *scull_unload* script is also available to clean up the*/dev* directory and remove the module. As an alternative to using a pair of scripts for loading and unloading, you could write an init script, ready to be placed in the directory your distribution uses for these scripts. As part of the scull source, we offer a fairly complete and configurable example of an init script, called scull.init; it accepts the conventional arguments start, stop, and restart and performs the role of oth scull_load and scull_unload. The Linux Standard Base specifies that init scripts should be placed in/etc/init.d, but some distributions still place them elsewhere. In addition, if your script is to be run at boot time, you need to make a link to it from the appropriate run-level directory (*i.e.*.../rc3.d).

If repeatedly creating and destroying/dev nodes sounds like overkill, there is a useful workaround. If you are loading and unloading only a single driver, you can just use rmmod and insmod after the first time you create the special files with your script: dynamic numbers are not randomized, and you can count on the same number being chosen each time if you don't load any other (dynamic) modules. Avoiding lengthy scripts is useful during development. But this trick, clearly, doesn't scale to more than one driver at a time.

Though certain kernel developers have threatened to do exactly that in the future. The best way to assign major numbers, in our opinion, is by defaulting to dynamic allocation while leaving yourself the option of specifying the major number at load time, or even at compile time. The scull implementation works in this way; it uses a global variable, scull_major, to hold the chosen number (there is also a scull_minor for the minor number). The variable is initialized to SCULL_MAJOR, defined in scull.h. The default value of SCULL_MAJOR in the distributed source is 0, which means "use dynamic assignment.

" The user can accept the default or choose a particular major number, either by modifying the macro before compiling or by specifying a value for scull_majoron the insmod command line. Finally, by using the scull_load script, the user can pass arguments to insmod onscull_load 's command line.

The init script scull.init doesn't accept driver options on the command line, but it supports a configuration file, because it's designed for automatic use at boot and shutdown time.

Here's the code we use in scull 's source to get a major number:

```
if (scull_major) {
dev = MKDEV(scull_major, scull_minor);
result = register_chrdev_region(dev,
scull_nr_devs, "scull");
} else {
result = alloc_chrdev_region(&dev, scull_minor,
scull_nr_devs,
"scull");
scull_major = MAJOR(dev);
}
if (result < 0) {
printk(KERN_WARNING "scull: can't get major %d\n",
scull_major);
return result;
}
```

Almost all of the sample drivers used in this book use similar code for their major number assignment.

SOME IMPORTANT DATA STRUCTURES

As you can imagine, device number registration is just the

first of many tasks that driver code must carry out. We will soon look at other important driver components, but one other digression is needed first. Most of the fundamental driver operations involve three important kernel data structures, called file_operations, file, andinode. A basic familiarity with these structures is required to be able to do much of anything interesting, so we will now take a quick look at each of them before getting into the details of how to implement the fundamental driver operations.

File Operations

So far, we have reserved som e device numbers for our use, but we have not yet connected any of our driver's operations to those numbers. The file_operations structure is how a char driver sets up this connection. The structure, defined in *<linux/fs.h>*, is a collection of function pointers. Each open file (represented internally by afile structure, which we will examine shortly) is associated with its own set of functions (by including a field calledf_op that points to a file_operations structure). The operations are mostly in charge of implementing the system calls and are therefore, named *open*, *read*, and so on. We can consider the file to be an "object" and the functions operating on it to be its "methods," using object-oriented programming terminology to denote actions declared by an object to act on itself. This is the first sign of object-oriented programming we see in the Linux kernel, and we'll see more in later chapters.

Conventionally, a file_operations structure or a pointer to one is called fops (or some variation thereof). Each field in the structure must point to the function in the driver that implements a specific operation, or be left NULL for unsupported operations. The exact behaviour of the kernel when a NULL pointer is specified is different for each function, as the list later in this section shows.

The following list introduces all the operations that an application can invoke on a device. We've tried to keep the list brief so it can be used as a reference, merely summarizing each operation and the default kernel behaviour when a NULL pointer is used.

As you read through the list of file_operations methods, you will note that a number of parameters include the string _ _user. This annotation is a form of documentation, noting that a pointer is a user-space address that cannot be directly dereferenced. For normal compilation, _ _user has no effect, but it can be used by external checking software to find misuse of user-space addresses.

The rest of the chapter, after describing some other important data structures, explains the role of the most important operations and offers hints, caveats, and real code examples. We defer discussion of the more complex operations to later chapters, because we aren't ready to dig into topics such as memory management, blocking operations, and asynchronous notification quite yet.

struct module *owner

The first file_operations field is not an operation at all; it is a pointer to the module that "owns" the structure. This field is used to prevent the module from being unloaded while its operations are in use. Almost all the time, it is simply initialized to THIS_MODULE, a macro defined in *<linux/module.h>*.

`loff_t (*llseek) (struct file *, loff_t, int);`

The *llseek* method is used to change the current read/write position in a file, and the new position is returned as a (positive) return value. The loff_t parameter is a "long offset" and is at least 64 bits wide even on 32-bit platforms. Errors are signaled by a negative return value. If this function pointer is NULL, seek calls will modify the position counter in the file structure in potentially unpredictable ways.

`ssize_t (*read) (struct file *, char _ _user *, size_t, loff_t *);`

Used to retrieve data from the device. A null pointer in this position causes the *read* system call to fail with -EINVAL ("Invalid argument"). A nonnegative return value represents the number of bytes successfully read (the return value is a "signed size" type, usually the native integer type for the target platform).

ssize_t (*aio_read)(struct kiocb *, char _ _user *, size_t, loff_t);

Initiates an asynchronous read a read operation that might not complete before the function returns. If this method is NULL, all operations will be processed (synchronously) by *read* instead.

ssize_t (*write) (struct file *, const char _ _user *, size_t, loff_t *);

Sends data to the device. If NULL, -EINVAL is returned to the program calling the *write* system call. The return value, if nonnegative, represents the number of bytes successfully written.

ssize_t (*aio_write)(struct kiocb *, const char _ _user *, size_t, loff_t *);

Initiates an asynchronous write operation on the device.

int (*readdir) (struct file *, void *, filldir_t);

This field should be NULL for device files; it is used for reading directories and is useful only for filesystems.

unsigned int (*poll) (struct file *, struct poll_table_struct *);

The *poll* method is the back end of three system calls: *poll, epoll,* and *select,* all of which are used to query whether a read or write to one or more file descriptors would block. The *poll* method should return a bit mask indicating whether non-blocking reads or writes are possible, and, possibly, provide the kernel with information that can be used to put the calling process to sleep until I/O becomes possible. If a driver leaves its *poll* method NULL, the device is assumed to be both readable and writable without blocking.

int (*ioctl) (struct inode *, struct file *, unsigned int, unsigned long);

The *ioctl* system call offers a way to issue device-specific commands (such as formatting a track of a floppy disk, which is neither reading nor writing). Additionally, a few *ioctl* commands are recognized by the kernel without referring to the fops table. If the device doesn't provide an *ioctl* method, the system call returns an error for any request that isn't predefined (-ENOTTY, "No such ioctl for device").

int (*mmap) (struct file *, struct vm_area_struct *);

mmap is used to request a mapping of device memory to a process's address space. If this method isNULL, the *mmap* system call returns -ENODEV.

int (*open) (struct inode *, struct file *);

Though this is always the first operation performed on the device file, the driver is not required to declare a corresponding method. If this entry is NULL, opening the device always succeeds, but your driver isn't notified.

int (*flush) (struct file *);

The *flush* operation is invoked when a process closes its copy of a file descriptor for a device; it should execute (and wait for) any outstanding operations on the device. This must not be confused with the *fsync*operation requested by user programs. Currently, *flush* is used in very few drivers; the SCSI tape driver uses it, for example, to ensure that all data written makes it to the tape before the device is closed. If *flush* isNULL, the kernel simply ignores the user application request.

int (*release) (struct inode *, struct file *);

This operation is invoked when the file structure is being released. Like open, release *can be NULL.*

Note that *release* isn't invoked every time a process calls *close*. Whenever a file structure is shared (for example, after a *fork* or a *dup*), *release* won't be invoked until all copies are closed. If you need to flush pending data when any copy is closed, you should implement the *flush* method.

int (*fsync) (struct file *, struct dentry *, int);

This method is the back end of the *fsync* system call, which a user calls to flush any pending data. If this pointer is NULL, the system call returns -EINVAL.

int (*aio_fsync)(struct kiocb *, int);

This is the asynchronous version of the *fsync* method.

int (*fasync) (int, struct file *, int);

This operation is used to notify the device of a change in its FASYNC flag. Asynchronous notification is an advanced topic and is described in. The field can be NULL if the driver doesn't support asynchronous notification.

int (*lock) (struct file *, int, struct file_lock *);

The *lock* method is used to implement file locking; locking is an indispensable feature for regular files but is almost never implemented by device drivers.

ssize_t (*readv) (struct file *, const struct iovec *, unsigned long, loff_t *);

ssize_t (*writev) (struct file *, const struct iovec *, unsigned long, loff_t *);

These methods implement scatter/gather read and write operations. Applications occasionally need to do a single read or write operation involving multiple memory areas; these system calls allow them to do so without forcing extra copy operations on the data. If these function pointers are left NULL, the *read* and *write*methods are called (perhaps more than once) instead.

ssize_t (*sendfile)(struct file *, loff_t *, size_t, read_actor_t, void *);

This method implements the read side of the *sendfile* system call, which moves the data from one file descriptor to another with a minimum of copying. It is used, for example, by a web server that needs to send the contents of a file out a network connection. Device drivers usually leave *sendfile* NULL.

ssize_t (*sendpage) (struct file *, struct page *, int, size_t, loff_t *, int);

Sendpage is the other half of *sendfile*; it is called by the kernel to send data, one page at a time, to the corresponding file. Device drivers do not usually implement *sendpage.*

unsigned long (*get_unmapped_area)(struct file *, unsigned long, unsigned long, unsigned long, unsigned long);

The purpose of this method is to find a suitable location in the process's address space to map in a memory segment on the underlying device. This task is normally performed by the memory management code; this method exists to allow drivers to enforce any alignment requirements a particular device may have. Most drivers can leave this method NULL.

`int (*check_flags)(int)`

This method allows a module to check the flags passed to an *fcntl(F_SETFL...)* call.

`int (*dir_notify)(struct file *, unsigned long);`

This method is invoked when an application uses *fcntl* to request directory change notifications. It is useful only to filesystems; drivers need not implement *dir_notify*.

The *scull* device driver implements only the most important device methods.

Its file_operations structure is initialized as follows:

```
struct file_operations scull_fops = {
  .owner = THIS_MODULE,
  .llseek = scull_llseek,
  .read = scull_read,
  .write = scull_write,
  .ioctl = scull_ioctl,
  .open = scull_open,
  .release = scull_release,
};
```

This declaration uses the standard C tagged structure initialization syntax. This syntax is preferred because it makes drivers more portable across changes in the definitions of the structures and, arguably, makes the code more compact and readable. Tagged initialization allows the reordering of structure members; in some cases, substantial performance improvements have been realised by placing pointers to frequently accessed members in the same hardware cache line.

The file Structure

struct file, defined in *<linux/fs.h>*, is the second most important data structure used in device drivers. Note that a file has nothing to do with the FILE pointers of user-space programs. A FILE is defined in the C library and never appears in kernel code. A struct file, on the other hand, is a kernel structure that never appears in user programs.

The file structure represents an *open file*. (It is not specific to device drivers; every open file in the system has an associated struct file in kernel space.) It is created by the kernel on *open* and is passed to any function that operates on the file, until the last *close*. After all instances of the file are closed, the kernel releases the data structure.

In the kernel sources, a pointer to struct file is usually called either file or filp ("file pointer"). We'll consistently call the pointer filp to prevent ambiguities with the structure itself. Thus, file refers to the structure and filp to a pointer to the structure.

The most important fields of struct file are shown here. As in the previous section, the list can be skipped on a first reading. However, later in this chapter, when we face some real C code, we'll discuss the fields in more detail.

`mode_t f_mode;`

The file mode identifies the file as either readable or writable (or both), by means of the bits FMODE_READ andFMODE_WRITE. You might want to check this field for read/write permission in your *open* or *ioctl* function, but you don't need to check permissions for *read* and *write*, because the kernel checks before invoking your method. An attempt to read or write when the file has not been opened for that type of access is rejected without the driver even knowing about it.

`loff_t f_pos;`

The current reading or writing position. loff_t is a 64-bit value on all platforms (long long in *gcc*terminology). The driver can read this value if it needs to know the current position in the file but should not normally change it; *read* and *write* should update a position using the pointer they receive as the last argument instead of acting on filp->f_pos directly. The one exception to this rule is in the *llseek* method, the purpose of which is to change the file position.

`unsigned int f_flags;`

These are the file flags, such as O_RDONLY, O_NONBLOCK, and O_SYNC. A driver should check the O_NONBLOCKflag to see if nonblocking operation has been requested; the other flags are seldom used. In particular, read/write permission should be checked using f_mode rather than f_flags. All the flags are defined in the header <linux/fcntl.h>.

`struct file_operations *f_op;`

The operations associated with the file. The kernel assigns the pointer as part of its implementation of openand then reads it when it needs to dispatch any operations. The value in filp->f_op is never saved by the kernel for later reference; this means that you can change the file operations associated with your file, and the new methods will be effective after you return to the caller. For example, the code for open associated with major number 1 (/dev/null,/dev/zero, and so on) substitutes the operations in filp->f_op depending on the minor number being opened. This practice allows the implementation of several behaviours under the same major number without introducing overhead at each system call. The ability to replace the file operations is the kernel equivalent of "method overriding" in object-oriented programming.

`void *private_data;`

The open system call sets this pointer to NULL before calling the open method for the driver. You are free to make its own use of the field or to ignore it; you can use the field to point to allocated data, but then you must remember to free that memory in the release method before the file structure is destroyed by the kernel.private_data is a useful resource for preserving state information across system calls and is used by most of our sample modules.

`struct dentry *f_dentry;`

The directory entry (dentry) structure associated with the file. Device driver writers normally need not concern themselves with dentry structures, other than to access the inode structure as filp->f_dentry->d_inode. The real structure has a few more fields, but they aren't useful to device drivers. We can safely ignore those fields, because drivers never create file structures; they only access structures created elsewhere.

The *inode* structure is used by the kernel internally to represent files. Therefore, it is different from the filestructure that represents an open file descriptor. There can be numerous file structures representing multiple open descriptors on a single file, but they all point to a single inode structure.

The inode structure contains a great deal of information about the file. As a general rule, only two fields of this structure are of interest for writing driver code:

`dev_t i_rdev;`

For inodes that represent device files, this field contains the actual device number.

`struct cdev *i_cdev;`

struct cdev is the kernel's internal structure that represents char devices; this field contains a pointer to that structure when the inode refers to a char device file. The type of i_rdev changed over the course of the 2.5 development series, breaking a lot of drivers. As a way of encouraging more portable programming, the kernel developers have added two macros that can be used to obtain the major and minor number from an inode:

```
unsigned int iminor(struct inode *inode);
unsigned int imajor(struct inode *inode);
```

In the interest of not being caught by the next change, these macros should be used instead of manipulatingi_rdev directly.

CHAR DEVICE REGISTRATION

As we mentioned, the kernel uses structures of type struct cdev to represent char devices internally. Before the kernel invokes your device's operations, you must allocate and register one or more of these structures. To do so, your code should include *<linux/cdev.h>*, where the structure and its associated helper functions are defined. There is an older mechanism that avoids the use of cdev structures (which we discuss. New code should use the newer technique, however.

There are two ways of allocating and initializing one of these structures. If you wish to obtain a standalone cdevstructure at runtime, you may do so with code such as:

```
struct cdev *my_cdev = cdev_alloc();
my_cdev->ops = &my_fops;
```

Chances are, however, that you will want to embed the

cdev structure within a device-specific structure of your own; that is what *scull* does. In that case, you should initialize the structure that you have already allocated with:

```
void cdev_init(struct cdev *cdev, struct
file_operations *fops);
```

Either way, there is one other struct cdev field that you need to initialize. Like the file_operations structure,struct cdev has an owner field that should be set to THIS_MODULE.

Once the cdev structure is set up, the final step is to tell the kernel about it with a call to:

```
int cdev_add(struct cdev *dev, dev_t num, unsigned
int count);
```

Here, dev is the cdev structure, num is the first device number to which this device responds, and count is the number of device numbers that should be associated with the device. Often count is one, but there are situations where it makes sense to have more than one device number correspond to a specific device. Consider, for example, the SCSI tape driver, which allows user space to select operating modes (such as density) by assigning multiple minor numbers to each physical device. There are a couple of important things to keep in mind when using *cdev_add*. The first is that this call can fail. If it returns a negative error code, your device has not been added to the system. It almost always succeeds, however, and that brings up the other point: as soon as *cdev_add* returns, your device is "live" and its operations can be called by the kernel. You should not call *cdev_add* until your driver is completely ready to handle operations on the device.

To remove a char device from the system, call:

```
void cdev_del(struct cdev *dev);
```

Clearly, you should not access the cdev structure after passing it to *cdev_del*.

Device Registration in Scull

Internally, *scull* represents each device with a structure of type struct scull_dev.

This structure is defined as:

```
struct scull_dev {
```

```
struct scull_qset *data;/* Pointer to first quantum
set */
int quantum;/* the current quantum size */
int qset;/* the current array size */
unsigned long size;/* amount of data stored here
*/
unsigned int access_key;/* used by sculluid and
scullpriv */
struct semaphore sem;/* mutual exclusion semaphore
*/
struct cdev cdev;/* Char device structure */
};
```

We discuss the various fields in this structure as we come to them, but for now, we call attention to cdev, thestruct cdev that interfaces our device to the kernel. This structure must be initialized and added to the system as described above; the *scull* code that handles this task is:

```
static void scull_setup_cdev(struct scull_dev
*dev, int index)
{
int err, devno = MKDEV(scull_major, scull_minor
+ index);
cdev_init(&dev->cdev, &scull_fops);
dev->cdev.owner = THIS_MODULE;
dev->cdev.ops = &scull_fops;
err = cdev_add (&dev->cdev, devno, 1);
/* Fail gracefully if need be */
if (err)
printk(KERN_NOTICE "Error %d adding scull%d", err,
index);
}
```

Since the cdev structure is embedded within struct scull_dev, *cdev_init* must be called to perform the initialization of that structure.

The Older Way

If you dig through much driver code in the 2.6 kernel, you may notice that quite a few char drivers do not use thecdev interface that we have just described. What you are seeing is older code that has not yet been upgraded to the 2.6 interface. Since that code works as it is, this upgrade may not happen for a long time. For completeness, we describe the older char device registration interface, but new code should not use it; this mechanism will likely go away in a future kernel.

The classic way to register a char device driver is with:

```
int register_chrdev(unsigned int major, const char
*name,
struct file_operations *fops);
```

Here, major is the major number of interest, name is the name of the driver (it appears in*/proc/devices*), and fopsis the default file_operations structure. A call to *register_chrdev* registers minor numbers 0-255 for the givenmajor, and sets up a default cdev structure for each. Drivers using this interface must be prepared to handle *open*calls on all 256 minor numbers (whether they correspond to real devices or not), and they cannot use major or minor numbers greater than 255.

If you use register_chrdev, the proper function to remove your device(s) from the system is:

```
int unregister_chrdev(unsigned int major, const
char *name);
```

major and name must be the same as those passed to *register_chrdev,* or the call will fail.

OPEN AND RELEASE

Now that we've taken a quick look at the fields, we start using them in real *scull* functions.

The) Open Method

The *open* method is provided for a driver to do any initialization in preparation for later operations.

In most drivers,open should perform the following tasks:

- Check for device-specific errors (such as device-not-ready or similar hardware problems)
- Initialize the device if it is being opened for the first time
- Update the f_op pointer, if necessary

- Allocate and fill any data structure to be put in filp->private_data

The first order of business, however, is usually to identify which device is being opened.

Remember that the prototype for the open method is:

```
int (*open)(struct inode *inode, struct file *filp);
```

The *inode* argument has the information we need in the form of its i_cdev field, which contains the cdev structure we set up before.

The only problem is that we do not normally want the cdev structure itself, we want the scull_devstructure that contains that cdev structure. The C language lets programmers play all sorts of tricks to make that kind of conversion; programming such tricks is error prone, however, and leads to code that is difficult for others to read and understand. Fortunately, in this case, the kernel hackers have done the tricky stuff for us, in the form of the *container_of* macro, defined in *<linux/kernel.h>*:

```
container_of(pointer, container_type, container_field);
```

This macro takes a pointer to a field of type container_field, within a structure of type container_type, and returns a pointer to the containing structure. In *scull_open,* this macro is used to find the appropriate device structure:

```
struct scull_dev *dev;/* device information */
dev = container_of(inode->i_cdev, struct scull_dev, cdev);
filp->private_data = dev;/* for other methods */
```

Once it has found the scull_dev structure, *scull* stores a pointer to it in the private_data field of the filestructure for easier access in the future. The other way to identify the device being opened is to look at the minor number stored in the inode structure. If you register your device with *register_chrdev,* you must use this technique. Be sure to use *iminor* to obtain the minor number from the inode structure, and make sure that it corresponds to a device that your driver is actually prepared to handle.

The (slightly simplified) code for scull_open is:

```
int scull_open(struct inode *inode, struct file
*filp)
{
struct scull_dev *dev;/* device information */
dev = container_of(inode->i_cdev, struct
scull_dev, cdev);
filp->private_data = dev;/* for other methods */
/* now trim to 0 the length of the device if open
was write-only */
if ((filp->f_flags & O_ACCMODE) = = O_WRONLY) {
scull_trim(dev);/* ignore errors */
}
return 0;/* success */
}
```

The code looks pretty sparse, because it doesn't do any particular device handling when *open* is called. It doesn't need to, because the *scull* device is global and persistent by design. Specifically, there's no action such as "initializing the device on first open," because we don't keep an open count for *sculls*.

The only real operation performed on the device is truncating it to a length of 0 when the device is opened for writing. This is performed because, by design, overwriting a *scull* device with a shorter file results in a shorter device data area. This is similar to the way opening a regular file for writing truncates it to zero length. The operation does nothing if the device is opened for reading.

We'll see later how a real initialization works when we look at the code for the other *scull* personalities.

The Release Method

The role of the *release* method is the reverse of *open*. Sometimes you'll find that the method implementation is called *device*_close instead of *device*_release.

Either way, the device method should perform the following tasks:

- Deallocate anything that *open* allocated in filp->private_data

- Shut down the device on last close

The basic form of *scull* has no hardware to shut down, so the code required is minimal:[7] [7] The other flavours of the device are closed by different functions because *scull_open* substituted a different filp->f_opfor each device. We'll discuss these as we introduce each flavour.

```
int scull_release(struct inode *inode, struct file
*filp)
{
return 0;
}
```

You may be wondering what happens when a device file is closed more times than it is opened. After all, the *dup*and *fork* system calls create copies of open files without calling *open;* each of those copies is then closed at program termination. For example, most programs don't open their *stdin* file (or device), but all of them end up closing it. How does a driver know when an open device file has *really* been closed?

The answer is simple: not every *close* system call causes the *release* method to be invoked. Only the calls that actually release the device data structure invoke the method hence its name. The kernel keeps a counter of how many times a file structure is being used. Neither *fork* nor *dup* creates a new file structure (only *open*does that); they just increment the counter in the existing structure.

The *close* system call executes the *release*method only when the counter for the file structure drops to 0, which happens when the structure is destroyed. This relationship between the *release* method and the *close* system call guarantees that your driver sees only one*release* call for each *open*.

Note that the *flush* method *is* called every time an application calls *close*. However, very few drivers implement*flush*, because usually there's nothing to perform at close time unless *release* is involved.

As you may imagine, the previous discussion applies even when the application terminates without explicitly closing its open files: the kernel automatically closes any file at process exit time by internally using the *close*system call.

SCULL'S MEMORY USAGE

Before introducing the *read* and *write* operations, we'd better look at how and why *scull* performs memory allocation. "How" is needed to thoroughly understand the code, and "why" demonstrates the kind of choices a driver writer needs to make, although *scull* is definitely not typical as a device.

This section deals only with the memory allocation policy in *scull* and doesn't show the hardware management skills you need to write real drivers. These skills are introduced. Therefore, you can skip this section if you're not interested in understanding the inner workings of the memory-oriented *scull* driver. The region of memory used by scull, also called a device, is variable in length. The more you write, the more it grows; trimming is performed by overwriting the device with a shorter file.

The scull driver introduces two core functions used to manage memory in the Linux kernel.

These functions, defined in <linux/slab.h>, are:

```
void *kmalloc(size_t size, int flags);
void kfree(void *ptr);
```

A call to kmalloc attempts to allocate size bytes of memory; the return value is a pointer to that memory or NULL if the allocation fails. The flags argument is used to describe how the memory should be allocated; we examine those flags in detail. For now, we always use GFP_KERNEL. Allocated memory should be freed withkfree. You should never pass anything to kfree that was not obtained from kmalloc. It is, however, legal to pass aNULL pointer to kfree.

kmalloc is not the most efficient way to allocate large areas of memory, so the implementation chosen for scull is not a particularly smart one. The source code for a smart implementation would be more difficult to read, and the aim of this section is to show read and write, not memory management. That's why the code just uses kmalloc and kfree without resorting to allocation of whole pages, although that approach would be more efficient.

On the flip side, we didn't want to limit the size of the "device" area, for both a philosophical reason and a practical one. Philosophically, it's always a bad idea to put arbitrary limits on data items being managed. Practically, scull can be used to temporarily eat up your system's memory in order to run tests under low-memory conditions. Running such tests might help you understand the system's internals. You can use the command cp/dev/zero/dev/scull0 to eat all the real RAM with scull, and you can use the dd utility to choose how much data is copied to the scull device.

In scull, each device is a linked list of pointers, each of which points to a scull_dev structure. Each such structure can refer, by default, to at most four million bytes, through an array of intermediate pointers. The released source uses an array of 1000 pointers to areas of 4000 bytes. We call each memory area a quantum and the array (or its length) a quantum set. A scull device and its memory areas are shown in Figure.

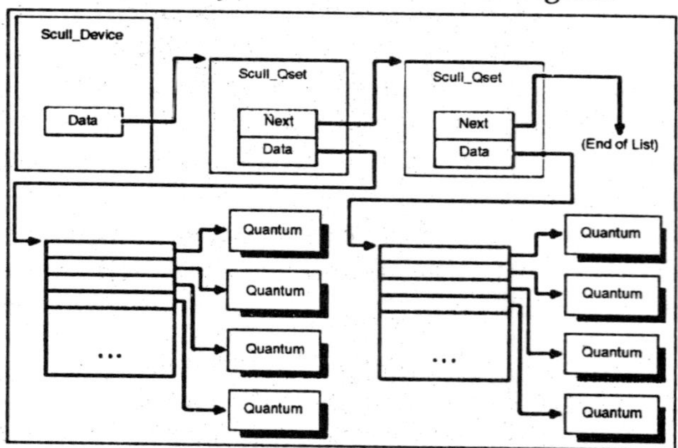

Fig: 3-1. The Layout of a Scull Device

The chosen numbers are such that writing a single byte in scull consumes 8000 or 12,000 thousand bytes of memory: 4000 for the quantum and 4000 or 8000 for the quantum set (according to whether a pointer is represented in 32 bits or 64 bits on the target platform). If, instead, you write a huge amount of data, the overhead of the linked list is not too bad. There is only one list element for every four megabytes of data, and the maximum size of the device is limited by the computer's memory size.

Choosing the appropriate values for the quantum and the quantum set is a question of policy, rather than mechanism, and the optimal sizes depend on how the device is used. Thus, the scull driver should not force the use of any particular values for the quantum and quantum set sizes. In scull, the user can change the values in charge in several ways: by changing the macros SCULL_QUANTUM and SCULL_QSET in scull.h at compile time, by setting the integer values scull_quantum and scull_qset at module load time, or by changing both the current and default values using ioctl at runtime.

Using a macro and an integer value to allow both compile-time and load-time configuration is reminiscent of how the major number is selected. We use this technique for whatever value in the driver is arbitrary or related to policy. The only question left is how the default numbers have been chosen. In this particular case, the problem is finding the best balance between the waste of memory resulting from half-filled quanta and quantum sets and the overhead of allocation, deallocation, and pointer chaining that occurs if quanta and sets are small. Additionally, the internal design of kmalloc should be taken into account. The choice of default numbers comes from the assumption that massive amounts of data are likely to be written to scull while testing it, although normal use of the device will most likely transfer just a few kilobytes of data.

We have already seen the scull_dev structure that represents our device internally. That structure's quantum andqset fields hold the device's quantum and quantum set sizes, respectively.

The actual data, however, is tracked by a different structure, which we call struct scull_qset:

```
struct scull_qset {
void **data;
struct scull_qset *next;
};
```

The next code fragment shows in practice how struct scull_dev and struct scull_qset are used to hold data. The function *scull_trim* is in charge of freeing the whole data area and is invoked by *scull_open* when the file is opened for writing. It simply walks through the list and frees any quantum and quantum set it finds.

```
int scull_trim(struct scull_dev *dev)
{
struct scull_qset *next, *dptr;
int qset = dev->qset;/* "dev" is not-null */
int i;
for (dptr = dev->data; dptr; dptr = next) {/*
all the list items */
if (dptr->data) {
for (i = 0; i < qset; i++)
kfree(dptr->data[i]);
kfree(dptr->data);
dptr->data = NULL;
}
next = dptr->next;
kfree(dptr);
}
dev->size = 0;
dev->quantum = scull_quantum;
dev->qset = scull_qset;
dev->data = NULL;
return 0;
}
```

scull_trim is also used in the module cleanup function to return memory used by *scull* to the system.

READ AND WRITE

The *read* and *write* methods both perform a similar task, that is, copying data from and to application code.

Therefore, their prototypes are pretty similar, and it's worth introducing them at the same time:

```
ssize_t read(struct file *filp, char _ _user *buff,
size_t count, loff_t *offp);
ssize_t write(struct file *filp, const char _
_user *buff,
size_t count, loff_t *offp);
```

For both methods, filp is the file pointer and count is the size of the requested data transfer. The buff argument points to the user buffer holding the data to be written or the empty buffer where the newly read data should be placed. Finally, offp is a pointer to a "long offset type" object that indicates the file position the user is accessing. The return value is a "signed size type"; its use is discussed later.

Let us repeat that the buff argument to the read and write methods is a user-space pointer. Therefore, it cannot be directly dereferenced by kernel code.

There are a few reasons for this restriction:

- Depending on which architecture your driver is running on, and how the kernel was configured, the user-space pointer may not be valid while running in kernel mode at all. There may be no mapping for that address, or it could point to some other, random data.
- Even if the pointer does mean the same thing in kernel space, user-space memory is paged, and the memory in question might not be resident in RAM when the system call is made. Attempting to reference the user-space memory directly could generate a page fault, which is something that kernel code is not allowed to do. The result would be an "oops," which would result in the death of the process that made the system call.
- The pointer in question has been supplied by a user program, which could be buggy or malicious. If your driver ever blindly dereferences a user-supplied pointer, it provides an open doorway allowing a user-space program to access or overwrite memory anywhere in the system. If you do not wish to be responsible for compromising the security of your users' systems, you cannot ever dereference a user-space pointer directly.

Obviously, your driver must be able to access the user-space buffer in order to get its job done. This access must always be performed by special, kernel-supplied functions, however, in order to be safe. We introduce some of those functions (which are defined in <asm/uaccess.h>) here, and the rest in the use some special, architecture-dependent magic to ensure that data transfers between kernel and user space happen in a safe and correct way.

The code for read and write in scull needs to copy a whole segment of data to or from the user address space. This capability is offered by the following kernel functions, which copy an arbitrary array of bytes and sit at the heart of most read and write implementations:

```
unsigned long copy_to_user(void _ _user *to,
const void *from,
unsigned long count);
unsigned long copy_from_user(void *to,
const void _ _user *from,
unsigned long count);
```

Although these functions behave like normal *memcpy* functions, a little extra care must be used when accessing user space from kernel code. The user pages being addressed might not be currently present in memory, and the virtual memory subsystem can put the process to sleep while the page is being transferred into place. This happens, for example, when the page must be retrieved from swap space. The net result for the driver writer is that any function that accesses user space must be reentrant, must be able to execute concurrently with other driver functions, and, in particular, must be in a position where it can legally sleep. We return to this subject.

The role of the two functions is not limited to copying data to and from user-space: they also check whether the user space pointer is valid. If the pointer is invalid, no copy is performed; if an invalid address is encountered during the copy, on the other hand, only part of the data is copied. In both cases, the return value is the amount of memory still to be copied. The *scull* code looks for this error return, and returns -EFAULT to the user if it's not 0.

The topic of user-space access and invalid user space pointers is somewhat advanced and is discussed. However, it's worth noting that if you don't need to check the user-space pointer you can invoke *_ _copy_to_user* and *_ _copy_from_user* instead. This is useful, for example, if you know you already checked the argument. Be careful, however; if, in fact, you do *not* check a user-space pointer that you pass to these functions, then you can create kernel crashes and/or security holes.

As far as the actual device methods are concerned, the task of the *read* method is to copy data from the device to user space (using *copy_to_user*), while the *write* method must copy data from user space to the device (using*copy_from_user*). Each *read* or *write* system call requests transfer of a specific number of bytes, but the driver is free to transfer less data the exact rules are slightly different for reading and writing and are described later in this chapter.

Whatever the amount of data the methods transfer, they should generally update the file position at *offp to represent the current file position after successful completion of the system call. The kernel then propagates the file position change back into the file structure when appropriate. The *pread* and *pwrite* system calls have different semantics, however; they operate from a given file offset and do not change the file position as seen by any other system calls. These calls pass in a pointer to the user-supplied position, and discard the changes that your driver makes. Figure represents how a typical *read* implementation uses its arguments.

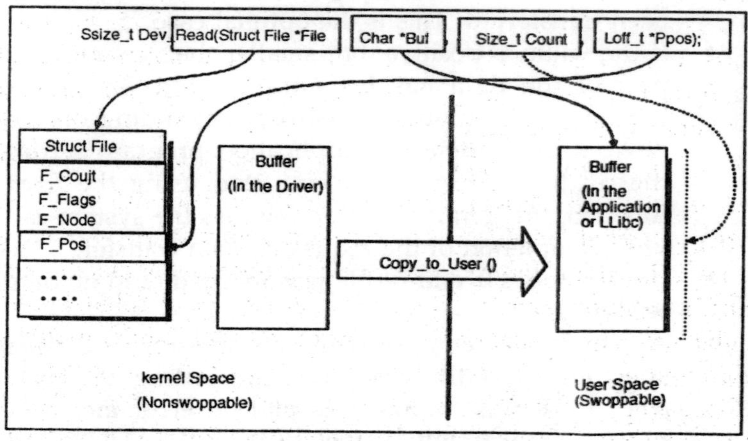

Fig: The Arguments to Read

Both the *read* and *write* methods return a negative value if an error occurs. A return value greater than or equal to 0, instead, tells the calling program how many bytes have been successfully transferred. If some data is transferred correctly and then an error happens, the return value must be the count of bytes successfully transferred, and the error does not get reported until the next time the function is called. Implementing this convention requires, of course, that your driver remember that the error has occurred so that it can return the error status in the future. Although kernel functions return a negative number to signal an error, and the value of the number indicates the kind of error that occurred (as introduced in programs that run in user space always see -1 as the error return value. They need to access the errno variable to find out what happened. The user-space behaviour is dictated by the POSIX standard, but that standard does not make requirements on how the kernel operates internally.

The Read Method

The return value for read is interpreted by the calling application program:

- If the value equals the count argument passed to the *read* system call, the requested number of bytes has been transferred. This is the optimal case.
- If the value is positive, but smaller than count, only part of the data has been transferred. This may happen for a number of reasons, depending on the device. Most often, the application program retries the read. For instance, if you read using the *fread* function, the library function reissues the system call until completion of the requested data transfer.
- If the value is 0, end-of-file was reached (and no data was read).
- A negative value means there was an error. The value specifies what the error was, according to*<linux/errno.h>*. Typical values returned on error include -EINTR (interrupted system call) or -EFAULT (bad address).

What is missing from the preceding list is the case of "there is no data, but it may arrive later." In this case, the*read* system call should block. We'll deal with blocking input. The *scull* code takes advantage of these rules. In particular, it takes advantage of the partial-read rule. Each invocation of *scull_read* deals only with a single data quantum, without implementing a loop to gather all the data; this makes the code shorter and easier to read. If the reading program really wants more data, it reiterates the call. If the standard I/O library (*i.e., fread*) is used to read the device, the application won't even notice the quantization of the data transfer. If the current read position is greater than the device size, the *read* method of *scull* returns 0 to signal that there's no data available (in other words, we're at end-of-file). This situation can happen if process A is reading the device while process B opens it for writing, thus truncating the device to a length of 0. Process A suddenly finds itself past end-of-file, and the next *read* call returns 0.

Here is the code for *read* (ignore the calls to *down_interruptible* and *up* for now; we will get to them in the next chapter):

```
ssize_t scull_read(struct file *filp, char _ _user
*buf, size_t count,
loff_t *f_pos)
{
struct scull_dev *dev = filp->private_data;
struct scull_qset *dptr;/* the first listitem */
int quantum = dev->quantum, qset = dev->qset;
int itemsize = quantum * qset;/* how many bytes
 in the listitem */
int item, s_pos, q_pos, rest;
ssize_t retval = 0;
if (down_interruptible(&dev->sem))
return -ERESTARTSYS;
if (*f_pos >= dev->size)
goto out;
if (*f_pos + count > dev->size)
count = dev->size-*f_pos;
/* find listitem, qset index, and offset in the
```

```
quantum */
item = (long)*f_pos/itemsize;
rest = (long)*f_pos % itemsize;
s_pos = rest/quantum; q_pos = rest % quantum;
/* follow the list up to the right position
(defined elsewhere) */
dptr = scull_follow(dev, item);
if (dptr = = NULL || !dptr->data || ! dptr-
>data[s_pos])
goto out;/* don't fill holes */
/* read only up to the end of this quantum */
if (count > quantum-q_pos)
count = quantum-q_pos;
if (copy_to_user(buf, dptr->data[s_pos] + q_pos,
count)) {
retval = -EFAULT;
goto out;
}
*f_pos += count;
retval = count;
out:
up(&dev->sem);
return retval;
}
```

The Write Method

write, like read, can transfer less data than was requested, according to the following rules for the return value:

- If the value equals count, the requested number of bytes has been transferred.
- If the value is positive, but smaller than count, only part of the data has been transferred. The program will most likely retry writing the rest of the data.
- If the value is 0, nothing was written. This result is not an error, and there is no reason to return an error code. Once again, the standard library retries the call to *write*. We'll examine the exact meaning of this case in where blocking *write* is introduced.

Bibliography

Bill, M.: *Learning Red Hat Enterprise Linux and Fedora,* Washington: CQ Press, 2002.

Bob, N.: *LINUX Assembly Language Programming,* Ann Arbor: University of Michigan Press. 1999.

Craig, H.: *Embedded Linux: Hardware, Software, and Interfacing,* N.J.: Erlbaum Publications, 1997.

Daniel, P.: *Understanding the Linux Kernel,* New York: Pergamon Press, 2003.

Ellie, Q.: *Linux System Programming,* NJ: L. Erlbaum Publications, 2005.

Gene, S.: *Linux Embedded Systems,* New York: Wiley Publications, 2003.

Jay, N.: *Linux Robotics: Programming Smarter Robots,* London: Rutledge Publications, 2003.

John, E.: *Linux on the Mainframe,* Boston: Houghton Mifflin, 2006.

John, L.: *Linux Kernel Development*, New York: Plenum Press, 1999.

Michael, S.: *The Linux Cookbook: Tips and Techniques for Everyday use,* New York: Holt, Rinehart, and Winston, 1998.

Mike, G.: *Linux and the Unix Philosophy,* New York: Wiley Publications, 2005.

Nate, C.: *Automating Linux and UNIX System Administration,* New York: Halstead Press, 2001.

Roderick, W.: *Linux in a Windows World,* IL: F.E. Peacock Publishers, 2008.

Computer